HUDSON'S

HUDSON'S
Hub of America's Heartland

by Jean Maddern Pitrone

A&M
Altwerger and Mandel Publishing Company
West Bloomfield, Michigan

Library of Congress Cataloging-in-Publication Data

Pitrone, Jean Maddern, 1920–
  Hudson's : hub of America's heartland / Jean Maddern Pitrone. —
1st ed.
    p.   cm.
  Includes bibliographical references.
  ISBN 1-878005-18-9 : $24.95. — ISBN 1-878005-19-7 (pb)
  1. J.L. Hudson Company—History. 2. Hudson Motor Car
Company-
-History. 3. Hudson family. 4. Department stores—Michigan-
-Detroit—History. 5. Automobile industry and trade—United States-
-History. I. Title.
HF5465.U6J256 1991
381'141'0977434—dc20   91-31033
                                                                  CIP
                                                                   AC

Copyright ©1991 by Jean Maddern Pitrone

Printed in the United States of America.

All Rights Reserved. No part of this book may be reproduced or
utilized in any form or by any means, electronic or mechanical,
including photocopying, recording or by any information storage and
retrieval system, without permission in writing from the publisher.
ISBN: 1-878005-18-9
First Printing.

A&M Publishing Company, Inc.
6346 Orchard Lake Road.
West Bloomfield, MI 48322

For my daughter
Jane Rossi
With appreciation
for her help in
researching this book

Contents

1 Hudson's Traditions and their Roots 1
2 The Mabley-Hudson Feud 15
3 Grand Opening 27
4 A New Century Dawns 39
5 "Crossing the Bar" 51
6 A Golden Decade 69
7 Dreary Days; Troubled Times 85
8 Drumbeats in the 1940s 97
9 Reaching an Apex 111
10 "The Ever Whirling Wheels of Change 131
11 The Decline 155
12 The Exodus—After 102 Years 171
Bibliography 191

Chapter 1

Hudson's Traditions and Their Roots

The J.L. Hudson store, its 49 acres of shopping floor-space rooted in one solid block of Detroit's Woodward Avenue, is still in its heyday in 1960. There is, as yet, scarcely a foreshadowing of the upheaval in social mores that lies just ahead—the renegade decade of hippies, protesters, the drug culture, a race to the moon, civil rights struggles, assassinations of political leaders, and the Vietnam War. The 1960 "Downtown Hudson's" is as much as a symbol of Detroit and Americana as "the old lady of Threadneedle Street" is symbolic of Britain. And like the Bank of England, the great department store in Detroit clings to stable and enduring traditions—its Midwestern heritage.

In no other metropolis in the country does one store represent a city in the singular way that the family-owned Hudson's represents Detroit. Ensconced at the hub of the automotive city's spoke-like streets, Hudson's roots reach five basements below Woodward Avenue. Its fifth subterranean-level digestive system ingests the sewage from the other four basements (including the two-floor "biggest in the world" Budget Store) into its bowels where giant sump pumps expel a steady flow of refuse back up to the city sewer level.

HUDSON'S: HUB OF AMERICA'S HEARTLAND

    The Motor City's main artery, Woodward Avenue, is the lifeline sustaining the city's heartbeat, regulated by the roaring or waning of blast-furnaces, the clanging of automated hammers, the flow of the assembly line. Hudson's, too, breathes with the pulse of the city's car factories. When the factory din subsides during recessions or model changeovers, the hulking downtown store strains for stamina to preserve the routine of its marketplace on 25 floors behind bronze main-entrance doors.

    The prize is merited by the struggle—the maintaining of Hudson's top sales-record reputation as the country's biggest rival of Macy's in New York City.

    The Detroit store sells more than one-half million commodities which include, according to a December 15, 1958 issue of *Life* magazine, "anything from jewelled dog collars to baby bumble bees preserved in soya sauce and sugar." Such esoteric items are not stocked in the capacious Hudson's Basement Store, but almost all other items—from can openers, fly swatters, and jewelry to clothing, furniture and sports equipment—can be purchased at competitive prices in Hudson's Basement, crowded with thrifty shoppers and bargain hunters.

    But in 1960, even the upper levels of the store are no longer the exclusive province of wealthy Junior Leaguers, Grosse Pointe dowagers, Bloomfield Hill matrons, and successful business and professional people. As long as factory assembly lines echo to the three-shift clanging of metal bodies dropping down to settle on steel frames, blue-collar workers' wives have money to spend freely.

    Like the factories that generate annual model changes for their sleek and powerful machines, the plant-workers' families disdain obsolescence. They come from tract houses on Kingsway Lane or Coventry Circle in the outlying and burgeoning cities of Warren or Livonia, Michigan, to walk Hudson's plush stretches of eighth-floor carpeting, examining furniture and accessories in the home decorator's shop.

    Other housewife-shoppers trek to Hudson's from older neighborhoods of Poletown, Dearborn and Royal Oak. When their men are working overtime in the plants, the women whisk charge cards from the depths of their genuine leather handbags and order the latest in camera equipment from the second floor . . . wide screen television consoles from the 13th floor music department . . . sets of copper cookware and incredibly delicate goblets as "shower" gifts for brides-to-be registered at Hudson's Bridal Shop.

The Hudson's-registered bride can remain completely unruffled when she unwraps duplicate sets of the incredibly fragile goblets or when she opens triplicate packages containing incisor-edged electric can openers, each guaranteed for lifetime performance. They can be returned at Hudson's for exchange. For credit. For cash refund. No questions asked. No sales slips required. Even if the gift was purchased at another store—a rival emporium or one of the fast growing "discount" stores—and returned in a J.L. Hudson Company box, the Hudson clerk is reassuring. "No problem," she says.

In reality, it is a problem that amounts to a loss of many millions of sales dollars each year—$25 million in 1960. But the liberal exchange policy is a Hudson tenet that reaches back to the base on which the founding Hudson built his business. It is doubtful that the base can be kicked away without a diminishing of customer loyalty and crumbling of the empire.

Legends have flourished from incidents related to the Hudson exchange policy. There is the story of the old lady who, while clearing out and sorting the belongings of her deceased sister, found a pair of bloomers, unused and still in a Hudson's box, with a 20-year-old sales slip. The woman came into the store, expecting the firm to take back the bloomers, and left a bit later, greatly pleased with her refund.

And so, Politeness remains the essence of Hudson policy. Helpfulness, the core of Hudson conduct. Friendliness, the mainstay of Hudson deportment.

Traditional Hudson fetish for friendly service is fostered, in 1960, by Joseph Lowthian Hudson, Jr., great-nephew of the store's founder and Prince Charming of the merchandise dynasty. "Joe" Hudson, he refers to himself in genial, folksy Hudson style. He is the heir apparent—a vice-president of the company for almost four years and slated to assume, very soon, the top leadership role as the first executive bearing the Hudson name to head the company since the founder's death in 1912.

At age 28, young "Joe" Hudson already fits the image of the

store as if he had been as much made-to-specification as the "special-order" automobiles that roll off the factory assembly lines. Six feet tall, handsome and trim at 173 pounds, he wears his good looks in a disarming manner. Newspapers claim he has done the necessary homework to step into the leadership role—graduating from Yale with a degree in Economics, serving his country as an Army artillery lieutenant for two years in Germany, working on the receiving docks and in the warehouses at Hudson's, then finally clerking in the Basement Store before moving into the office.

He also has moved into a leadership role in Detroit's civic affairs, living up to the Hudson ethic of returning to a community the favors of wealth and position received from that community . . . of continuing traditions established by the company's founder, the original Joseph Lowthian Hudson.

Like the store's founder, young Hudson supports his church (Presbyterian,) does not smoke (nor even drink coffee,) and is a Republican who avoids any hint of a flamboyant lifestyle. He takes pride in his expansion of the company's long established employee-relations department which assists Hudson workers with unusual medical, financial, or personal problems, and helps retain the non-unionized status of most Hudson employees.

Although Joe Hudson is innovative enough to have recently installed a fine wines shop in the store (departing from the practices of his cousins and great-uncle who would not allow alcoholic beverages within the sacrosanct bronze portals,) the younger Hudson is practical enough to recognize the importance of certain classic Hudson traditions to the people of Metropolitan Detroit.

There are many such traditions, including the annual unfurling of 1500 pounds and more than 24,000 square feet of stars and stripes on Flag Day (June 14) and displaying of "The Largest Flag in the World" across the store's Woodward Avenue visage . . . the mammoth Hudson's parade (vying with Macy's for the title of oldest in the country) each Thanksgiving morning to the accompaniment of 18 blaring, thumping, high stepping bands and concluding with a colorful Santa Claus float that delivers the rotund "real" Santa to the Hudson's marquee where the mayor of Detroit awaits his arrival.

Few people know that a second, extra Santa Claus, complete

with costume and beard, is stashed into close quarters under the seat of the glittering float, hidden there in the event—heaven forbid—that the visible Santa meets with a misfortune. The services of an understudy, however, have not been necessary for many years, and the resplendent visitor from the North Pole always steps smartly onto the marquee with the assistance of a high-low tractor lift. He walks majestically through a specially prepared window into the store where he and his clones will reign over Hudson's Toyland, receiving hordes of visitors throughout the holiday season.

For out-of-towners visiting the Motor City, a visit to Hudson's store is a must at any time of the year. Checking coats and parcels, visitors travel long flights of automated stairways to treasures on every floor. Or they step into walnut-panelled elevators where neatly uniformed operators press buttons and call out floor numbers in courteous, well modulated voices.

The elevators disgorge clusters of women at the fourth floor, the location of spacious and well appointed rest rooms, and mirrored powder rooms with lounges. In the elegantly equipped children's sections, mothers may feed their babies or change their diapers on dressing tables while more self-sufficient tots use child-sized facilities and drink from handsome brass fountains placed at convenient heights. Rest room attendants, mostly black females wearing crisp uniforms and fluted caps, move about unobtrusively—mopping, polishing, replacing soaps and towels and tissues, trailing lemon and lilac antiseptics in their wake.

Visitors have a selection of dining rooms; there are four attractive restaurants within the Hudson complex. In one of the restaurants, a black teen-age girl clears dirty dishes from tables and carts them back to the kitchen, her skinny, bony figure hardly camouflaged by her starched and striped bus-girl's uniform. The teen-ager works part time at Hudson's, after school, as do many of her peers. But as she leaves the store and returns to the east-side public housing project where she lives, her visions are not of stacks of dirty dishes and half-eaten leftovers. Instead, she is preoccupied with visions of an attractive dress that drapes the form of a pale, sophisticated-looking Hudson mannequin—an effigy of the elegant and patrician women who are long-term Hudson customers.

HUDSON'S: HUB OF AMERICA'S HEARTLAND

The teen-ager's great dark eyes have absorbed the details of the costume displayed in the store's chic "Woodward Shop," so that she can try to recreate the dress on her own sewing machine at home. Clothes are her passion. Singing, also, is her passion. The bus-girl's name is Diane Ross — yet to become the Supreme (Diana) who will, within a few short years, change from designer costume to designer costume in the course of a single stage performance . . . who will spin, with the turning of the Motown platters, into a world of wealth and glamour and celebrities.

But Diane Ross is still an unknown in 1960, and Joe Hudson is saying, in that same year, that he is concerned with the plight of the underprivileged and jobless and of the minority groups in Detroit. He gives orders to hire these people in greater numbers at the majestic Hudson store.

The editors of *Fortune* magazine are predicting great prosperity in the 1960s, accompanied by the elimination of poverty in the United States. They forecast the introduction of marvelous mechanical and technical inventions that will change the world for the better. Despite such predictions in the pages of that peerless publication, young Hudson senses that the changes of the sixties may bring their own problems and burdens to his company and to Detroit.

Neither Joe Hudson nor other prominent and civic-minded Detroiters, however, can conceive of the traumatic and overwhelming changes which will occur in the coming decade. The changes will have powerful effects on the J.L. Hudson Company. On Detroit. On the entire nation.

Some 80 years earlier, back in 1881, the birthing of Detroit's J.L. Hudson store had not been without peril. The city, smaller than Cleveland, Ohio, or Buffalo, New York, in that early era, had a population of 130,000 with Germans surpassing the French as the largest ethnic group. A magnificent clock tower, rising from a City Hall built ten years earlier, overlooked a flourishing downtown area. Visitors could make a circular climb of an iron stairway to the top of the tower, looking out on the Detroit River to the south, thick woods to the north, and down to the roofs of many mercantile establishments surrounding City Hall. The establishments included the thriving dry-goods and clothing stores of C.S. Mabley, H.G. Milward & Son, J. Congdon & Co., August Rasch & Co., J. Steinfield, and others.

Competition was keen among Detroit merchants when 35-year-old Joseph Lowthian Hudson opened the doors of his first store. He was only one of many entrepreneurs trying to run a mercantile business in the city where the firmly entrenched emporium of Newcomb, Endicott and Co. was attracting customers with its gaudy delivery wagons, decorated in red and gold.

Joseph L. Hudson, however, was determined to succeed despite the fierce competition. Struggles and adversities in his early life had served as a whetstone, honing his spirit of endurance, sharpening his sense of discipline, and edging his resolve with splendid visions of the future.

His father, Richard Hudson, had been a merchant striving to keep solvent in the tea, coffee and spice trade when Joseph was born in October of 1846 at Newcastle-upon-Tyne, England. This second child and second son was almost seven years old when his father left England for Canada to find prosperity in the New World. Two years later, Richard's wife, Elizabeth, and the couple's four children — the youngest only one year old, joined him in Hamilton, Ontario, where Richard had found employment with the Grand Trunk Railroad.

Young Joseph, nine years old in the year of his arrival at Hamilton, immediately was enrolled in school. By the time he completed an eighth grade education, he, also, was working for the Grand Trunk Railroad as a telegraph messenger boy. Shortly thereafter, 13-year-old Joseph took a steady job at five dollars per month as a grocer's helper. There would be no further schooling for him. His five dollar contribution to his family evoked a response from his gentle mother that was a source of pride to the boy. Her son was now "a young man" who could have butter on his bread, Elizabeth Hudson said.

The demands of the work-world took their toll of the boy's endurance as he worked the dawn-to-dark hours expected by his employer. His daily deliveries of groceries, often by wheelbarrow, along Hamilton's dirt roads were his toughest assignments—

especially the trips up St. James Street to the top of a steep hill where stood the home of Joshua Freeman, barrister and outstanding citizen among the city's 27,000 residents. When the barrow was loaded with a bushel of potatoes and sundries, St. James hill loomed mountainous to Joseph Hudson as he struggled with his cumbersome, almost vertical, load.

After the move from England, Richard Hudson was restless in Canada. When, in 1860, he decided he might find better opportunities in Grand Rapids, Michigan, as the gypsum industry began to thrive there, he moved his family to the U.S.A. The move did not turn out to be a fortuitous one. Young Joseph worked on a Grand Rapids farm at first. Many years later, he frequently would recall the bitterness of a cold Michigan winter as he—a boy of 14—walked the lengths of Canal and Monroe streets with his father, both searching without success for employment.

After a year of unrelenting poverty in Grand Rapids, Richard Hudson decided to move his family eastward—across the state to Pontiac, north of Detroit. Because, while living in Canada, he had become acquainted with the Mabley family, now he hoped to find employment at the Pontiac store of 25-year-old Christopher R. Mabley.

Like most immigrant groups, Cornish employers tended to choose their own countrymen as employees. The Mabley family, who had emigrated from Cornwall, England, to Toronto when Christopher Mabley was a child, had established a clothing store in the Canadian city. At age 23, young Mabley had come to Pontiac and set up his own store, parlaying a flair for flamboyance combined with a native shrewdness into a thriving $25,000-a-year business.

Soon after the Hudson family's arrival in Pontiac, Richard Hudson began working for Mabley. His son, 15-year-old Joseph, also was hired as a clerk at four dollars a week. Mabley, who quickly recognized the dependable and scrupulously honest qualities of young Hudson, doubled Joseph's salary after one month.

When Mabley decided to expand his business with the purchase of a second store in the small farming and lumber community of Ionia, Michigan—west of Pontiac, he sent Richard Hudson to manage the Ionia business. Elizabeth Hudson, who had followed her husband from England to Canada to two cities in Michigan, now followed him to still another home in the village of Ionia. But it must have been difficult for her because home and property were important to Elizabeth, who was the daughter of land owners in "the old country." Her family—the Lowthians, of Penright—had not approved her marriage to the tradesman, Richard Hudson. But Elizabeth Lowthian, at age 28, married 22-year-old Richard, nonetheless.

Although his parents and siblings moved to Ionia, Joseph Hudson remained in Pontiac with Mabley, living at the Mabley home where he was provided with three meals a day in addition to a salary which gradually increased to $800 a year. The finances of the Hudson family finally were improved. This was fortunate, since three more children had been born to Elizabeth after she came to Canada. One young child had died in infancy, but there were remaining seven Hudson brothers and sisters.

In 1863, only shortly after moving to Ionia, Elizabeth Lowthian Hudson died at age 49—exhausted by child-bearing and the family's struggles for survival. Seventeen-year-old Joseph, devastated by the death of his gentle mother, remained in Pontiac, determined to learn from his employer how to become as successful as Mabley.

Although the eldest son, named Richard for his father, helped with the work at the Ionia store, he continued attending school in the hope of soon beginning university studies. But Joseph, the tradesman's apprentice, was able to help the family, financially, to a point where the senior Richard Hudson bought an interest in Mabley's Ionia store.

According to two of the oldest items in the Hudson historical collection at the Detroit Public Library, the upturn in the fortune of the Richard Hudson family was attributed to a modest investment made in the slave trade in the early 1860s, before the death of Elizabeth Hudson. The same items claim that the return on this investment provided a profit which Richard Hudson applied to the purchase of a flour mill and pine lands to the north of Ionia as the lumbering industry boomed. In later biographical data taken from the original information, the slave trade references are omitted—possibly because they cannot be substantiated.

It was true that many merchants, usually east-coast tradesmen, were secret investors in the voyages (or a single voyage) of clipper ships which brought slaves to the western hemisphere. But even before 1860, slave trade on the high seas was considered piracy. And although, in that same year of 1860, the interstate slave trade still flourished in the southern states of this country, and an occasional illegal importation of slaves from Cuba occurred, the chief issue of the 1860 presidential election in the United States was that of the extension or prohibiting of slavery.

Although great numbers of Northerners were totally opposed to slavery, many other Northerners scorned abolitionists as fanatics. Richard Hudson was a God fearing Methodist who occasionally served as a lay preacher to congregations who also were divided on the issue of slavery. And since, on the heels of Abraham Lincoln's inauguration as President, the Civil War began in April, 1861, it seems unlikely that Richard Hudson would have made this kind of investment anytime near this period.

The time of Hudson's purchase of his partner Mabley's share in the Ionia clothing store is less ambiguous. February of 1866. Richard's son, 19 years old, then left Mabley's Pontiac store to come to Ionia and work for his father. They proudly renamed the Ionia store, R. Hudson & Son.

The village of Ionia had begun its slow growth with the 1857 arrival of the railroad—and railroad cars drawn by horses over wooden rails from Detroit and Pontiac at that early date. Only a few years after the R. Hudson & Son store had been established on Main Street, Ionia's leading citizen, George Webber, complained that it was "getting so crowded around here that a man's got to put up fences to keep the neighbors' cows off his property."

Later, the Webber family would be connected closely to the Hudsons by business interests and with the marriage of George Webber's son, Joseph T. Webber, to the Hudsons' second daughter, Mary Eleanor. But Mary Eleanor was not yet 14 years old when her brother Joseph came to Ionia to work with his father in the store in which they now shared complete ownership. Joseph's sister Anna was 16 years old and Eliza was the baby of the family.

In the absence of the oldest son, Richard, who began his studies at the University of Michigan in 1867, the second son, Joseph, continued to take as much responsibility as did the father for the welfare of the younger Hudson children. Their hard work in the Ionia store kept the business profitable for seven years, rising in profits from $4,000 that first year.

In 1869, the Ionia post office displayed a list of names of citizens who had to pay taxes, in accordance with the first national income tax levied by Congress during the Civil War (and continued for several years afterwards to pay a government debt of nearly $3 billion.) The names of Richard Hudson and Joseph L. Hudson, whose store was now known as the New York Clothing store, were prominent among those of Ionian taxpayers. The amount on which each Hudson had to pay taxes was $1,250 — the income remaining after a $1,000 deduction, plus "other lawful deductions."

The Hudsons then expanded their business into the neighboring village of Portland by setting up the younger brother, teen-age James, in a mercantile partnership there — Smith & Hudson. But the increasing inflation of the post-Civil War years soon led to the Panic of 1873, which rapidly depressed the economy, forcing 89 railroads into the hands of receivers and closing nearly half the nation's iron and steel plants.

Ionia sawmills whined to a halt in 1873, and a distraught Richard Hudson, worried about business failure and about his investment in pine lands, died that same year. The Hudson business, owing money to suppliers, now was the responsibility of 27-year-old Joseph — half owner, and trustee of the remaining 50% for the rest of the family. He took a loss on the flour mill, and lost another $8,000 when a local lumber dealer failed in business, owing money to the Hudson's.

Despite his personal financial difficulties, Joseph L. Hudson was elected City Treasurer when Ionia became a city in April of 1873. For three more years, he struggled unsuccessfully to keep the Ionia store solvent, finally settling with his creditors for 60 cents on the dollar. Then, leaving the Ionia store under the management of his younger brother, James B. Hudson, Joseph came to Detroit in 1877 to meet with his former employer, Christopher R. Mabley, at the six-story Russell House — Detroit's leading hotel.

Mabley had opened a Detroit clothing store on Woodward Avenue, right next to the popular Russell House, in 1870. Six years later, he built a new and larger store on the same site, expanding into women's and children's clothing and notions, then into furniture and appliances at 15 and 17 Monroe Avenue. Mabley had not forgotten the dependable qualities of his former apprentice, and now offered Joseph Hudson a job as manager of his new store's clothing department at $50 a week. Hudson started working immediately—on the same day that 14-year-old Robert B. Tannahill also began working, under Hudson's supervision, for Mabley.

In the following four years of Hudson's employment by Mabley in Detroit, both men benefitted from their alliance. Hudson learned a great deal about public relations and sales promotions from his employer, a natural showman who conducted pie-eating contests in the show-windows and high-wire walking exhibitions across Woodward Avenue in front of the store.

With Hudson "minding the store," it was possible for the gregarious Mabley to freely indulge his own taste for jovial company and hard liquor by means of a private door which the store owner ordered built into a wall leading directly from the Mabley emporium into the Russell House bar. When he was in the bar, his employees were instructed to warn him of any unexpected arrival of the redoubtable Mrs. Mabley, who aspired to the kind of elegance and status that she felt were threatened by her husband's affinity for alcohol.

When Joseph Hudson first came to Detroit to work for Mabley, he lived in his employer's home at the corner of Woodward and Holden. He soon decided, however, to move into a rented room at the plush Russell House. When, as frequently happened, Mabley disappeared from the environs of the store and his home for a two or three-days' span, his wife invariably sent a message to Joseph, at the store or at the Russell House, asking him to locate her husband and return him to the Mabley mansion.

By way of these searches, Hudson soon became acquainted with his employer's haunts, quickly returning the store owner to Mrs. Mabley who appreciated the discreet behavior of her husband's employee in handling her inebriated spouse. Hudson, a nondrinker, became an even more dedicated teetotaler as he experienced the reversal of authority roles between the store owner and employee when Mabley was under the influence of alcohol.

HUDSON'S TRADITIONS AND THEIR ROOTS

After working in Detroit for one year, Hudson was provided with a one-fourth share of Mabley's annual profits, and a guarantee of $7,500 per year. With his family in mind, Joe Hudson then bought a home in Detroit at 14 Madison Avenue. The home was large enough to accommodate his younger brother William, who moved in as he, too, began to work for Mabley. Joseph's two unmarried sisters, Anna and Eliza, also lived with their older brother and managed his household.

By 1880, Mabley was not in good health. Knowing that his store would be managed capably by his trusted employee, Mabley decided to take an ocean voyage to England. He was accompanied by Joseph Hudson's older brother, Richard, who had graduated from the university in 1871, served as a minister in the Methodist Episcopal Church for eight years, and had recently begun teaching history at the University of Michigan.

Before his departure, Mabley gave specific instructions to Joe Hudson for acquiring free advertising for the store. He told Hudson to erect a huge sign at the side of the Mabley house — a sign that would attract the attention of throngs of people as they walked into the fairgrounds to attend the annual State Agricultural Association Fair set up on property stretching away from the Mabley mansion.

Following orders, Hudson had a giant billboard erected, 60 feet long and 15 feet high, next to the imposing Mabley home. As painters prepared to letter the sign with bold advertising, an aghast Catherine Mabley stormed out of the house, insisting that the name Mabley was not to appear on the sign.

Still determined to carry out his employer's orders, Hudson had his workers remove the sign, place it on a vacant lot right next to the Mabley property, and paint the Mabley advertising message in large, vivid letters. When Hudson found the sign hacked apart and chopped into kindling wood the following day, he immediately had his workers build a second sign of similar proportions. After the new sign was erected and painted, he hired two guards to stand watch at the site.

If Joseph Hudson thought that was the end of the matter, he was wrong. Mrs. Mabley's horse-drawn carriage soon clattered south on Woodward Avenue and downtown to the entrance of the Mabley store where her coachman assisted her from the carriage. The

13

store-owner's wife swept angrily into Hudson's private office, all thoughts of haughty elegance forgotten as, according to a *Detroit News-Tribune* report, "she sprang at Hudson, attacking him with her fingernails" while she "poured abuse" on the store manager.

Hudson's calm self-control, which Catherine Mabley previously had admired, now inflamed her to even greater rage. As she picked up a spittoon to hurl at the store manager, Hudson acted quickly, seizing her arms to avoid violence. Then he forced her to sit on a sofa until she agreed to leave the store, still threatening him with discharge from the employ of Mabley. But the garish sign remained under guard on the vacant lot.

Although Joseph Hudson was able to oppose his employer's wife and to withstand her display of violent temper, Christopher R. Mabley had no stamina for thwarting the strong will of the contentious Catherine. When the store owner returned from his three-month vacation, Mrs. Mabley met him at the pier in New York, launching into her tale of Joseph Hudson's shocking behavior. Mabley's attempt to defend Hudson was feeble. He soon perceived that it was impossible to placate his wife without chastising Hudson. On his return to the store, he was forced to support Catherine Mabley's biased version of her clash with his employee. The relationship between the two men rapidly disintegrated.

Before leaving C.R. Mabley's employ, Joe Hudson and his brother James bought the Toledo, Ohio, store owned by Mabley's brother, William. As James Hudson went to Toledo to reorganize William Mabley's former business, Joe Hudson's fancies of setting up his own business in Detroit began to crystallize. He determined to set up a J.L. Hudson store in Michigan's largest city . . . a store that would become a bigger and more prestigious establishment than that of Christopher R. Mabley.

2

The Mabley-Hudson Feud

With $60,000 accumulated in less than four years of working for Mabley in Detroit, Joseph Hudson was ready to open his own business within three months of his separation from his former employer. In March, 1881, Mabley's chief competitor—Newcomb, Endicott & Co.,—moved from its first-floor headquarters in the handsome Detroit Opera House to a new five-story building ("lofty" the newspapers gushed) at 190–198 Woodward. To most Detroit merchants, Newcomb, Endicott's move to the $110,000 Renaissance-style building seemed impractical, since the new location was north of the bustling downtown area reaching from Jefferson Avenue, near the Detroit River, to Campus Martius.

At this point, Mabley was concerned less about his traditional adversary, Newcomb, Endicott, than about his former protege, Joseph Hudson, who rented Newcomb, Endicott's vacated Opera House headquarters, just off Woodward, for his new business. Although Mabley may have thought of his former protege as an ungrateful young upstart, Hudson was 34 years old when he opened his store—J.L. Hudson, Clothier. He looked even older because of his most prominent feature—his large head, dome-shaped and already balding. Everything else about Joseph L. Hudson met the definition of average: his height, slightly above medium; his weight, 160 pounds; his blue eyes and medium brown eyebrows and mustache.

The feisty little Cornishman, C.R. Mabley, was already entertaining considerable regret that he had divested himself of the services of Joe Hudson. In so doing, he now discovered that he also had unwittingly divested himself of the services of many other trusted employees, including 18-year-old Robert Tannahill, who were induced to join Hudson at his new store. Mabley's embarrassment at the loss of so many employees was compounded when Hudson ran a grand-opening newspaper advertisement for his store, slated to open for business on Saturday, April 2, 1881. The top of the giant advertisement boasted a listing of twenty experienced salemen, cutters and fitters who would staff the store. Sixteen of these names were followed by the phrase, in bold-faced type, "Formerly with C.R. Mabley." Joseph L. Hudson's younger brother William was one of the 16. William, who had been promoted to department manager in Mabley's Detroit store, had organized the mass exodus of Mabley employees.

The rest of the Hudson advertisement, announcing opening-day hours that ran until eleven p.m., copied the florid style consistently used by Mabley. The ad invited visitors to receive "polite attention" from the "Gents Furnishing Department" staff, to visit the "handsomely furnished and beautifully stocked Children's Clothing Department," to enjoy "Free Promenade Concerts" in the morning, afternoon, and evening performed by the Detroit Opera House Orchestra conducted by Professor R. Speil. The announcement included an entertainment listing—three separate programs of marches and overtures.

Mabley certainly held no monopoly on newspaper advertising, but because he had been the first businessman to run a full-page advertisement in a Detroit paper, he had a proprietary zeal for this mode of promoting his store. At the time he tried to run his original newspaper ad after opening a Detroit store in 1870, he found it necessary to threaten to file a lawsuit when newspaper management was unwilling to accept business ads of a garish type. Now, in 1881, Mabley bought newspaper space to run his flamboyant advertising right next to the equally grandiose ads of J.L. Hudson. "We will undersell all competitors," the Mabley ad claimed. "We do not care what prices they name on goods, we will discount them . . . If it is in Merchant Tailoring, we will nearly double discount every time and on Furniture, we will leave them in the shade."

Mabley offered the toughest, but not the only, competition to Hudson. Among newspaper stories of suicides, murders, and alienation-of-affection suits, and mixed with bits of homespun humor, puns, small ads for Cuticura, elixirs, and popular cures for catarrh, were the advertisements of J. Steinfield, Newcomb, Endicott and Co., and others. The smaller Steinfield refused to be eclipsed by larger stores such as that of C.R. Mabley with its pompous claim of "occupying 3,500,000 cubic feet" of space. Steinfield took up the challenge by boasting of "occupying 203,515,200 cubic inches of room." But the struggle between Hudson and Mabley was more heated than the competition among other business rivals. It mushroomed into a personal obsession for mastery on the part of both businessmen.

On the Saturday of the Hudson store opening, carriages "in waiting" blocked Woodward Avenue and incoming streets as ladies, in large plumed hats and long full skirts that swept the wooden streets, moved in and out of the J.L. Hudson store, on to the C.R. Mabley emporium, and to other business places within the crowded few blocks of the central shopping area. Mingling with the grander ladies of the carriage trade were middle class people who arrived on Detroit's streetcars, drawn along strip rails by teams of horses clopping over cobblestones spread between the rails so the horses would have better footing. Dismounting passengers carried the odor of horses and the stench of dirty streetcars in the folds of their skirts and cloaks as they joined the crowds moving into Hudson's store—described by the *Detroit Free Press* as "a crowd which swelled to almost suffocating proportions."

The same newspaper described the men's furnishings department at Hudson's . . . the fine fabrics of its "customs" section, its "handsome upper and counter showcases" and some 30 tables "loaded with a fine assortment of ready-made clothing." The description went on to boast of a slight elevation at the rear of the store with "departments devoted to custom tailoring for children, to the ladies' toilet, and to retiring rooms for gentlemen and children."

17

HUDSON'S: HUB OF AMERICA'S HEARTLAND

The new store, its painted walls absorbing the carbon smell of its gas lights, had neither a telephone nor typewriter. These handy gadgets were in existence in 1881, the first Detroit telephone having been installed in 1877, but J.L. Hudson, Clothier, relied on messenger boys and hand-written missives and ledgers in the early years of its presence in Detroit — as did most other businesses.

On opening day, the great bell in the City Hall tower clanged its measure of the passing hours as Detroiters clustered near the store to hear the Opera House Orchestra perform its morning concert . . . afternoon concert . . . evening concert. And when the sounds of horns and cymbals and drums faded at the conclusion of each march or overture, the sounds of other horns and cymbals and drums resounded from the C.R. Mabley store, where Hudson's pugnacious rival had hired Professor Gardner's Detroit Band to boom a megablast of band music, coaxing customers to Mabley's doors. The Hudson-Mabley battle intensified as, on April 3 and 6, Hudson ran a thank-you notice in the newspaper.

> "I desire to return my hearty thanks to the people of Detroit and vicinity who thronged my new establishment in such large numbers on the day of its opening, and gave such cordial expression to their congratulations and good wishes for the success of the enterprise . . .
>
> . . . I shall sell goods at such figures that no one can afford to undersell me. Goods have been marked in plain figures, and a strictly one-price system has been adopted, so that the money of the poor man will go as far as that of the rich . . ."

Because dickering and bargaining between customer and clerk had been the standard method of buying and selling merchandise, which had been deliberately left unmarked, this advertised "one-price" policy became associated in many customers' minds with Hudson as its originator. Some customers, unwilling to buy without bargaining, simply walked out of the Hudson store when they discovered they could not dicker with the clerks or owner.

C.R. Mabley, however, had been advertising and employing the one-price policy even before Hudson went into business for himself. Now, as Hudson advertised "plain figures and a strictly one-price system" in his thank-you notice, a resentful Mabley told his friends that he would give the Hudson store "three months to exist."

To help hasten the expected failure of the Hudson store, Mabley plastered signs advertising his own store on barns and fences. Hudson did the same, until it seemed that every barn or fence within a radius of 100 miles flaunted either a Mabley or Hudson sign—sometimes both.

The Hudson store continued to flourish as the 1881 Christmas holiday season approached and the downtown stores began staying open until ten p.m. So many shoppers crowded Woodward Avenue between Campus Martius and Grand River during the holidays that policemen stood at crosswalks to escort ladies and children across the cedar-block avenue to prevent pedestrians from being run down by horses and carriages, drays, or streetcars.

When the Hudson store continued to draw customers in 1882, Mabley stepped up the pace of his newspaper ads. Hudson retaliated, claiming "the most extensive, elegant, and attractive men's, boys' and children's spring clothing stock in the state." Mabley's adjoining ad boasted of "the most natty styles in children's hats ever shown in Detroit," promising that "every boy buying a hat of us this week will be presented with a baseball or bat; ladies buying furnishing goods for their gentlemen friends will receive a 'companion' (printed plaque) to those distributed last week."

Hudson responded with printed promises of baseball-schedule books to men customers, "Sure Pop Whips" to boys, and "neat little cylindrical boxes, containing the Best Quality of Court Plaster" to general customers, prompting Mabley to launch a fierce price war. Advertising "fearful low prices," Mabley claimed that "we have marked every dollar's worth lower than ever known since the Creation, or since man's apparel has exceeded the dimensions of a fig leaf." A later Mabley ad was more strident. *We Want Money* it proclaimed. *Money We Must Have. To Get It, we must Slaughter! Slaughter! Slaughter!*

Hudson not only survived Mabley's ad campaign, but he competed with Mabley in a price slashing duel in which Hudson promised free Waterford watches to the purchasers of certain suits. Similar ads attracted swarms of customers to the Hudson store for a gigantic sale in June, 1882. As the doors opened at seven a.m., women grabbed at $5 suits for their husbands, racks swaying as they frantically searched for their choices in patterns and sizes. Men snatched vests and coats, and rummaged through piles of trousers as frenzied clerks struggled to prevent chaos.

In one day, 900 suits sold. But the crush of people and disarray of merchandise grew to such proportions that Hudson had to close the doors of the store until order was restored. At the close of each sale day, exhausted clerks tried to sort and arrange scattered and mixed merchandise as Hudson's department managers returned to the store with more supplies from wholesalers to replace broken stock.

Business hours on ordinary days were as lengthy as sales-day hours. Seven a.m. until eight p.m. for five months a year—July through December. A nine p.m. closing from April through June, and a seven p.m. closing in the winter months—January through March. On Saturday nights, hours were extended, frequently to eleven p.m.

Young boy employees (under 14 year of age) received weekly wages of $3.50 to $4.50 for working the same long hours as adults. Hudson clearly remembered his own youthful labors as a delivery boy struggling with a loaded wheelbarrow. He had a good deal of empathy for messenger boys, cash boys, and parcel boys who delivered Hudson packages on foot. But the general employer view of such youthful workers was that the younger they were, the more tractable, and the better service an employer could expect from them.

Many years later, William A. Petzold—a parcel boy who came through the ranks to become secretary-treasurer of the company—would recall the antics of another young parcel boy named Freddie Rick. The brash, red-headed Freddie, assigned to carry a few parcels to the Hudson home at 14 Madison, left the store at closing time. Ahead of him, J.L. Hudson was walking up the street. Freddie sprinted to catch up with his employer. "Are you going home, Mr. Hudson?" the boy asked. "Would you mind taking these along with you?"

With a mixture of surprise at the request and admiration for the

THE MABLEY-HUDSON FEUD

enterprising youngster, Hudson took the parcels and carried them to his home.

In an era when there were no child-labor restrictions, the child worker in a dry goods store conceivably considered himself a good deal more fortunate than the wispy, pale-faced children at work in mills, coal mines, garment factories and manufacturing plants. Such plants multiplied in Detroit in the 1880s, turning out boots and shoes, clothing, tobacco, cigars, and mostly iron and steel products. The number of manufacturing jobs in Detroit more than doubled during the 1880s, and as jobs and population increased, more shoppers poured into the downtown stores.

Finally resigning himself to having a Hudson store as a thriving competitor, Mabley turned his considerable strategic talents to enhancing his own business and his image as an entrepreneur. The first Detroit business to install Edison incandescent lights was Metcalf Bros., dry goods store, in January, 1883, but shortly before the end of 1883, Mabley illuminated his store with a U.S. Electric Light Company system.

In the same year, citizens of Detroit were dazzled by the brilliance of the city's first electric-arc streets lights erected at Jefferson and Woodward. More of these bright lights soon were placed in various parts of the city — built on lofty grids, some of which towered 60 feet high; others more than 150 feet. Like the lights at Jefferson and Woodward, they illuminated the heavens but left the town shadowed.

In 1883, Hudson still did not have electric lights in his store. But he introduced other innovations to attract customers. That fall, he outfitted 25 members of a brass band, formed by his employees, with bright red coats, navy trousers with white stripes at the sides, and with helmets with red plumes. The uniforms, made by Hudson tailors, gave a spiffy "spit-n-polish" image to the band, which performed not only at the store but also at the Princess Roller Skating Rink and at ceremonial events about town.

Although Joseph Hudson did not install a telephone in his Detroit store until 1887, he began expanding his business after sales for 1883 rose to $234,600 at the Detroit store. In 1884, he bought a 50% interest in Symington Carpets & Upholstery Goods store at 141-145 Woodward Avenue. The carpet and upholstery goods store then became known as Hudson & Symington. And in January, 1885, Hudson purchased a large clothing store in Cleveland, Ohio—Stein, Hirsch & Co.

Mabley observed the start of Hudson expansion in 1884-85 with a dawning realization of his former protege's inevitable success. Although Mabley already had expanded his own business into two Ionia stores and into stores in Baltimore, Louisville, Toledo, and into a Cincinnati store featuring a skating rink, he was unwilling, now, to be upstaged by Hudson. Mabley began to visualize plans for a spectacular building that not only would showcase the Mabley emporium, but also would provide a magnificent tribute to the Mabley name.

He knew that Detroiter Frank Hammond's meat-packing plant in Indiana was being sold for three-quarters of a million dollars, and that Hammond was proposing to build Detroit's first skyscraper with the money. Determined to surpass any skyscraper that Hammond would build, Mabley spent $700,000 for choice property at the corner of Michigan and Woodward, intending to build a Mabley skyscraper that would house his store in a taller and more magnificent high-rise building than the structure planned by Hammond.

Neither man lived to see his vision of a skyscraper become a reality. When Hammond died in 1886, however, his widow carried out his plans. She had a ten-story, red brick building erected at Fort and Griswold, with marble fireplaces for heating. Its official opening in 1890 was celebrated by a state holiday featuring a high-wire artist who wore baskets on his feet as he pushed a wheelbarrow across a wire stretched from the Hammond building rooftop to the tower of City Hall.

When the Hammond Building sagged six inches shortly after its gala opening, its prestige was scarcely marred. Henry B. Joy, later to become an automotive magnate with the Packard Motor Car Company, was only one of many tenants—mostly lawyers—who occupied the highly desirable office space in the towering building.

Christopher R. Mabley, who died in June, 1885—a year earlier than Hammond's death, must have had a premonition that he might not live to observe his fiftieth birthday. In 1884, he had reorganized his business and formed a new firm, Mabley and Company, making stockholders of his faithful department managers. Mabley's attorney, Henry Wisner, was also Joseph L. Hudson's attorney. And, at the time of Mabley's death, Wisner spoke of the two men as "business enemies." A *Detroit News* article quoted Wisner. "Socially, they were not on amicable terms, but they let each other alone. The popular idea that Hudson's is a branch of Mabley's business is erroneous."

Such a "popular idea" vexed the normally even-tempered Hudson who had employed Mabley's younger brother, John, since 1884. And, as Joe Hudson soon would discover, he still was to be involved in the affairs of the late C.R. Mabley.

Seven months following Mabley's death, his 49-year-old widow, Catherine, was married in New York City to William J. Spiers, a 25-year-old Detroit minister and a private tutor to the Mableys' only son—a seven year old. A court battle immediately erupted over the distribution of the Mabley fortune as the two adult Mabley daughters publicly wrangled with Catherine Mabley-Spiers who struggled to retain guardianship of her four minor children.

Their mother, the older daughters claimed, had an "ungovernable temper" and treated her children cruelly. Young Spiers, they insisted, was a fortune hunter.

Newspapers headlined the affair in purple prose, as Catherine Mabley-Spiers denied that the young minister had married her for any reason other than true love. "The Furious Devotion of Mr. Spiers for Mrs. Mabley" one headline read. "Spiers' Uncontrollable Passion" another proclaimed.

Mabley's brother John testified in defense of his sister-in-law; his employer, Hudson, testified on behalf of the older daughters. Under oath, Hudson said that he had formerly been a Mabley partner and had lived in the Mabley home. He had observed Mrs. Mabley's "violent temper" and gave his opinion that she was "not a fit person" to have charge of the children.

"You have quarreled with Mrs. Mabley, have you not?" the widow's lawyer asked.

"No, sir, she quarreled with me," Hudson replied, adding that he was "kicked out of the business" after Mrs. Mabley came into the store and "excitedly assaulted" him.

The personal bitterness between the two sides was partly

assuaged when Catherine Mabley admitted being in such "poor health" that she wanted her attorney to take over her guardianship of the minor children, as well as management of her business affairs. With this concession, public interest in the proceedings declined as only the two opposing lawyers continued the maneuvering to determine which attorney would retain the most power in the estate.

Regardless of any public embarrassment engendered by the court hearing, a second Mabley brother, Thomas, joined the Hudson sales force in 1886, followed by his brother Fred the next year. And as Hudson advanced John Mabley to manager of the men's clothing department, Miss Maude Mabley, eldest of the minor Mabley children, and Warren Mabley also became Hudson employees.

The house that Joseph L. Hudson had bought at 14 Madison Avenue, only a short distance from his store in the Opera House building, had become a family home for various Hudsons. The unmarried sisters, Anna and Eliza, still managed the house for their brothers, Joseph and William. Through the Hudsons' association with Frederick Clay, treasurer at the Opera House, Eliza Hudson met Clay's brother William, a railroad clerk. When 28-year-old William Clay and Eliza Hudson were married in 1884, the newlyweds lived at the comfortable Madison Avenue home of Joseph Hudson, who also gave his new brother-in-law a job, clerking at the store.

Despite Joe Hudson's strong teetotaler beliefs, his equally strong sense of family loyalty restrained his intolerance of the fondness that Eliza's husband displayed for alcohol. Such fondness for drink was easily indulged in Detroit where saloons flourished.

The Webbers, who still lived in Ionia with their son, six-year-old Richard, and their two-year-old daughter Louise, became parents once again in January, 1886. This time, Mary Eleanor Hudson Webber gave birth to twin boys, named Joseph Lowthian and James Benson Webber by the proud parents. The children's Uncle Joseph Hudson dutifully came to Ionia by train to visit his infant nephews. As they lay in their cradles, the red-faced twins were rechristened in one of Joe Hudson's rare flashes of dry humor. "I think you ought to call them 'Tom and Jerry'," the prohibitionist

Hudson joked. Even his jokes were taken seriously, and the twins were known, thereafter, as Tom and Jerry Webber.

In that same year, the twins' older brother, Richard, became his Uncle Joseph's protege, spending much of his time at the Hudson home in Detroit. At age seven, the boy accompanied his uncle to New York City on a buying trip. It soon became clear to everyone in the family that young Richard Webber was being groomed by Joseph L. Hudson to become his aide and, eventually, his successor.

In 1887, when the Detroit Opera House underwent remodeling, Joe Hudson moved his store and its entourage from the Opera House into the six-story Woodward Avenue building occupied by Hudson & Symington, on the west side of Woodward between Michigan and State. Hudson & Symington moved north to 225-229 Woodward, and Joe Hudson planned to build a new and larger Hudson store. First, however, there were certain obligations—moral, but not legal—that he wanted to discharge.

Former Eastern creditors, who had accepted a settlement of 60 cents on the dollar at the time Hudson had gone backrupt in Ionia eleven years previously, were amazed in August of 1888 when they received Joseph Hudson's checks for the additional 40% plus compound interest. In return, they sent gifts and letters of appreciation for what the E.H. Van Ingren & Co. of New York termed as Hudson's "high sense of commercial honor . . ."

When Joe Hudson learned, a year later, that the First Presbyterian Church at Gratiot and Farmer would be sold, he immediately offered to purchase the nearly 13,000 square feet of property as a site for the store he wanted to build. The church congregation soon moved farther out Woodward Avenue, away from the business area, and Hudson bought the vacant property for $71,000. Looking to the future, he also bought two adjoining Farmer Street lots, an area of approximately 5,900 square feet, for an addtional $39,000. On March 1, 1890, he began razing the old buildings on the property to make way for an eight-story Hudson store, which would be built with $242,000 borrowed from David Whitney.

Business leaders and friends offered unheeded advice. The new Hudson store would be doomed, they said, by its obscure, side-street location. It was impossible, they counseled, to draw trade away from Woodward Avenue competition.

But as the Presbyterian Church was dismantled and then leveled, Joseph L. Hudson could envision a new and splendid Hudson edifice, fronting 210 feet on Farmer Street and 100 feet on Gratiot Avenue, rising from the rubble. Still, it was not likely he imagined, at that early date, that the Gratiot-Farmer building would become only a nucleus of the great Hudson mart at the core of a vigorous, vital Detroit.

3

Grand Opening

Detroit's Gay Nineties were as buoyant and animated as those in any of the fourteen larger cities in the country. Bicycling became a craze at the middle of that decade with replacement of the high-wheel cycle by the "drop frame" type, with pneumatic tires, that women could ride. Wearing divided skirts, high laced shoes, and sailor hats set squarely on their heads, women decorously pumped their bicycles down Woodward Avenue. Their more unladylike counterparts, who were likely to ascribe to the suffragette movement and might dare to engage in such coarse behavior as whistling in public, pumped much faster, bent over the handlebars in what was considered an unbecoming imitation of male wheelsmen, known as "scorchers."

"Scorchers"—so named because of their penchant for racing about recklessly—whizzed past the assortment of carriages, wagons, and pedestrians on the streets of Detroit in the mid-1890s. Between 1886 and 1891, electric trolleys had replaced all the stinking horsedrawn streetcars on Woodward Avenue, kindling a new, slick image for the city as the "electrics" clattered and clanged along their routes, startling pedestrians and frightening horses pulling drays and carriages. Only the intrepid "scorchers" dared to challenge the trolleys, weaving around the "electrics" as the cars, powered by magical antennae, swayed down the avenue. Skittering pedestrians stepped lively to dodge helmeted policemen, furiously pedaling their own cycles in pursuit of madcap "scorchers."

But high wheel cycles, ridden only by young men, were still in vogue at the end of July 1891, when workmen were varnishing and garnishing and furbishing the interior of the new eight-story J.L. Hudson building in preparation for its grand opening. At this same time, Detroiters looked forward to an unprecedented celebration by the GAR (Grand Army of the Republic) observing its silver anniversary with an encampment in Detroit the first week of August.

Hudson's Band, blaring the strains of Sousa's "Washington Post" march, was one of 122 bands from across the nation participating in the celebration. Many prestigious visitors, including former President Rutherford B. Hayes and Clara Barton, were among some 100,000 people who poured into Detroit for the festivities. Hayes, Barton, and other eminent guests were housed at the Russell House, its vividly canopied windows now merged into a riot of color—swathes of bunting and an aggregation of flags decorating the hotel.

A huge parade of Union veterans of the Civil War provided a magnificent spectacle of mounted police and cavalry army units in resplendent dress uniforms as they rode prancing horses, setting the pace for marchers over a three-mile parade route. Spectators at the back of crowds lining the route heard the beat and blare of martial music and caught glimpses of shiny brass-buttoned coats. Black wide-rimmed hats. Gold-corded trousers. Of dignitaries swinging canes and wearing tall silk hats.

The J.L. Hudson Company, not yet in its new building, joined in the celebration by offering a Civil War historical book to each veteran who came to the store and bought a ten dollar suit. Despite gloomy predictions by other Detroit businessmen, it now was reported that the Gratiot-Farmer property on which the new Hudson store was being built, had nearly doubled in value since its purchase less than two years previously. And as the final brass-toned notes of trumpet and trombone faded at the close of the GAR anniversary week, the attention of Detroiters focused on the handsome, 123-foot-high, J.L. Hudson building, its slim pillars and rows of gracefully arched windows encasing still unrevealed aisles of pyramided treasures behind its vaulted and locked doors.

In the few weeks previous to the September Grand Opening of the new store, Joseph Hudson conferred frequently with the 27-year-old man who would manage his Detroit store—E.J. Hickey. Like his employer, Hickey was a self made man who had scrambled for jobs since he had left school at age nine to work as a cash boy for George Peck & Co. In his teens, Hickey managed to get some more schooling, while also working as cash boy in C.R. Mabley's hat department. When he joined the ranks of those leaving Mabley's employ to work at Hudson's Opera-House store, Hickey was promoted to package wrapper, then to cashier, bookkeeper, and finally to manager.

Both Hudson and Hickey cultivated thick mustaches. But Hudson's chin now was beardless, although he grew mutton-chop whiskers which, in company with his thick eyebrows, constrasted strangely with his large and hairless head. Young Hickey was a handsome fellow with not only a mustache and beard, but also a full head of hair that must have been the envy of his employer.

Fred Saxby, a former manager of C.R. Mabley's tailoring, was to manage the first floor tailoring department in Hudson's new store. Recessed into a gallery just above the tailoring department were four offices—the first, boasting an elegant Venetian clock, was the domain of head honcho Joseph L. Hudson. Manager Hickey's office adjoined that of Hudson. The third office housed Hudson's advertising manager and "writer," the fourth, Hudson's head bookkeeper.

Among Detroit businessmen, the main topic of discussion was Joe Hudson and the money he had spent to equip his new store with the latest in modern technology. A $25,000 expenditure for engines and pumps and boilers to provide energy for his own lighting, heating, and power. For the lighting—large switchboards and automatic Sperry Dynamos, "five of them being 40-arc light, one 200-light automatic Fisher incandescent," a Detroit newspaper reported. For heating—air blown into a superheated reservoir with a large fan and conducted under the floor over heated pipes, and then pumped throughout the building by an Atlas engine. For the powering of four elevators to run from basement to eighth floor — three Laidlaw & Dunn pumps with a capacity of 1000 gallons of water per minute, providing pressure powerful enough to "send the elevators a distance of 125 feet in 15 seconds." And for the maintenance of the equipment — an engineer, a fireman, and a electrician.

On opening day, September 17, Hudson's nephew — 12-year-old Richard Webber — held the key to open the doors of the new store. As his sister, Louise, watched him turn the key in the lock, curious Detroiters crowded into Hudson's aisles, coming through the Gratiot entrance into the men's furnishing department — rich with oaken fixtures and expanses of plate glass. Apart from a few female employees such as Miss Conway of the millinery department, the clerks and department managers — all male — wore dark suits, white shirts, bow ties, and high stiff collars. Although the unbearded look recently had come into fashion, a clean-shaven upper lip was considered the mark of immaturity. Few Hudson clerks were bearded, but all wore mustaches.

The disorderly grand opening of the first Hudson store had no reverberations in the circumspect procession of visitors through the lofty Hudson's of 1891. From behind the clear-paned showcases of derby hats, neatly arranged displays of pointy-toed shoes, and carefully sorted dark, or faintly-striped, wools in the dry goods department, relentlessly smiling, impeccably courteous male clerks were clearly in command — directing visitors through the tailoring department and on toward the elevators and the grand staircase of quartered oak; writing sales slips by hand in elaborately ornamental Spencerian script.

The elegance of the huge store was impressive enough to subdue any uncivil behavior. One particularly gracious feature was the ladies' reception room located at the staircase landing, with a view of the busy first floor. Women, whose tightly laced corsets allowed for only shallow breathing, could stop to rest at the reception room, furnished with comfortable chairs and with tables, magazines and, even, stationery. There also were water closets on the second, third, fourth and fifth floors, shoppers learned with considerable appreciation.

From the reception room, women lifted the hems of their full skirts over their high shoes to walk on up to the L-shaped ladies' furnishing department. Here, Miss Conway assisted in fitting unwieldy bonnets on heads wound with thick braids or sporting coils or puffs of hair. She helped customers select feathers, flowers, bows and veilings to embellish their bonnets, then directed them to the dressmaking and the cloak departments.

In the close confines of the swooshing, vibrating elevators, male passengers stood stiffly, removing their derby hats and holding them against their chests as if the Hudson Band had struck up "The Star Spangled Banner." Female passengers tried to prevent their bustles from being crushed against the wall panels and to guard their taffeta dust ruffles from the tread of others' shoes. Such opening day discomforts did not diminish store-patrons' appreciation of the Hudson & Symington fourth-floor display of lush carpets and draperies, or the Hudson & Symington array of furniture on the fifth and sixth floors, presided over by Campbell Symington.

The seventh floor, visitors were told, would be outfitted with children's toys and holiday accessories for the Christmas season. And the eighth floor was the domain of storerooms and workrooms for carpenters, painters, cobblers and carpet makers. Above the eighth floor, a roof-top observatory accommodated visitors who could view most of the City of Detroit from the Hudson roof, although the 11-story Hammond Building loomed three stories higher than the Hudson store.

Hudson's seventh floor assortment of toys, dolls, and "fancy goods" attracted an abundance of shoppers from Detroit's population of more than 200,000 that first holiday season of 1891. They bought cylindrical records for their Gramophones, Kodak box cameras, shaving mugs, and Uneeda Biscuits which could be purchased neatly packaged instead of being scooped from open barrels.

Although there were less than 1,124 blacks listed as employed in the Detroit City Directory of 1890, J.L. Hudson advertised for customers in a Detroit black newspaper, *The Plaindealer*. He welcomed its readers to his store and invited them to "Walk about, look about, you'll attract no attention."

Detroit shoppers flocked to the J.L. Hudson sewing-machine department where New Home and Standard machines whirred in crescendo or diminuendo, dependent on the operator's speed, or lack thereof, in applying foot to treadle. For less expensive gifts, shoppers wandered through the crockery department, admiring displays of kitchen utensils and decorative items referred to as "art pottery." The "Art Room" featured a dining table, its linen cloth a snowy background for cut-glass pieces, fine china, and gleaming silverware — a handsome model for the kind of gracious living that was becoming accessible to more upper middle-class families.

By this time, ten years from the date he started his first business in Detroit, Joe Hudson had opened stores in five more cities in addition to Toledo and Cleveland — Sandusky, Ohio; Grand Rapids, Michigan; St. Louis, Missouri; St. Paul, Minnesota; and Buffalo, New York. He sent his brother William to oversee the Buffalo store.

The family's former store in Ionia had been sold after being managed for a few years in the 1880s by Joseph T. Webber, husband of Joe Hudson's sister, Mary Eleanor. The remaining Hudson's stores achieved a combined sales volume of $2 million in 1891 along with public recognition of Hudson's as the biggest retailer of men's clothing in America.

Although millions of Americans traveled to Chicago in 1893 to see the World's Fair futuristic city built at the shores of Lake Michigan, they returned to hometowns already caught up in the Panic of 1893. Since 1890, the plight of American farmers had worsened steadily because of savage droughts, declining production, and increasing mortgages that led to foreclosures. At the same time, with the passage of the Republican Silver Act devaluating silver, American capitalists were gripped by terror for two reasons . . . dwindling gold reserves and emerging labor problems as workers began to strike for better wages and union representation.

Banks closed across the country in 1893, including the Third National Bank of Detroit of which Joe Hudson was an inactive director. Going to Washington D.C. with Michigan's bank examiner, Hudson was give permission, as the bank's appointed receiver, to liquidate the bank as soon as funds could be raised for this purpose. The store-owner immediately pledged $265,000 of his own money to subsidize depositors' losses as he and Captain William H. Stevens secured enough additional pledges to cover the deficit.

Although Hudson's main store in Detroit — apart from Hudson & Symington — had achieved a sales volume of $972,000 in 1892, the Panic of 1893 put an end to escalating sales. During the next twelve years — while presidential candidates and Congress argued about preservation of the gold standard and how to deal with coal mine strikes and numerous revelations of corporate fraud — sales at Hudson's main store wavered, reaching a low point of $660,679 in 1898. Still, Joseph Hudson retained faith in his ability to succeed, after having incorporated his business in 1895.

In 1895 he decided to expand his store by taking over Hull Brothers Grocery and the grocery company's delivery service by horse-drawn truck. In that same year, he moved from his residence at 14 Madison to a handsome Victorian home on elm shaded Alfred Street, close to Woodward.

Joe Hudson's youngest sister, Eliza, continued living with her husband, William Clay, in the home of her brother even after the Clays' first child, Josephine, was born in 1891. The oldest sister, Anna Hudson — four years younger than Joseph, was still unmarried in her late thirties.

Although Joseph L. Hudson was a bachelor, and apparently quite content with that status, he considered it his obligation to make sure that his sister did not remain an "old maid." Ever since the Hudson store had opened its doors to Detroiters, Robert B. Tannahill had been a trusted employee. In 1892, with his advancement to advertising director, the 29-year-old Tannahill married his employer's 40-year-old sister, Anna. A year later, the Tannahills, who also lived in the Hudson residence, became parents of a son — Robert Hudson Tannahill.

The Mabley empire was no longer a threat to Joseph L. Hudson. When C.R. Mabley died in 1885 at age 49, the Mabley business had begun to languish. Its deterioration accelerated with the Panic of 1893. At that point, the store was known as Mabley & Co. Bazaar and Shoe House, with "gents furnishings."

By October of 1896, Mabley & Co. was only a tenant on the first floor of a magnificent new building — at 14 floors, a skyscraper that dwarfed the Hammond Building and occupied the most valuable downtown property, located at Woodward and Michigan. Still, the letter *M* on the building's capstones and brass doorknobs carried the imprint of the flamboyant Cornishman entrepreneur who had planned his Mabley Building as a memorial to his success.

At C.R. Mabley's death, stockholders in the Mabley company had tried to carry out the founder's dream for his memorial, but were hampered by financial problems. When a new building company had taken over plans for the unfinished skyscraper ten years after Mabley's death, the magnificent building was completed and named the Majestic in tribute to its marble and dark-mahogany grandeur, and to make use of its M imprints. From a railed observatory at dizzying heights above the fourteenth floor of the Majestic Building, visitors could look down at small figures on the J.L. Hudson rooftop. But within a few years, the Mabley enterprises were moved out of the Majestic as Pardridge and Blackwell took over the first eight floors of the building for its department-store business.

It was Joseph L. Hudson's habit to come into his store early every morning. When he encountered an employee who was also an early arrival, the store owner invariably greeted the employee by name. "You and I are the first ones here this morning," he would say, nodding his large bald head in commendation of such zeal to begin work.

Seated in a barber chair in the "tonsorial shop" he had set up in the basement of his store, Hudson appeared to require privacy, holding a newspaper in front of his face while the barber skirted the mutton-chop whiskers with a straight-edged razor. Once whiskers and mustache were trimmed properly, Hudson liked to walk about his store, quietly observing his managers and clerks as they worked.

On one occasion, as he inconspicuously surveyed the third floor men's department, he spotted an ambitious clerk pushing the sale of a $15 suit to a customer who appeared to be charmed by the sharply creased trousers (creases being a recent addition to men's fashions) but unaware that the suit coat was too short in the sleeves. Joseph Hudson walked quickly to the customer's side. Pointing out diplomatically that the coat did not fit as well as it should, he took the time to search for a more suitable jacket. Hudson's wanted only satisfied customers, he reprimanded the clerk when the suit-buyer left.

GRAND OPENING

Boarding one of the four "plunger" elevators, Hudson frequently visited the busy seventh floor where, in one section, buggy carriages were stocked and sold. In another section, little boys toted baskets and armloads of customer-purchases marked for home delivery. The boys dumped their loads on tables where workers sorted them for the seven drivers employed by Hudson in 1895. These teamsters backed their horses and wagons to the Farmer Street curb, swung iron weights—each weight attached to a horse's bridle with a length of strap—to the street to hold the horses in position, then loaded the packages into the wagons and set about making their deliveries.

Joseph L. Hudson needed no horse and carriage to get to Sunday morning services at Central Methodist Episcopal Church. He could walk up Woodward to the church, accompanied by his younger sister, Eliza Clay, who promenaded to their pew with a swishing of layers of taffeta petticoats embellished with ribbons and lace beneath a long gored skirt. Eliza's enormous hat flaunted veilings, flowers, feathers and birds (the handiwork of a taxidermist) from Hudson's millinery accessories.

Because the Clays still lived in the Hudson home, Joseph was a devoted uncle to his young niece, Josephine. When the Clays' second daughter, eight-month-old Esther, died in 1895, Hudson shared Eliza's grief. The birth of a third daughter, Eleanor Lowthian Clay, in 1896, brightened the lives of all occupants of the Alfred Street home.

The ties of family loyalty, forged in the store owner's youth, remained strong in these later years of his financial success. The bachelor Hudson was warm and affectionate, also, to the children of his other sisters . . . the daughter and four sons, including the youngest—Oscar, of Mary Eleanor Webber, and the young son of Anna Tannahill. He planned for all five male nephews to work at the Hudson store, learn the business, and take over its management.

For a time, in 1896, however, Detroiters received the impression that the future of Hudson's store was uncertain. Newspaper accounts claimed that J.L. Hudson was "financially embarrassed" and forced to ask his suppliers for an extension of credit from 30 days to two years.

HUDSON'S: HUB OF AMERICA'S HEARTLAND

Although the Hudson business actually had a surplus of $753,638, the store owner sought "the indulgence" of his creditors, since he could not convert his "large surplus" into cash in time to meet deadlines on his obligations to creditors. His reputation for honesty paid off, as creditors recalled Hudson's earlier repayment of the Ionia store's suppliers in full. They sent telegrams to the Detroit store, assuring its owner that they would wait for their money. Hudson's store survived the crisis, which stemmed from effects of the Panic of 1893 and the failure of Third National Bank of Detroit, and the owner retained faith that his business could be handed down to his family's descendants—to carry on the Hudson name and traditions.

One of these traditions sprang from Joseph Hudson's belief that a business man should assume civic responsibilities that would help improve the city from which he garnered his profits. Hudson assumed a major civic responsibility when he became a member of Harper Hospital's board of directors. The hospital, organized during the Civil War to care for wounded Michigan soldiers and for Detroiters stricken with deadly illnesses—consumption, cholera, heart failure—needed money for expansion to meet the rising health needs of the city's growing population.

At the end of the short-lived Spanish-American War in 1898, wounded and fever-plagued soldiers from Michigan's Thirty-First Volunteer Infantry were shipped back to Detroit. When the train carrying the disabled soldiers steamed into Detroit, J.L. Hudson's seven delivery wagons, temporarily converted into ambulances bearing large *Harper Hospital* signs, waited at the depot. As soon as the veterans were moved from the train into the wagons, the Hudson drivers flicked their reins over the horses' rumps. The animals began clopping along Detroit's streets to the hospital where each man's care was paid for by the state at a dollar-a-day rate.

Among J.L. Hudson's periodic financial contributions to Harper Hospital was a donation for a "perpetual free bed." The "free bed" plan, devised to raise $110,000 for the hospital, was a kind of insurance venture. The donor, who paid $7,500 to $10,000, was then entitled to hospital care at Harper for the rest of his life, without payment, if such care was required.

Apart from his business, his family, and his pet charities, Hudson had two main interests. Known as a baseball "crank" (the 1890's term for "fan,") he had regularly attended Detroit Wolverines' games at Recreation Park until the major-league Wolverines disbanded and a team called the "Tigers" formed in 1895, playing at Bennett Field. Equally fervent in his support of the Anti-Saloon League, Hudson became one of the League's chief financial contributors in the state of Michigan.

Before the end of the Gay Nineties, Carry Nation was in the forefront of the National Woman's Christian Temperance Union with her harmonica, hymns, and hatchet assaults . . . playing the harmonica for hymn singing in front of the saloons, and bursting into taverns to smash bottles and fixtures with her hatchet. Because the temperance movement also promoted woman suffrage, the labor movement, vegetarianism, stricter immigration laws, and other ideas labeled "radical," Joseph L. Hudson threw his support to the more sedate Anti-Saloon League boasting such prominent members as Andrew Carnegie, John D. Rockefeller, and S.S. Kresge.

At a time when physicians prescribed generous doses of the "bitters" for most ailments, and when Lydia Pinkham's Vegetable Compound and a host of tonics and elixirs—all liberally dosed with alcohol—were taken for everything from gout to heart disease, druggists and patent-medicine manufacturers vigorously opposed the temperance movement. So, too, did German brewery owners who resented the thunderings of Methodist preachers against "The Devil's Broth Factories." And since a large percentage of Detroit's population was made up of newly arrived southern-European and Slavic immigrants, this group, along with French, German, and Irish Detroiters, was antagonized by the Anti-Saloon League and its backers.

Because of his strong Methodist background, Joseph Hudson neither smoked nor drank, and he prided himself on absolute honesty in business practices. So, even though some Hudson customers were lost because of the owner's association with the League, others—also opposed to the League—continued to shop at Hudson's because of the owner's reputation for scrupulously fair business dealings. And then there were the Protestant Church people who supported Hudson's stance and his store, and who gathered in great numbers when evangelist Dwight Moody came to Detroit in 1899 to preach against the evils of breaking the laws of the Sabbath and against the temptations of wine, women, and song.

By the end of the 1890s, the sale and delivery of groceries, scooped from open barrels, made up a large part of the J.L. Hudson Company's business. Eggs sold for twenty cents a dozen. Sugar for six cents a pound. The margin of profit was small, but wages for the average laborer were equally small — $1.62 a day.

Hudson now placed his brother-in-law William Clay, formerly manager of the grocery store division, in charge of a cafe included in the Hudson store as early as 1897 — the same year that Joe Hudson expanded his store by adding 33 feet to the north side of the Farmer Street building. Leading citizens of Detroit began to patronize the cafe, which also sold apples pies and cakes to customers who lined up at the counter on Saturdays to buy Sunday dinner desserts.

A new century was on the horizon. Wireless messages were being transmitted across the English Channel, and there was the promise of many innovations and labor saving devices to come in the twentieth century. Detroit was growing — a brawny, lusty, muscular town where skilled machinists were already setting up shops equipped with forges and lathes to fire and mold and shape the engines and transmissions that would soon transform Detroit into the Motor City of the world.

4

A New Century Dawns

Americans looked forward to celebrating the birth of the twentieth century as they anticipated wondrous technological advances — advances that were expected to change their lives and offer unprecedented opportunities to the children of working-class parents. Like other Americans, Detroiters could not agree when they should observe the beginning of the new century. Some people insisted on ringing in the arrival of January 1, 1900, with whistles and noisemakers. But most Detroiters waited for the passing of midnight, December 31, 1900, to create a thunderous arrival for the year 1901 with bands blaring, firecrackers blasting, and skyrockets flaring over the Detroit River and lighting the heavens above the skyscraper memorial to Christopher R. Mabley — the Majestic Building.

Lights gleamed from every window of Hudson's store to enhance Detroit's downtown area where every major building was illuminated. No Detroit merchant looked forward to twentieth century progress with greater expectation than did Joseph Lowthian Hudson whose 19-year-old nephew, Richard Webber, had become his uncle's aide and, often, his spokesman at the store. The older man and the nephew were, as Richard Webber later would recall, "inseparable."

Although many boys, who started working as cash or parcel boys at Hudson's when they were as young as ten or twelve years of age, came up through the ranks to take positions as department managers, Webber's predetermined rise to Hudson's upper echelons was much swifter. And as the new century began, Joseph Hudson, at age 55, began to relegate to his aides some of the responsibilities he always had assumed. In 1901, store manager E.J. Hickey, likely observing the meteoric rise of young Webber, left Hudson employ to go into business for himself.

The average life expectancy in the United States, in 1900, was 49 years, and both Eliza Clay and her brother were aware that Joe Hudson already had lived several years longer than had his mother and father. At the Hudson home, Eliza urged her brother to moderate the pace of his workday—to get out of bed a little later in the morning and to enjoy a good breakfast at home before going to the store.

When he finally acquiesced to these changes in his routine, it became the duty of 12-year-old William Murphy, newly employed at the store in 1904, to take a report of the previous day's "door sales" figures to Mr. Hudson each morning. Because Hudson could not relax and enjoy his morning meal until the sales figures were in his hand, young Murphy was hurried on his way from the store with a nickel supplied for trolley fare. The enterprising Murphy— who eventually became general superintendent for operations at Hudson's—always saved the nickel and ran, as hard as he could, the several blocks to the Hudson home. There, his employer greeted him with a pleasant "Good morning, Willie," then returned to the table to digest the sales report along with his breakfast.

Two years after the youthful messenger began this morning ritual, sales figures for Hudson's main store began to mount steadily, after a plateau of 13 years. $953,000 in 1905; $1,162,000 in 1906. The demands of Hudson's grocery business forced the store owner to rent four "special" wagons and extra drivers to take care of the overload of deliveries. The "specials" frequently delivered groceries from the main store as late as 10:30 p.m.; occasionally as late as midnight.

A NEW CENTURY DAWNS

For the past six years, Joe Hudson had eagerly anticipated this breakthrough in sales volume as Detroit's turn-of-the-century population of some 286,000 people boomed with the arrival of many more Italian and Slavic immigrants. Michigan farm boys also flocked to Detroit by train and bicycle, seeking work in the city's machine shops and in its embryonic automobile factories.

The one-cylinder Oldsmobile, brain-child of Ransom Olds and the first gasoline-powered car manufactured in quantity, already was wobbling, on bicycle-type wheels, along Detroit's streets by 1900. In 1903, Henry Ford's two-cylinder, eight-horsepower Model A — a sturdier car built from Ford's plans by the red-haired Dodge brothers — rattled its way around the city and soon was challenged by Leland's classy Cadillac. By Packard. And by various other automobile companies that brought recognition to Detroit, in 1905, as the foremost automotive city — recognition formerly credited to Indianapolis.

But Henry Ford was still a struggling, nearly penniless mechanic in April, 1901, when — as Ford biographer Robert Lacey relates in his book on the Ford family — Henry brought his 35-year-old wife, Clara, to Hudson's store to buy a pair of women's patent leather shoes and black silk stockings. A short time later, the young Fords returned to Hudson's to exchange Clara's shoes for a more suitable pair. When they could not find a satisfactory exchange, Hudson's refunded the money for the shoes in accordance with the store's policy.

Although Henry Ford's finances reached a low point in 1901, the persistent tinkerer looked ahead with optimism to his own future in Detroit and to the success of the commercial motor car he wanted to manufacture. Joseph L. Hudson, a teetotaler like Ford, shared the struggling car-maker's optimistic outlook for the future of Detroit — and for the future of his store, well stocked with starched white blouses, Ascot scarves, sailor hats, and silk parasols for ladies enamored of the Gibson Girl look. With traditional three-piece, blue serge suits for men, who wore jackets even in the summertime. With high, stiff collars and cuffs that buttoned onto men's shirts. And with the latest in young men's fashions — peg-top trousers.

Because men always wore hats out of doors, Hudson's had done a brisk business in hat sales ever since the store's 1881 beginnings, centering on its haberdashery departments. Silk hats for executives who wore them, with frock coats, to their offices. Derbies. Straw hats for summer. Caps and straw sailors for boys in knee-pants or knickers.

Shoppers in the furniture department could find a number of major items that sold for less than five dollars each. An ice-box. A mahogany table for the parlor. A bed, with brass trimming. And as clerks rang up sales on cash registers, the salespeople frequently would call out "cash boy" and expect to see youthful employees scurrying toward the registers to bring or collect bills and coins.

In 1903, Hudson's sister, Mary Eleanor Webber, moved with her husband and children from Ionia to Detroit where her husband, J. T. Webber, became a Hudson store employee. Mary Eleanor's youngest son, Oscar, began high school studies in Detroit while his 17-year-old twin brothers, Tom and Jerry, took jobs in Men's Clothing at their uncle's store. The twins ran errands, unpacked crates and arranged stock, wrapped parcels, and did jobs as unglamorous as polishing brass cuspidors as they gradually worked their way up to salesmen, floor walkers, and then into buying.

At age 20, Tom went to Toledo to help manage the Hudson store in that city for one year. Two years later, in 1908, a fire destroyed the Toledo store and it was not rebuilt. Since the larger Detroit store on Woodward Avenue was the company's showplace and top moneymaker, with rapidly expanding departments, there was opportunity for all five Hudson nephews—Tannahill and the four Webbers—to work and advance into management at the bustling Detroit store. The youngest of the five, Oscar Webber, came to work in his after-school hours, on Saturdays, and during vacations.

At this early time, the Detroit store was stocked from orders taken by traveling salesmen, except for merchandise bought by Joseph Hudson and his nephew Richard on weekend trips to Cleveland. Years later, Richard Webber would recall leaving the store on Saturday nights to board a Cleveland-bound boat, selecting merchandise on Sundays as arranged by appointment, and then returning in time to work at the store on Monday mornings.

On some Saturday nights after the store closed at 10 p.m., the uncle and nephew enjoyed a late dinner at the Cadillac Hotel, then played a game of pool before going home. But that happened only when there were no weekend inventories to be taken or no buying trips to Cleveland already scheduled.

Although the Webbers had settled into a Detroit home on Ferry East, the eldest son, Richard, continued to live at his employer-uncle's home at 445 Woodward Avenue. Hudson had moved to the new address to provide more spacious quarters for the large "live-in" family he had acquired—his nephew Richard, his sister Anna Tannahill and her husband and son, the Clays and their two daughters.

Anna Tannahill's husband was now a Hudson store vice-president. And young Eleanor and Josephine Clay attended Detroit's most prestigious day school for girls to receive traditional Liggett School training in etiquette and decorum. Their devoted uncle also sent his nieces to Annie Ward Foster's dancing school to mingle with the sons and daughters of Detroit's "Four Hundred" set.

Joe Hudson had equal concerns for his sisters, encouraging then to select fashionable clothing from, or through, his store. A December, 1906, invoice for one broadtail Persian scarf and matching muff from Wm. H. Miller & Co., Furs, billed "J.L. Hudson (personal)" for $37.50 "at exact cost" for Mrs. J.T. Webber.

For the store owner, "Work and plenty of it" continued to be a favorite motto. From his desk, he could look up to a pen and ink drawing displayed on the office wall . . . a drawing of a pick-ax, the sharp end pointing to the words: "If there's a way, I'll find it." At the blunt end: "If there is none, I'll make one."

He found a way to anchor the State Fair in Detroit by persuading three other prominent Detroiters to join him in buying 135 acres of land east of Woodward between 7 1/2 and 8 Mile Roads, then deeding the land to the Michigan State Agricultural Society for one dollar in April, 1905. That same year, the acreage was the site of the State Fair, which would continue to flourish on the same, but expanded, land for more than 80 years to the present date.

Hudson's motto and creed conformed with the public image of the serious minded store owner, who served as president of Detroit's Municipal League until that civic organization received a letter, sent by its secretary, Anthony Pratt, accusing the League, while under Hudson's leadership, of abandoning the principles of government by the people. Joseph Hudson, who considered the letter an insulting attack on his integrity, immediately resigned from the presidency, despite pleas from other members to retain his office. Pride appeared to be the only weakness in the strong moral character of the store owner . . . an ego which would not allow him to belittle himself by defending his integrity, but demanded uncompromising rejection of an attacker. In the wake of Hudson's resignation, Pratt came under pressure from other board members and he, too, resigned.

The attack by Pratt had little impact on Detroiters' perception of J.L. Hudson as a philanthropist and a strong supporter of many charities and organizations such as the Young Men's Christian Association. But the store owner's participation in a mock trial, held on the stage of the YMCA hall in 1906, seemed to be out of character. Posing as the defendant in a simulated breach-of-promise suit, Joe Hudson took the part of the "wretch" being sued for "heart balm" by tearful plaintiff "Miss Jerusha Perkins."

Newspapers picked up the story with captions of "Weird Oaths in Hudson Case" as Detroit's Mayor-Elect Thompson and other prominent citizens, serving as the jury, were warned that " . . . (if) you are directed by the court to vocalize, you will do so in long meter, short meter, or meet her by moonlight . . . " Witnesses received equally waggish orders: " . . . the evidence you shall give in the case shall be part of the truth, any of the truth, or as little of the truth as you please."

Detroit women apparently took no offense at the ungallant "testimony" of Joe Hudson, who stated that "I would not marry the plaintiff if she were the last woman on earth." As the beautiful Miss Perkins wept copiously, Hudson added that he wanted "a wife that knew as much as an oyster—to keep its mouth shut."

"J.L. Hudson is 'Guilty' and Must Pay Fine of $11.48" one newspaper reported the "verdict," adding that "Jury soaks him for trifling with the affections of Miss Jerusha Rugg Perkins"—a most attractive and fashionable young woman. In private life, the bachelor, Hudson, had no interest in Miss Perkins, but retained a great

A NEW CENTURY DAWNS

deal of interest in stocking the latest fashions in his store and in employing people instructed to be courteous and helpful.

In 1906, Miss Carrie Sloan came to work in "Ribbons," strategically located in the first-floor center aisle where it served as a magnet to feminine shoppers who could not resist its wares. Miss Sloan, who customarily wore a huge bow ribbon at the back of her head—pinning a cluster of curls hanging to her shoulders, was an attractive addition to the Ribbons display which included many accessories . . . embroideries, leather goods, trimmings and jewelry.

Cosmetics, except for face powder, still were taboo for any woman who did not wish to be mistaken for a prostitute. But the decorous Gibson shirtwaist took on a seductive look with the introduction of embroidered perforations. And at the arrival of the tight hobble-skirt, a flash of the wearer's ankles was exposed through a slit that made it possible for a woman to walk.

Hobble-skirts became very popular at Hudson's store in the 1905-1910 period, even though women who wore the stylish garments put themselves at risk to cross Woodward Avenue. On Woodward, pedestrians had to sidestep clanging trolleys, careening bicycles, sputtering motor cars, and snorting horses frightened by the clamor of unregulated traffic . . . equally frightened by the sight of hobble-skirted women, feather boas flowing from their shoulders and ostrich plumes fluttering from huge hats, mincing across the avenue and dodging the nervous delivery horses.

Stimulated by rising sales and by Detroit's rapid population growth, Joe Hudson had a 35-foot, eight-story building erected on Farmer street in 1907, extending the Hudson store to the north. In the same year, Pardridge and Blackwell moved from its spacious quarters in the Majestic building to Farmer and Gratiot, becoming Hudson's across-the-street neighbor and rival in the mercantile business. Two years later, Crowley, Milner and Company would take over the Pardridge and Blackwell firm, but Joe Hudson already had learned that such rivals did not hurt his business; the additional stores helped to attract more customers around the corner to off-Woodward emporiums.

In October, 1908, Joe Hudson finished remodeling the main part of his store, removing its four elevators and replacing them with seven new Otis elevators. He installed better lighting, heating, and ventilation systems and moved the store's delivery department into the basement.

Joe Hudson had hired Captain James H. McConnell as chief detective at his store to protect the merchandise from thieves. When McConnell caught someone stealing an item from a counter, he escorted the shoplifter into the office of the store owner, who, depending on the nature of the attempted theft and the kind of sob-story the shoplifter could muster, was likely to lecture the person and release him.

Hudson's sales had continued to expand in early 1908 when, in February, Joe Hudson's brother-in-law, William Clay, died at age 51. Since the Clays' two young daughters, Josephine and Eleanor, had always lived in the Hudson home, their father's death brought few changes in their accustomed way of life except a difficult adjustment to the loss of a father. Their Uncle Joseph, who always had been very close to his nieces, now became an even more important father-figure to the girls. He even entertained the notion that the strong-willed Josephine Clay—now nearly 17 years old—could take her place among the all-male directors of the Hudson store in a few years.

The widowed Eliza Clay observed the traditional mourning period for her husband, wearing black "widow's weeds" for two years during which she withdrew from social activities. Struggling to find her own identity at this period in her life, she fussed about the name she had never liked—Eliza. She changed it, first, to Elna. Then to Lillie. To Janet. And, eventually, back to the familiar Eliza.

In October, 1908, the product of Henry Ford's inventive genius, the Model T Ford automobile, went on the market and gave Detroit undisputed claim to the title, Motor City. The Ford factory was flooded with orders for the sturdy, four-cylinder car with its one-piece cylinder block and planetary transmission. Ten thousand Model T's sold within the first year of production, while prospective buyers waited for the Detroit factory to manufacture more of the cars that could survive rutted gravel roads, potholes, mud and encounters with tree stumps and boulders.

Ford's hometown soon swarmed with Model T's rattling and

A NEW CENTURY DAWNS

coughing their way about the downtown hub and along Woodward and Jefferson Avenues to outlying areas where farmers, too, became proud owners of the homely, but reliable, motor cars. With the introduction of the Model T, Henry Ford carried out his plan to change the exotic status of the automobile, formerly owned only by the wealthy, to a plebian ordinariness that would make the car available to the common working man.

Ford's success encouraged other entrepreneurs to invest in the automobile business, including Joseph Lowthian Hudson. A new motor car, the "Model 20," recently had been designed by Howard E. Coffin, assisted by Roy D. Chapin and Roscoe B. Jackson—all formerly employed by Ransom Olds and now working for the Chalmers-Detroit Company. When Chalmers needed more money to finance the car, Roscoe Jackson—husband of J.L. Hudson's only Webber niece, Louise—came to his wife's uncle for help. Joining several other investors, Joe Hudson risked $90,000 to produce an automobile that would bear his name as he became president of the newly incorporated Hudson Motor Car Company.

Setting up production in a small factory at Mack and Beaufait in 1909, Jackson and his associates began manufacturing a four-cylinder, 20 horsepower Hudson—the first automobile to offer a selective sliding-gear transmission featuring three forward speeds. By 1910, Chapin took over the presidency of the company, Jackson became general manager, and Hudson, who took no active part in the business, reigned as chairman of the board.

Enchanted with the handsome, solidly built Hudson car, Joseph Lowthian invited five guests to accompany him on a chauffeur-driven tour through Ontario, Canada, and up to Montreal, Quebec, in August, 1909. As the chauffeur drove the automobile along a narrow road parallel to the St. Lawrence River near Montreal, the car ran into a pocket of sand and lurched sideways. Grazing a telephone pole, the machine tilted and stopped at the edge of an embankment. The shaken passengers abandoned the car, leaving it to be extricated by workmen while Hudson and his guests went on by boat to Quebec City before returning to Detroit through the state of New York.

Although, in 1910, a saleswoman in a Hudson's store department such as "China" considered $15 to $20 in her sales book as a gratifying amount for one day, the multiplicity of such sales added up to $2,203,000 for Hudson's main store that year . . . double the sales of three years earlier. Triggered by a booming Motor City prosperity, J.L. Hudson Company profits prompted Joseph Hudson to buy a fine mansion on East Boston Boulevard, just off Woodward, among the handsome homes of wealthy Detroiters. Purchased from Alex Malcomson, one of Henry Ford's earliest business partners, the three-storied home of red brick and shingles, next door to the mansion of the John Dodge family, boasted a round-windowed tower extending from the third floor at the front of the house. Hudson moved his family—the Tannahills, the Clays, and his nephew-protege, Richard Webber—into the Boston Boulevard home which encompassed six family bedrooms and four baths, servants' quarters, and a four-car garage with accommodations for a chauffeur. Because Hudson strictly observed the principles of John Wesley—founder of the Wesleyan Methodist Church—he was shocked by periodic newspaper reports relating the drunken escapades of his neighbor, John Dodge. Nonetheless, the Dodges' two daughters, Winifred and Isabel, who attended Liggett School with Josephine and Eleanor Clay, soon became close friends of Hudson's nieces.

By 1910, Joseph Hudson was more active than ever before in the Anti-Saloon League and in its campaign to promote "dry" counties in Michigan under the county-option law of the state. The League printed literature calling attention to martyrs who had died for the cause of temperance . . . to the cases of a judge and a physician shot and killed because of their leadership in elections that turned certain counties "dry" . . . to an Ohio businessman and League promoter whose home and business were wrecked by dynamite. It published articles on the relationship of saloons to insanity; on the unsavory connections between liquor and "houses of ill fame."

Hudson's uncompromising loyalty to the Anti-Saloon League provoked many letters of protest from brewers, including Klein Brothers Distillers of Cincinnati who sent their protests to the Hudson Motor Car Company. The letter accused Hudson of "making warfare against the business we are interested in." It complained that "the nature of your business is no more a necessity than ours . . ."

A NEW CENTURY DAWNS

From other companies came sarcastic suggestions that Hudson should refrain from soliciting distillers' business (i.e., trying to sell them Hudson automobiles or merchandise from the J.L. Hudson store) and from accepting "tainted money."

Ignoring the protests, Joe Hudson made increasingly generous donations to the Anti-Saloon League. He also continued contributing money to Harper Hospital—where he had served as president of the board of directors since 1901, and to the YMCA and other charitable organizations on whose boards he served . . . McGregor Institute, Associated Charities, Florence Crittenton Mission, Central Methodist Episcopal Church, and the d'Arcambal Association for Discharged Prisoners. He never had swerved from his opinion that a businessman owed a percentage of his earnings to the community in which he lived and worked in the same manner that a churchman tithed to support his church.

Hudson's community—Detroit—reached a population of 465,766 in 1910, with 39,000 people employed by automobile manufacturers and another 19,000 by the manufacturers of motor car accessories. Detroit also was known, in 1910, as the home of the largest rubber works in the world, and had been long recognized as the world's major manufacturer of stoves. The city was expanding fast, and Joseph L. Hudson became obsessed with the idea of annexing another building to his store in a breakthrough to Woodward Avenue.

Chapter 5

"Crossing the Bar"

Detroit became the ninth largest city in the country in 1910. Its economy boomed as a railroad tunnel was completed under the Detroit River—the busiest inland water channel in the world, connecting Detroit to Windsor, Canada. Although women workers in garment factories were earning as little as eight cents an hour, the fashion business also boomed with the introduction of full, gathered, shorter skirts. Style-conscious Detroit females abandoned hobble skirts and their daring slits for the shorter creations, as high as six inches from the floor, which permitted women to board streetcars with much less difficulty.

On Woodward Avenue, which boasted a one-mile, outlying section paved with concrete since 1909, Detroiters gathered in large groups to wait for streetcar transportation. When wintry winds gusted along Woodward, chivalry was forgotten as passengers scrambled to get aboard the cars as they clanged to a stop. Men had no time for ogling feminine ankles revealed by the shorter hemlines. Instead, they scrambled and shoved for places to stand in crowded aisles or on front or rear steps from which they clung to the overloaded Woodward Avenue cars.

The siren call of heavily trafficked Woodward Avenue lured

Joseph L. Hudson to make his breakthrough to the city's central corridor in 1911. He had purchased the Benson Building in 1910, ordered it razed, and then constructed a new ten-story building, fronting on both Woodward and Gratiot. The new building was connected, at the rear, to the older eight-floor Hudson store by direct passages extending over the alley on the second to the eighth floor.

Handsome granite facades, on Woodward and Gratiot, rose to the third floor of the new building, its higher floors faced with brown tapestry brick and terra cotta trim. Within the building, a steel frame was fireproofed with concrete, and an enclosed iron staircase was protected with fireproof barriers. The modern heating and ventilating systems in the building included air washers and vacuum cleaners operated by basement machinery.

When the new building opened in October, 1911, three large elevators whisked passengers from the basement to top floors, and an open staircase ran from the basement to a mezzanine, enclosed with ornamental iron railings, which circled the building. Only six months later, eight-year-old Archie Smith, of Windsor, Canada, fell to his death from one of Hudson's elevators. Riding up to the seventh floor of the building at nine p.m., accompanied by two Windsor women who had taken the child shopping, the boy plunged through open grillwork and down the shaft from the fifth floor to the basement before the elevator operator, Earl Bisso, could stop the car. The two women claimed that the car lurched and pitched the boy forward, trapping his head between the grating and the elevator cage. But Bisso said the child reached out and grasped the screening so that he was propelled down the shaft.

Deaths in elevator shafts were not uncommon. Many workers, especially child employees, fell to their deaths in this way. In 1904, Hudson's neighbor, the Newcomb, Endicott department store, had attracted the kind of publicity no store owner wanted when Katherine Shearer Russel, a society woman and mother of three young children, fell backwards into one of the store's elevator shafts and was killed.

Mary Elizabeth Ketzmiller, hired at $8 a week in 1909 by Hudson's brother-in-law, J.T. Webber, worked happily in Yard Goods, wearing the required "uniform"—dark skirt and white, long-sleeved, high-necked blouse, its collar held in place by stays sewn into the fabric. Following the example of other clerks, she tied paper around her cuffs to keep them clean. Yard Goods was a busy department, and when customers waited for service at Mary Elizabeth's counter, J.T. Webber worked alongside her—measuring and cutting from bolts of material.

Like most employees at the store, Mary Elizabeth felt that working at Hudson's was being "part of a family." This feeling was reinforced for the Yard Goods clerk when, during a period of hospitalization, Mary Elizabeth was surprised by a personal visit to her bedside from her "boss"—Joseph L. Hudson.

Even before the new Hudson building on Woodward opened in 1911, Joe Hudson bought a brick mansion near Walkerville, Ontario. He hired workmen to renovate the mansion into a summer resort for his female workers—a resort where thirty "women and girls," could come on their vacations, free of charge, for two weeks at a time. Hudson named the manor "Halcyone Hall" and ordered the construction of tennis courts, croquet grounds, and a pier extending out into the lake. And with the opening of the new store, Hudson included rest rooms and a comfortable women's lounge area for employees, plus a self-serve lunch room with meals offered at cost to workers.

The Hudson home on East Boston Boulevard overflowed with family in 1911 as Joseph's older brother, Richard, retired from the University of Michigan, where he had been Dean of literary studies, and came to live at the East Boston manor. At age 65, Richard "Buddy" Hudson still had many things to occupy him—travels abroad and, as the scholar in the family, manuscripts on English history that he was researching and writing.

Joe Hudson, who always had wanted to travel to England and visit his birthplace, had never taken time away from his store and civic responsibilities, as the shopkeeper in the family, to do much traveling. *Soon perhaps*, he told his nephew Richard Webber, who had become a vice president of the J.L. Hudson Company in 1911 and now encouraged his uncle to take a trip to England. *Soon*, he promised Eliza Clay and Anna Tannahill, the sisters who shared his home and scolded him for working much too hard. *Very soon*, he told his sister, Mary Eleanor Webber, who assured him that Richard and her other sons would do a fine job of managing the store while their uncle was away.

Hudson certainly trusted his nephews, and he also trusted his brothers-in-law, Robert Tannahill and J.T. Webber—all of whom helped with the Hudson business. But times were changing rapidly, and the new Woodward Avenue building had to be launched—its departments filled with the finest and most modern stock. Kathleen Norris' novels occupied considerable space on the shelves of the book department. The latest in peg-top, tiered, and draped skirts filled racks in the women's clothing department. The most modern of bathroom fixtures—tubs with white enameled linings—were moved into the bath department along with toilets that only now were beginning to replace outhouses for lower, middle-class families.

By April of 1912, Hudson decided that his enlarged store employed so many people, approximately 1,000, that he should make arrangements for medical treatment for employees who became ill while at work. The decision stemmed from Hudson's own experience when he had contracted typhoid fever and a nurse, Miss Etta Russell, had given him excellent care. Now, he sent for Miss Russell, hired her as a nurse at the store, and set aside a "hospital room" on the ninth floor, which Etta Russell furnished with two beds, a medicine cabinet, and an assortment of medical supplies.

By this time, Joseph Lowthian Hudson had been elected a national officer of the Anti-Saloon League, which was flexing its muscles with effective results. In Michigan, 39 of the state's 83 counties already had become "dry" under the country option law. 1912 was also a busy year of changeover for the Hudson Motor Car Company with the introduction of the first six-cylinder Hudson, the handsome Model Six-54. Still, Joseph Hudson carried out the promises he had given his sisters by leaving on a sea voyage to England in the latter part of June.

For months, as J.L. Hudson Company workers noticed that

their employer's face looked drawn and that he was losing weight, rumors circulated in Detroit that the store owner was unwell. Long-term employee William Wilson, concerned about Joe Hudson's poor health, felt compelled to offer his advice to "take a good rest" when he heard that his boss was leaving for England. "Don't come back until you get that 42-inch waistband again," Wilson urged, expressing the prevailing opinion that an ample paunch was evidence of good health. "You never will be well with a 36-inch waist measure."

Admitting only to a troublesome throat problem, Joe Hudson left Detroit in the company of Dr. R.A. Studer, a physician and secretary of the Detroit YMCA—to which Hudson had made a major financial contribution for the organization's new headquarters. When, in late June, the two men sailed from New York aboard the *Kron Prinz*, it became apparent to Dr. Studer, who had advised the store owner to take the trip in an attempt to regain his health, that Joseph L. Hudson was losing strength during the sea voyage. Encouraged by Studer to take exercise, Hudson shuffled listlessly up and down stairs and along the decks.

When the steamship finally approached England's shores, Studer escorted Hudson up to the deck. "This is England," Joseph Hudson said quietly. "The land where I was born. The land which I have never seen since I was a boy. And the land to which I am now coming back—to die." He bowed his head on the rail and, according to Dr. Studer's report, "wept like a child."

In London, as the two men were driven about the city by a hired chauffeur, Dr. Studer made an appointment for Hudson to see one of the city's renowned physicians. When the specialist recommended taking Hudson to a seaside resort, Studer accompanied the store owner to Worthing—a resort just west of the busy seaside town of Brighton.

The sea air did not slow Hudson's decline. On July fourth, just six days after his arrival in England, he would not eat when his nurse tried to feed him. Dr. Studer brought a cup of broth to the bedside and begged the ailing man to drink it.

"I would do anything in the world to please you," Joe Hudson managed to say as he sipped the broth. But these were his last words before he sank into a coma. He remained unconscious the next morning, close to death as the stirring strains of a military march played by a band, outside, penetrated the sickroom.

Later that morning, Dr. Studer wired a cablegram to Richard Webber in Detroit. "Mr. Hudson just passed away. Pneumonia. Return earliest possible moment with body." After receiving the cablegram, Vice President Webber walked quietly about the store, seeking out department heads and informing them, first, of his uncle's death.

On Wednesday, July 17, Richard Webber and his two uncles—Richard Hudson of Ann Arbor and Detroit, and William Hudson of Buffalo—went to New York, with delegates from the Detroit Board of Commerce, to meet the steamship *Oceanic*, bearing the body of Joseph L. Hudson, as it arrived from Southampton.

No customers went in or out the door of the J.L. Hudson store on Friday, July 19. A simple, black-bordered card on each door noted the one-day pause in the store's 31 years of business in Detroit. "Closed on account of the death of Mr. Joseph L. Hudson, President of the J.L. Hudson Company." Early that morning, 300 members of the Detroit Board of Commerce formed two columns reaching from the Michigan Central train shed out to the curb at Third Street. There, the honor guard awaited the nine a.m. arrival of the train transporting an oxidized metallic casket, covered with a blanket of flowers and bearing the body of Detroit's "Merchant Prince."

Escorted by Hudson's nephews—Tannahill and the four Webbers—plus Louise Webber Jackson's husband, the coffin was placed in a waiting motor hearse and taken to Hudson's East Boston Boulevard home. There, the distraught family awaited the arrival of the man who had counseled each member of the extended Hudson clan, provided homes and jobs for most of them, and who was responsible for the family's prosperity. Eliza Clay's daughters, 21-year-old Josephine and 16-year-old Eleanor, were inconsolable at the loss of the uncle who was like a father to them.

For the next few hours, the casket reposed at the East Boston Boulevard home, tastefully decorated with carefully selected artworks and paintings befitting Hudson's appointment as a trustee of the Detroit Institute of Arts. After a short prayer service, the Webber brothers, Robert Hudson Tannahill, and the son of Joseph's brother William, from Buffalo, carried the heavy casket back into the hearse for the drive to Central Methodist Church, its galleries filled with spectators.

Outside the church, mounted Detroit policemen patrolled Woodward Avenue and kept the street clear of people who stood in Grand Circus Park, across from the church, even though Hudson store employees had been requested not to attend their employer's funeral services because of the overflow crowd. Richard Webber had suggested that the employees should "try to make the day one of real benefit and rest" to themselves.

Bishop F.D. Leete came to Central Methodist to give the funeral eulogy for Joseph L. Hudson, who had served as a trustee for the church and was frequently referred to in print as "a businessman of phenomenal ability and spotless character." Newspaper stories also lauded Hudson as a philanthropist—citing his recent, hefty contributions for a new YMCA building and to Harper Hospital for a new building which would cost $450,000 when completed and equipped. In November, 1911, Hudson, as president of Harper's board of directors, had pushed a shovel into the earth to turn the first piece of sod for construction of the new Harper building. At his death, the edifice was named the Hudson Memorial Building, and Richard Webber succeeded his uncle on the hospital's board of directors.

Now, with the conclusion of the Bishop's prayer, the reading of the scriptures and a talk by Dr. Studer, friend and companion of J.L. Hudson in his last days, Joseph Hudson's favorite hymns, "Crossing the Bar" and "Abide With Me," resounded through the church. The six nephews picked up the casket once again and carried it outside for its trip to the Hudson crypt in Woodlawn Cemetery. The 33-year-old bachelor nephew, Richard Webber, knew, as he helped carry the coffin, that he was to take his uncle's place as the person who would be accountable for the Hudson family and civic responsibilities, and for directing a store with annual sales that would soar to $3.4 million during 1912.

HUDSON'S: HUB OF AMERICA'S HEARTLAND

Joseph L. Hudson had carefully prepared his nephew to take charge of these responsibilities. After several years in various store departments as clerk, buyer, and then manager, Richard Webber had been a board of directors member since 1908; a company vice president since 1911. His younger brothers Joseph L. and James B., along with Oscar—who recently graduated, Phi Beta Kappa, from the University of Michigan with a degree in business administration—were already department managers and would become co-directors of the store within a year. The Webber brothers' 19-year-old cousin Robert Hudson Tannahill (whose father was a Hudson vice-president) now was named vice-president of the Hudson Motor Car Company—an honorary appointment requiring minimum effort from young Tannahill, more interested in art than business, and who, a newspaper reporter commented, "was under no pressure to work."

A few days after the funeral, J.L. Hudson's will made Richard Webber the recipient of 51% of the Hudson estate, valued conservatively to reporters by Webber at "more than $1 million." The balance of the estate went, in equal shares, to Joseph Lowthian Hudson's six brothers and sisters, all of whom recognized that it would be Richard Webber's duty to act on his uncle's behalf, as family patriarch, and to be accountable for philanthropic obligations—including pensions for former employees and widows of former employees—entrusted to him by his uncle.

Shortly after the death of Joseph Lowthian Hudson, the Anti-Saloon League of Michigan passed a resolution commending the store owner as the "first man of position and wealth in this state to lend his time and efforts" to fight the saloons. At this time, both the anti-saloon and temperance movements were forcing politicians to take sides in an ongoing, heated battle between these organizations and those opposed to prohibitionist legislation.

The same year, for the first time in 20 years, a Democratic victory in the November presidential election ousted the Republican Old Guard when Woodrow Wilson defeated both President Taft and the Progressive Party nominee, Theodore Roosevelt. Predictions of "a new era" seemed believable, even to reluctant Republicans, when the entire country was occupied with imaginative ideas designed to move America forward into a better and innovative future.

Detroiters now could boast of their city-owned, electric-lighting system, encompassing more than 18,000 poles for 5,409 arc lamps that looped the city like multiple strands of a diamond-studded necklace. At night, blazing electrical signs illuminated the Campus Martius, turning it into a promenade for male "dandies," sporting derbies and canes, and for women teetering along on four-inch French heels, the fashion craze of 1913. At the center of Campus Martius traffic, a glittering Detroit Opera House marquee and vaudeville billing at the Temple Theater advertised the names of famous Broadway stars who, while appearing in Detroit, stayed in suites at the lush Pontchartrain Hotel, only a few steps from the Campus.

Although customers crowded into the book department of the Hudson store to buy that best-selling chronicle of sweet innocence, Eleanor H. Porter's *Pollyanna*, the aura of change from Victorian-age mores seemed to be sparked by the electrical illumination of America. The 1912 unveiling of the painting "September Morn" introduced the idea of artistic nudity to the general public. Daring young Americans abandoned genteel ballroom dancing to take up more energetic dance fads—the tango, the turkey trot. The clergy railed at such excesses, but the opening of the Lincoln Highway— the first coast-to-coast paved road—in 1913, provided a new freedom for the increasing number of people who owned automobiles. Auto theft then became a major problem as many of those who did not own motor cars appropriated vehicles parked on the streets— often for a night of joyriding; sometimes for permanent use.

Detroiters who felt safe enough in their own homes to leave their doors unlocked at night now resorted to chaining their cars' steering wheels when they parked their automobiles. The city's growing population and changing mores were blamed for the auto theft problem.

In January, 1914, Henry Ford's announcement of $5 a day for workers brought floods of unemployed men to Detroit from across the Midwest. Some found work. Others, unable to get jobs, joined lines of jobless immigrants, speaking a hodgepodge of foreign languages as they plodded from the gates of one factory to the next, eager to get work in the "Automotive City" where the Woodward Avenue windows of Hudson's store displayed a tantalizing panorama of the 1914 "American Dream."

For the 35-year-old Richard Webber, new president of Hudson's, 1914 was a year when he surrendered his bachelor status to marry Eloise Jenks. Store employees, who respected the quiet-spoken "Mr. Dick" as much as they had respected his uncle, contributed to a wedding-gift collection and presented the newlywed Webbers with a large silver punch bowl. Although Richard's visions of the "American Dream" included a wife and children, they did not include continuing to operate Hudson's grocery and meat departments. Supported by his three brothers, Richard closed Hudson's grocery business in May, 1914. The Webbers already had ambitious plans for enlarging their store to keep pace with Detroit's growth as the automotive industry boomed. The brothers promptly erected a second Woodward Avenue structure, called the Brooks Lewis Building, giving Hudson's 60 additional feet of frontage on Woodward in 1914, and extending Hudson's frontage up to the neighboring Himelhoch's store.

In April of the same year, the Webbers bought a large building on Library Avenue, just behind Hudson's store, where the brothers wanted to set up their own music store. The six-storied building housed Weil & Co., sellers of huge, nickel-plated, steel cookstoves for $35 and five-piece, silk-damask covered parlor sets, with carved mahogany finished frames, at $26.50. Weil & Co. moved to another address as the Webbers renovated the building and moved their own heavy piano-players, victrolas, and stacks of piano rolls, sheet music, and records into the newly decorated, and separate, Hudson's Music Store—also known as the J.L. Hudson Piano and Victrola Store.

The "American Dream" scarcely quivered when, that summer of 1914, major European nations plunged into a nightmarish conflict—World War I. As Detroit factories began manufacturing munitions, in addition to automobiles, more jobless men went to work and soon had money to spend. Hudson's annual sales in

Detroit, exclusive of its piano store, zoomed past the $4 million mark in 1914; past $6 million in 1915.

The Hudson Motor Car Company was also profiting from proliferating automobile sales. In November, 1914, the company introduced its "1915 Hudson Six-40 Landau Limousine," priced at $2,700, advertising "Luxury and Distinction Without Extravagance."

A second Hudson brother, 66-year-old James Benson Hudson of Cleveland, Ohio, died in December, 1914, leaving a widow but no children. In partnership with his brother Joseph L., he had directed operations of the Hudson store in Cleveland until his death. Two months later, the eldest of the Hudson brothers, bachelor Dr. Richard Hudson died at the Biltmore Hotel in New York, where he had gone to receive medical treatment for what was described as "an ailment of the throat." Only the youngest brother, William Hudson, who managed a Hudson store in Buffalo, New York, now survived.

Of the three Hudson sisters, Mary Eleanor—mother of the Webber brothers—still lived with her husband in Detroit. Anna Tannahill, her husband, and their son, Robert, continued to live in the Boston Boulevard home of the deceased Joseph Lowthian Hudson, as did the youngest sister, Eliza Clay, and her two daughters.

In November, 1916, a quiet wedding ceremony at the Hudson home on Boston Boulevard united Eliza's younger daughter, Eleanor Clay, to Henry Ford's only son, 22-year-old Edsel Ford. The liaison linked the Ford automotive fortune to the social-register listing of the Hudsons, whose shopkeeping background was much less of a deterrent to "Blue Book" inclusion than was Henry Ford's gasoline-tainted wealth. Eliza's older daughter, Josephine, soon married Ernest Kanzler, an ambitious and aggressive attorney who, as a brother-in-law of the unassuming Edsel Ford, became an executive for Ford Motor Company.

Although the deaths of the three Hudson Brothers, Joseph L., James and Richard, facilitated the rise to prominence of the names Webber and Tannahill, the Hudson persona remained indelibly imprinted on the bustling city of Detroit—not only by the commanding presence of the J.L. Hudson store, but also with the introduction of the 1916 Hudson motor car. Sales of this handsome 4/5-liter "Super Six" automobile elevated the Hudson Motor Car Company into the top ranking of independent automobile companies.

Among the four Webber brothers, the youngest, Oscar, already had taken a star role as an innovator with his "store within a store" idea . . . a concept of a basement store to meet the needs of newly prosperous Detroit workers. Oscar stocked the first basement level with collections of men's, women's, and children's clothing so that bargain-hunting shoppers could find economically priced merchandise backed by Hudson's guarantee of customer satisfaction. In March, 1915, the 25,000 square foot Basement Store opened to the public with a blitz of advertising. "Growing Girls' Corsets — 50 cents to $2.00." "Women's Factory Dyed Shoes, finest Russian calf and kid — $1.00." "1,000 pairs of men's shoes — $2.45 a pair."

Customers crowded the aisles of "Hudson's New Basement Store" for its opening and in the months that followed. First year sales for the Basement Store added up to a hefty million dollars. In 1916, Basement Store sales contributed to a total Detroit Hudson's sales of more than $8 million, with a gross profit of 32.9%.

Although the Webber brothers shrank from personal publicity, their quiet reserve did not restrain them from devising ingenious ways of promoting the Hudson store and finding new ways to expand their business. In 1916, the Webbers joined with a group of department stores, including Filene's and Dayton's, to form the Retail Research Association. Two years later, the association formed the country's first cooperative buying group, Associated Merchandise Corporation, with offices in the U.S. and abroad for mass buying of merchandise to stock the retail dry goods stores making up the group's membership. The cooperative-buying venture saved millions of dollars for the individual stores participating in the association.

While the Webbers helped set up the cooperative-buying association, they also forged ahead with their plans to expand Hudson's Woodward frontage. In 1917, they built a ten-story haberdashery section on the other side of Himelhoch's, giving their store a total 220 feet on Detroit's main thoroughfare.

"CROSSING THE BAR"

By 1919, Detroit's downtown intersection of Woodward and Michigan would be recognized officially as one of the busiest in the world as more than 16,000 motor cars and more than a half-million people passed this location each day. Policemen, stationed at such intersections, tried to manage the jumble of horses, automobiles, bicycles, and pedestrians while, as early as 1914, the front pages of Detroit newspapers were glutted with reports on the perils of traffic pileups on Woodward Avenue. *Many Are Hurt In the Streets. Falls Keep Ambulances On The Jump. Bicycles Hit By Autos. Pedestrians Hit. Auto Collisions.*

Traffic congestion seemed to entice even more people to come downtown where Hudson's, including its Music Store, was the mecca of attraction. But at Hudson's, the Webbers did not permit the sale of popular sheet music—only classical and teaching music could be purchased there. Shoppers had to go elsewhere to buy copies of "St. Louis Blues" to place on their heavy, upright pianos that stood, covered with fringed scarves, against the parlor walls of average, middle-class homes. Daily newspapers delivered to these homes contained lurid headlines of atrocities committed in the European war, but the personal lives of most Detroiters remained untouched by the reality of war at a time when an expanding prosperity was improving the lives of Detroit workers.

"Growing with Detroit" continued to be the slogan for Hudson's store as the Webber brothers introduced a system of "tubes and rands" that eliminated the need for employing young boys to run about buildings, collecting cash from registers and bringing their collections to the cashiers' room—then returning from the cashiers with supplies of coins. Since 1910, the accelerated efforts of state legislatures and reform groups had begun to show results in formulating restrictions against the exploitation of young children working in coal mines, mills, and factories. Although few of these measures affected the employment of little boys in stores, the change in America's social conscience had its impact. Gradually, the idea of an employer being charitable by paying wages to young children was reversed to a perception of an employer being manipulative of child-workers by using them to enhance his profits.

Bert Robertson, who had come to work for J.L. Hudson in 1893 as a cash boy in men's furnishings, had won rapid promotion to assistant cashier because of his quick arithmetic and competence in handling money. When, soon afterwards, he became cashier, he had three office people working for him. By 1915, he directed 160 people in the cashier's department—a number that was reduced with the introduction, that same year, of Hudson's modern system of "tubes and rands."

Hudson's cashed more checks, at this time, than any bank in the city of Detroit. Every cent of the cash that came into, or out of, the store, went through the cashier's department. And, on paydays, Hudson's gray pay envelopes, containing two-dollar bills and coins, were issued by the cashier's office for distribution to the store's employees.

In that bastion of up-to-date technology, the "Tube Room," a cash drawer was placed in front of each female employee as she sat on a wooden chair in front of an array of tubes, soon numbering 112. The tubes funneled small red and white carriers, and their contents of sales slips and money, through the hollow cylinders on powerful air currents from a blower system that swiftly suctioned or propelled the air-borne carriers to their destinations.

Behind the "tube girls," who uniformly pinned their long hair up off their necks or in coils at the ears, the Tube-Room supervisor, Mrs. Crittenden, kept constant surveillance of their performance, posture, and deportment. At the other, cash-register end of each tube, floor managers reminded clerks that they must wait several seconds between placing carriers in a tube to avoid entanglement of one carriage-basket with another. If such enmeshment occurred, the supervisor or floor manager quickly summoned an electrician to clear the tube or make repairs.

With the declaration of war by the United States against Germany on April 6, 1917, Detroit men began to enlist in the armed forces. One of the early enlistees from Hudson's was floor manager Jenkins, separating himself from his Trimming and Ribbons department to serve in the U.S. Navy. Known to the Ribbons "girls" as "Mr. Jenkins," the courteous and smiling floor manager had been the first Hudsonian to greet customers with a "good morning" as they came into the store. Now as he departed for Navy training in May, he wore a new wristwatch—a gift from the clerks in Trimming and Ribbons.

Hudson's store immediately launched a variety of patriotic enterprises, including a Hudson Soldier Shop presided over by a Mrs. Davenport who offered advice and counsel to soldiers and sailors. Beneath a painting of Joan of Arc, "Women of America" were urged to buy war savings stamps. At meetings of the women's "Hudsonian Club," organized as early as 1914, the members knitted socks and mittens for "the boys." The store circulated the addresses of former employees now at Camp Custer or overseas in France and England, and urged employees to write to the growing number of men who were serving their country after the draft began in July, 1917.

In turn, letters from servicemen arrived at Hudson's store. "I took out $10,000 insurance for my mother," Cecil Allen wrote. "I think it is cheap considering the chances you take. It only costs me $6.40 a month."

Former employee Stewart Webster, hospitalized with scarlet fever in a U.S. army camp, wrote of his experiences in the cavalry. "I have to ride without reins and stirrups, and it is hard to stay on." He concluded his letter with an apology. "Excuse my writing as I am in bed and can't see to write very well—and my pen is broken besides."

Hudson's opened its doors at 8:30 a.m., a half hour early, on April 6, 1918 for its observance of the first anniversary of America's entrance into the war. The ceremonies began when employees massed on the main floor of the store to listen to buglers blaring an introduction for assembly singing of "The Star Spangled Banner" as Hudson's launched its third Liberty Loan Drive.

In the absence of so many Detroit men, the first women mail-carriers appeared on the streets of the city, and women conductors began working on streetcars. A growing independence for women, as they took jobs formerly held only by men, was reflected in dress styles. The one-piece chemise, with a narrow belt at the hip, became popular—allowing greater freedom of movement for the wearer.

The continuing war across the ocean and the growing number of American "doughboys" shipped overseas to fight in France scarcely tinged the kind of innocent buoyancy pervading Detroit as automotive factories hired more workers to manufacture munitions and ambulances. Detroiters flourished their patriotism at songfests and war bond rallies as they endured, with varying degrees of cheer, home-front hardships—"heatless Mondays" and food shortages.

Exuberance only gradually became edged with anxiety as newspapers published American casualty lists. At Hudson's store, word passed quickly from one shocked employee to another as notification arrived of the first war casualty to claim the life of a former Hudson worker—handsome Jack Townley—in France.

But by October, 1918, an influenza epidemic was spreading out from the East coast, spewing its deadly fury into American cities across the nation and quickly—often within 48 hours—claiming the lives of its victims . . . killing 22 million people, worldwide, within a year. The shocking effect of war casualty lists paled by comparison.

In Detroit, as in other cities, theaters closed. Schools closed. People went about wearing gauze masks. Desperately ill citizens were denied admittance to under-staffed hospitals already overflowing with patients. Many doctors and nurses previously had left Harper Hospital to care for flu victims in army camps, where the disease flared through the barracks. Before the epidemic faded in the early winter months of 1919, three Harper nurses were among more than 1/2 million Americans who died of influenza.

Still, when the Armistice was announced on November 11, 1918, Detroiters roused themselves to pour into the streets and celebrate the Allied victory. Workers put down their tools and clerks deserted offices and stores to join the crowds gathering in front of city hall. Under effigies of the Kaiser, hanging from telephone poles, the crowds cheered, clapped, and began dancing on Woodward Avenue to celebrate a new era of peace.

Coinciding with the war's end, women's hemlines lifted to daring new heights—six inches below the knee. Hudson's sold the new, short, peg-top dresses, cut full at the waist and hips, to women who, just two years later, would hike their skirts still higher and become known as "flappers." Large hats remained popular, but the newest styles in millinery had brims set at the eyebrow line.

Mr. Jenkins, former Hudson's floorwalker in Ribbons, returned to the store where he was assigned to Hosiery, and life in Detroit settled into an accelerated period of postwar prosperity as the influenza epidemic subsided. No one guessed that it would return the following winter to plague Detroiters who had not yet built up an immunity to the disease.

In the flush of postwar prosperity, the Dodge Brothers approached directors of Hudson Motor Car Company, proposing a merger with Dodge that would include a takeover of Timken-Detroit Axle Company and Continental Motor Company. The Dodges wanted to acquire a more expensive car, and they also wanted control of the other three companies. Since Hudson Motor Car Company was already doing very well and had no desire to come under Dodge control, the plan was dropped.

The flourishing Hudson store checked the performance of its thirty "Tube Room girls" during the busy Christmas season of 1919—with what was termed "remarkable" results. Each "girl" could receive one of the red and white carriers, make necessary change, and return the carrier through the tube in an average 14 seconds.

By this time, Hudson's had acquired 25,000 charge customers whose names were listed on "rands" in the Charge Tube Room. There, workers checked their files ("rands") for credit customers' records, although the more experienced workers were so familiar with names of reliable credit customers that they approved many transactions without bothering to check.

By 1920, Detroit's population had more than doubled its 1910 census count to nearly a million people, becoming the fourth largest city in the United States. Three years earlier, the Detroit Board of Commerce directors had met to discuss providing proper housing for "Negroes" who were flooding in from the South to find work in the Motor City. The meeting would be only a faint stirring of the winds of discontent that would, in time, gust through the city, shaking its traditions and the complacency of its foremost citizens.

When Detroit installed the nation's first electric traffic signal at the busy downtown intersection of Woodward Avenue and Michigan Avenue in 1920, it symbolized the public's growing concern to have the potpourri of rushing traffic regulated; to have the free-wheeling motor car harnessed so that city streets would no longer be a no-man's land where citizens must scramble and skirmish for survival.

At the turn of the century, Mayor William Maybury had envisioned Detroit as "a quiet city quietly governed." Some current civic leaders, of the same temperament as the late, and staunchly Methodist, Joseph L. Hudson and his strait-laced Webber nephews, resolved to change Detroit's split-personality . . . to erase its earthy image as a lusty, brawling, grease-stained city of unlettered immigrants and replace it with the more gracious image of towering churches, a downtown shopping hub presided over by the cosmopolitan Hudson's store, a symphony orchestra and an art museum, and charming neighborhoods with tree-shaded boulevards and solidly built, attractive homes.

Both images mirrored the Detroit of 1920. Although Joseph L. Hudson had not lived to have the satisfaction of seeing Michigan turn "dry" in May, 1918, and the entire country turn "dry" in January, 1920, neither did he live to experience disillusionment as thousands of saloonkeepers continued to do business in Detroit by simply drawing curtains across their windows and selling bootlegged liquor. More than 500 whorehouses, including a thriving "red light" district on Detroit's lower east side, and an abundance of opium dens and gambling haunts continued to exist despite reformers' protests.

The automated traffic light at the heart of the city may have signified law and order, but the widely accelerating growth of Detroit was racing past the limits of disciplined and orderly containment into the "Roaring Twenties."

Chapter 6

A Golden Decade

The postwar economic boom brought another surge in Detroit's population, but the boom subsided as the country suddenly fell back into a period of business recession—the Panic of 1920. By 1922, production accelerated once again and the stock market began to climb. A new Hudson Motor Car Company was incorporated at that point, with 1,200,000 shares of no-par value stock, one-third of which went on the market as Hudson Motor's first public offering. Roscoe Jackson, the husband of Louise Webber, became president of the prospering automobile company which now produced both the larger Hudson car and a newer, low-priced Essex automobile.

As more working-class Americans found jobs in 1922, they began satisfying their aspirations to own automobiles, player pianos, phonographs and radios. The static-ridden radio reception of the early 1920s did not dampen the eagerness of an American public—lured by department store promotion of credit terms—to hear championship fight reports, news items, and election returns on their own radio sets. Hudson's sold quantities of radios in 1922, elevating its sales for that year—including sales from Hudson's

Piano Store—to nearly $26 million. 1923 sales topped the $30 million mark.

Theater entertainment attracted crowds to see Harold Lloyd, Mary Pickford and Jackie Coogan perform on the silver screens of new, lush motion-picture palaces furbished with velvet and marble, and suffused with the glorious resonance of cadenzas, arpeggios, and full-throated chords from tiered-key theater organs ringed with rainbow lights. Hudson's sold stacks of hats, with copies of Mary Pickford's signature inside, to women enamored of "America's Sweetheart." In its 1922 Christmas advertising, the store featured a Mary Pickford page headed with a photograph of the actress reading the story of Christmas to a group of children, accompanied by sketches of the sweet-faced Pickford in various screen roles.

In the early 1900s, Hudson's had ended its sponsorship of the J.L. Hudson Band to represent the store by marching in parades. The Webbers chose to have the store represented by a French horn quartet, a woodwind trio, and a dignified Hudson's Concert Band, with 40 instruments, which toured the state along with singing groups. Hudson's men's quartet wore identical suits, white bow ties, and stiff celluloid-like collars which may have helped the tenor stretch his neck for high notes but precluded the bass from scooping down for low tones. Hudson's "women's quartette" was a winsome group, wearing sleeveless, all-white dresses, belted low with a bloused waist effect. Blessed with a second soprano named May Flower Cowperthwaite, the four women regularly performed at schools, ladies' aid societies, and civic activities.

Hudson's Director of Musical Affairs was responsible, too, for 15 minutes of "inspirational singing of the highest type" in which J.L. Hudson employees joined each morning, on the first floor of the main building. The Webbers believed that a sing-along helped employees to "start the day off right."

Among the many engagements filled by the music director and his instrumental and singing groups was a performance at the Detroit Statler Hotel for the 23rd annual meeting of the American Booksellers' Association in May, 1923. Although most of Hudson's female employees were unmarried, since young ladies of the 1920s customarily left their jobs for the joys of housekeeping when they acquired husbands, the head of Hudson's book department was a Mrs. Morris. For each of the four days of the booksellers' convention, Mrs. Morris appeared at the Statler to meet publishers and the popular author, Irving Bachellor.

At Hudson's Book Shop, Mrs. Morris stocked an array of Zane Gray's novels in response to customer demand. Hudson's salesgirls crowded the book department on their lunch breaks, buying copies of current and very popular love stories . . . *Trodden Gold, The Vision of Desire, The Enchanted April* . . . and envying the glamorous jobs of clerks who worked in "Books" and had access to celebrated writers who came for autograph sessions.

Lanky, red-headed Sinclair Lewis breezed into the Book Shop in November, 1922, to autograph copies of his latest novel, *Babbitt*, only two years after *Main Street* brought him great success with its portrayal of small town smugness and intolerance contrasted with big-city sophistication. It is doubtful that Lewis would have included the Midwestern city of Detroit, now fourth largest in the country, as a desirable cosmopolis. But as Detroit grew from 21 square miles in 1918 to 139 square miles by 1927 when its assessed value reached more than $3 million, the Motor City gleaned a number of glowing tributes from such prestigious sources as the *New York Times*.

The *Times* lauded Detroiters as "the most prosperous slice of average humanity that now exists or ever has existed," while magazines described the city as "shockingly dynamic," complimenting Detroit for its high wages and short hours, and for schools which "are a boast of American education." New skyscrapers, including the 47-story Penobscot Building, added spectacular dimension to the Detroit skyline of the 1920s, and the handsome, 29-floor Book Cadillac Hotel, with 1,200 guest rooms and a staff also numbering 1,200 — including 100 French cooks, was built in 1924 and hailed as the tallest hotel in the world.

When the patrician, and church-going, John C. Lodge became the city's mayor in 1922, he worked tirelessly to enhance Detroit's positive image. The Webber brothers, following their uncle Joseph L. Hudson's anti-saloon stance, took satisfaction in announcing that sales of candy at Hudson's were proliferating in the wake of Prohibition, contributing to annual confectionery sales of $1 billion, nationwide. These results, Hudson's newsletter pontificated, "ought to convert us all to sweets and make a return to booze forever impossible." Stroh's ice cream became a Detroit by-product of Prohibition's arrival as the huge, red-brick Stroh's Brewery shut off the flow of beer to its great vats and began churning out frozen, sweetened cream in a variety of flavors.

But Detroit had not rid itself of its split personalilty. The poisonous oozing from the city's soft, rotten underbelly fermented as the 1920s became a heyday for Detroit rum-runners who operated flourishing businesses by transporting Canadian liquor across the Detroit River in high-powered boats. Gang wars erupted when liquor supplies, trucked to bootleggers in cities across the Midwest, were hijacked by other gangsters, armed with machine guns and sawed-off shotguns.

Beer flats, complete with entertainment, criss-crossed the city of Detroit. Speakeasies—known locally as "blind pigs" and ranging from plush nightclubs to hole-in-the-wall saloons—attracted throngs of thirsty, pleasure-seeking Detroiters. The flagrancy of this illicit liquor trade brought condemnation to the Motor City in those same years of the early 1920s that had drawn praise from the New York press. A Rockefeller Commission issued a statement that Detroit was the "wickedest city" in the country. *Life* magazine described the automotive city as "soused and serene."

Hudson's emporium, a reservoir of serenity, rose grandly from crowded Woodward Avenue, shielded from the city's corruption and carousing as effectually as the store's thickly carpeted floors and glossy fixtures were separated from the sewer pipes that ran through its subterranean levels. Large, gleaming automobiles, driven by liveried chauffeurs, delivered ladies of wealth to Hudson's Farmer Street entrance where a uniformed doorman deferentially assisted them from their motor cars to the store's red-carpeted entrance.

Near the more crowded Woodward entrance, the noisy snarl of clattering traffic was tamed at the city's hub where the police department kept an officer stationed at the intersection near Hudson's. Beginning in 1924 and continuing for the next 25 years, patrolman Courtney "Jack" Coombs served as ringmaster at the crossing, beckoning pedestrians across the avenue with one white-gloved hand while holding back the surge of traffic with the other hand, occasionally tipping his white cap to ladies while staring forbiddingly at drivers who dared edge forward as Coombs blew shrill warning-blasts on his whistle. When, years later, Officer Coombs was still a fixture at Detroit's hub, downtown merchants converged on the patrolman's station one Christmas Eve and piled gifts at the policeman's feet as traffic stopped and pedestrians stared at the mid-intersection pageant.

Hudson's delivery men wore natty attire—puttees and knickers, long string-ties, and caps—which rivaled that of patrolman Coombs. As the Hudson employees drove about the city in trucks with open front seats, the drivers frequently were hailed by citizens who seemed to regard the white J.L. Hudson Company lettering on the sides of the trucks as Red Cross insignia. Encouraged by the Webbers to be responsive to the needs of Detroiters, Hudson drivers were known to pick up stranded motorists and to rush them to train stations or hospitals, to return lost children to their mothers and lost dogs to their owners, to deliver perishables and place them in ice boxes when there was no one home, and to follow instructions left in notes on kitchen tables . . . notes that might ask a driver to please remove a pan of baked beans from the oven, or to take a written message to a neighbor.

At the store's Delivery section—a building at Beacon and Beaubien, back of the store—a White tractor-trailer combination shuttled between the store and Hudson's sub-station, transporting packages for sorting. The sub-station also housed Hudson's own print shop.

Within the store itself, stocked with the latest fashions in clothing and furnishings and with the most recent labor-saving devices, an air of Victorian gentility and decorum prevailed . . . a courtly tranquility that the Webbers had committed themselves to maintain. They set up employee training programs emphasizing the need for clerks to be polite, pleasant and helpful to customers, and to be neatly dressed in the dark skirt, white blouse quasi-uniforms prescribed by the Webbers' esteemed uncle, J.L. Hudson.

When a customer, as reported in a 1923 Hudson newsletter, selected a spool of thread, charged it, and asked to have it delivered, the clerk smiled and complied. The smile encouraged the customer to remove her muddied galoshes and to ask if the clerk would also include the galoshes with the delivery.

Floorwalkers and supervisors, who strolled about the store, made note of clerks who did not smile, rouged their cheeks, or used such forbidden terms as "Girlie," "Dearie," or "Little Lady" to address customers. These clerks were summoned upstairs, to inner offices, where they were questioned and reprimanded.

Detroit's black community, which had muliplied to 41,000 in 1920 and to twice that number by the middle 1920s, was represented among Hudson employees — mostly as maids, janitors, and elevator operators. A black woman, known to store employees as "Johnny," wore a dark uniform with a wide white collar and white headband, with scalloped edges, set low on her forehead for her work in "Infants." When a clerk sold infant furniture, it was "Johnny's" responsibility to clean the furnishings of any finger marks or dust before delivery from "Infants" where a registered nurse displayed her professionalism by demonstrating the use of modern "Vanta" garments — teaching customers to dress babies without buttons or pins.

Dr. Clyde Chase reigned over Hudson's "Hospital," now equipped with four beds and 25 cots and treating from 80 to 100 people each day. The department also employed two visiting nurses who went, in Hudson Motor Cars, to the homes of employees reporting illnesses — calling on an average 20 to 25 workers each day.

Both men and women ran the store's elevators — the men wearing bell-hop type caps, the women in high-necked uniforms with long skirts and long sleeves, their hair pulled back severely from their faces. A steady stream of female customers poured out of the elevators on the seventh floor in the early twenties, crowding into the beauty salon to sacrifice their long tresses to the new fashion — bobbed hair. Some Hudson clerks were among those who were sheared of their long hair in the beauty shop, exciting comments in the pages of the store's in-house magazine. Such comments were variations on "the girls in 'ribbons' are oohing and aahing over Miss McGinchy's short hair" type of theme.

Each store department contributed chatty items to Hudson's little monthly publication — news of which employee owned a new dog . . . comments on Miss Dunlap having "a new Ford Sedan and taking special lessons in driving" . . . playful jibes about Miss Skidmore having "her head in the clouds; Leonard must have called her." Most issues carried the names of women employees who were taking leaves of absence to care for "sick mothers," or teasing references to clerks who were "taking the rest cure," quickly explained as taking time off for housecleaning.

Other pages of the magazine reported on the current status of the "Girls' Bowling League" and the "Men's Bowling League," and offered glowing reports of which female employee was sporting a diamond ring or filling a "hope chest"—and which hapless male employee ("fallen brother") was surrendering his freedom to the chant of "another good man gone wrong." This sort of waggishness accompanied frequent printings of Edgar Guest's poems, vacation suggestions, proverbs of "the man who sticks to the beaten path usually make a rut of it" type, and accounts of amusing customer-clerk incidents at the store.

The last-mentioned incidents included the tale of the "lad" who asked for "some of that stuff that opens and closes"—meaning elastic, the clerk discovered. Such enigmatic requests were not always interpreted correctly, since many foreign-born customers, who had recently come to work in Detroit's factories, shopped at Hudson's. For that reason, the very proper "Waspish" Webbers like to hire clerks who were fluent in a second language.

When, several years after the innovation of the bobbed-hair vogue, the boyish "shingle" came into fashion along with the flat-chested, flapper look, the Webbers announced that the "shingle" was not permissible for Hudson female employees. Clerks at Hudson's were encouraged to wear their hair parted in the center with neatly marcelled waves covering their ears. Some of Hudson's customers, those as strongly traditionalist as the Webber brothers, continued to resist the bobbed-hair fad and to patronize Miss Wein's Hair Goods department—offering hairnets, snoods, rats, jeweled hairpins, aigrettes, and "real hair" switches. But less inhibited young women crowded the seventh floor Beauty Shop which expanded to include 85 employees—17 barbers, 40 hairdressers, 16 manicurists, and a dozen clerks.

The Webbers' traditonalist instincts were no impediment to their plans for major expansion of the store in the prosperous 1920s. The same decade brought a series of changes to the closely knit Hudson-Webber family. On October 25, 1921, "Mr. Dick" Webber kept the store closed until noon in observance of funeral services for Joseph L. Hudson's eldest sister, Anna Tannahill. Anna had died at the Hudson home on East Boston Boulevard, leaving her husband—Robert B. Tannahill, her 28-year-old son—Robert Hudson Tannahill, two sisters—Eliza Clay and Mary Eleanor Webber, and a brother—William Hudson of Buffalo.

In early June, 1923, the Webbers closed the store for the funeral for their 71-year-old mother, Mary Eleanor Webber, known for her work for Detroit charities. Mary Eleanor left $5,000 to her maid for "faithful service," jewelry and personal effects to her daughter, Louise, and willed $10,000 and the family home on Iroquois to her husband, J.T. Webber, until his death when it would become the property of the eldest son, Richard. The rest was divided equally among the other children.

Two years later, Anna Tannahill's husband, Robert B., died after a two-year illness which had forced him to resign as a vice president of the J.L. Hudson Company. Since the day he had started working at Mabley's store—on the same day that Joseph L. Hudson began working for Mabley in Detroit—Tannahill's life had been closely linked with the Hudson family. His funeral service, like that of his wife, was held at the East Boston Boulevard residence that had been his home ever since Joe Hudson bought the house.

Only the son, Robert H. Tannahill, and his aunt, Eliza Clay, remained in the huge Hudson home, rattling around in the house that had been filled with family a few years previously. Young Tannahill, who was much more interested in collecting art than in aspiring to his father's position as vice-president of the J.L. Hudson Company, was not urged to join, or compete with, his cousins—the Webbers. He continued to live with his Aunt Eliza until the Hudson house was sold. Then he moved, with his aunt, into the spacious Indian Village district home on Iroquois Avenue, in which Eleanor Clay Ford and her husband, Edsel, had lived until they moved to a two-acre East Jefferson Avenue estate and, in 1929, to Grosse Pointe.

A GOLDEN DECADE

The Indian Village home was one of four on Iroquois Avenue occupied by the close-knit Hudson-Webber family shortly before 1920. One of the other three manors, all designed by architect Leonard B. Willeke, had been built by Eliza Clay as a wedding present for her older daughter, Josephine Clay Kanzler. Louise Webber Jackson and her husband, Roscoe, built their elegant home next door to the Kanzlers. The senior Webbers owned the fourth home in the handsomely designed enclave which, the Hudsons recognized, was a public reflection of the artistic tastes of a family whose Woodward Avenue store dominated Detroit . . . a store featuring a prestigious interior design department reigned over by Mrs. Sidney Corbett, Jr.

In March, 1922, Richard and Eloise Webber, who now lived in Grosse Pointe, became the parents of a baby boy, their third child. They named the child, their only son, Joseph Hudson Webber—for the uncle revered by Richard. This son, they hoped, would preserve family traditions in the flourishing department store engraved with the uncle's name.

There was ample room for the four stocky, blue-eyed Webber brothers in the bustling department store business. But Richard turned most often to his youngest, energetic brother, Oscar, for the kind of ideas that would spark his own vigor and inventiveness.

"Mr. Dick and "Mr. Oscar" had conferred with Joe Mills, hired by Richard in 1914 to direct Hudson's public-relations department, in planning the program for Hudson's fortieth anniversary of the 1881 date when the "House of Hudson" was founded in the Detroit Opera House. The anniversary program began on August 30, 1921, with a free performance for Hudson employees at Orchestra Hall where "Hudson's 40th Anniversary Minstrels" presented the kind of "black wig and burnt cork" minstrel show popular at that time, complete with "60 blackface artists, 4 end men, and 10 high salaried soloists." Mills also brought in "vaudeville acts from New York," including that of Joe Jackson—the "Tramp Bicycle Rider," to entertain Detroit audiences.

A storewide Fortieth Anniversary Sale attracted crowds of shoppers who then walked up Woodward to the Madison Theatre where Hudson's had built a runway out from the stage center. Hudson models pranced along the stage and down the runway, presenting a review of costumes of 1880, 1885, and every fifth-year period through 1920, capped with the modern bride of 1921—all to the accompaniment of "Sweet Alice Ben Bolt" and music appropriate to the individual era.

By the spring of 1923, the Webbers were ready to extend their Woodward Avenue frontage to close a gap between their Woodward building and their men's store—a gap still occupied by Himelhoch's. The brothers bought the Himelhoch building, razed it, and added thousands of feet of floor space to Hudson's as they constructed a connecting building of ten floors to solidify their Woodward facade up to the neighboring stronghold of Newcomb, Endicott—Hudson's longtime competitor. In 1924, they completed two additional stories over the entire Woodward unit.

Joe Mills' public relations' exploits attracted 15,000 people to Woodward Avenue near Hudson's on Armistice Day, 1923, when Mills arranged for the Quantico U.S. Marine Band to play "The Star Spangled Banner" in front of the store in a Hudson's salute to America's veterans. Uniformed Boy Scouts stood at attention as Hudson workers unfurled "The World's Largest Flag"—a 900 pound "Stars and Stripes"—across a 230-foot expanse of the store's facade, above the bronze doors and marble entrances. When the flag was unrolled to its full length, the clear, brassy tones of the national anthem echoed up and down Woodward Avenue.

As the Christmas holidays approached, the Webbers hired additional clerks until, on the busiest pre-Christmas sales days, as many as 1,650 salespeople worked at Hudson's store. The store's in-house magazine warned salespeople of "things that displease customers," which included workers calling each other by first names in the presence of customers, using slang or "unpolished language," talking to someone else while serving a customer, or criticizing other stores.

An Old Newsboys' Goodfellow Booth, set up in Hudson's Toys department in the pre-Christmas season of 1924, was stacked with packets of dolls to be handed out to "any woman or child who wishes to dress one or more dolls to gladden the heart of some child on Christmas." Hudson's advertised its undressed dolls until several thousand had been handed over or sent to people who would sew

A GOLDEN DECADE

costumes for them. As the dolls were returned, each named by its costume-designer, they were arranged in a massive display in the store's Woodward Avenue windows until prizes were awarded for the costuming and the dolls were distributed to needy youngsters. Never had the name "Betty" been so popular as in 1924 when 2/3 of the dresser-named dolls flaunted "Betty" tags.

The glorification of Hudson's twelfth floor Toyland as Santa Claus' Detroit headquarters was another of Joe Mills' ingenious projects in the early 1920s. Mills arranged for Santa to officially "arrive" at the big Woodward store in a razzle-dazzle of publicity that swelled into the first Hudson-sponsored Thanksgiving parade down Woodward Avenue in 1925. Three hundred male employees, all from Hudson's offices, volunteered to take part in that first parade — 18 of them walking under an 85-foot-long green covering that made up an enormous caterpillar, weaving down Woodward Avenue. The Detroit Creamery Company loaned its hefty horses and milk wagons to transport Santa and to pull 26 other floats built from wooden frames, chicken wire, and *papier mache.*

Inside an old tabernacle at Antoinette and Cass, where Billy Sunday once had shouted his fiery sermons, parade participants milled about on the sawdust floor as they got into their costumes and waited for the signal to line up for the march down Second Avenue, around Cass Park to Elizabeth Street, and down Woodward to Hudson's store. When the signal was given, the creamery horses and wagons lumbered past a crowd of more than 150,000 people lining the streets, their cheering drowned in the roar of a dozen police-motorcycles, three bands, and several iron-wheeled hay wagons pressed into service to augment the milk drays.

Among the cheering spectators were one thousand orphans, brought to Detroit by Hudson's from other parts of the state, screaming excitedly from their reserved grandstand as they watched a horse-and-wagon-drawn Mother Goose float, 18 feet long and 15 feet wide, rumble past behind the motorcycle division. Behind Mother Goose came a retinue of nursery-rhyme floats and a 20-foot-long Goozlebug, one of only a few built on a tractor that crawled, snakelike, along Woodward.

Spectators held children on their shoulders to see the live elephant, named "Toto" to represent a stuffed toy in demand at Hudson's toy department. They held the children still higher when Santa Claus, on the last float, climbed the steps to Hudson's marquee where Acting Mayor Bradley waited to hand the North Pole visitor the key to the city. At that point, the parade watchers returned to their high, boxy automobiles, parked on Second Avenue, or lined up for streetcar transportation to their homes. The next day, thousands of them returned to join crowds of people shopping in Hudson's Christmas wonderland as a Hudson's tradition was established that would last for almost 60 years.

For the Webbers, the apex of the Golden Decade, the 1920s, was achieving their dream of expanding a modern Hudson's store over most of one solid block at Detroit's shopping hub. In 1924, the brothers boasted that Hudson's was the first department store to have air-conditioning after the Webbers purchased a centrifugal refrigeration system for cooling the Basement Store. Sales zoomed as increasing numbers of Detroiters came to shop where they could find relief from the city's sultry summer heat.

By September, 1924, the Webbers were embarking on the biggest financial gamble of their lives as they moved all their stock and equipment out of half of the nine-floor Farmer Street building — the store built by Joseph Lowthian Hudson in 1891. With 108,000 square feet of space vacant as stock and fixtures were carted into other departments and temporary quarters, the empty half-building was torn down and replaced in 1925 by a new 16-story edifice constructed of concrete with steel framework and steel columns, each weighing from 15 to 36 tons. The strength of the foundation and frame would allow for the erecting of five more stories on top, whenever the brothers decided to have additional space.

In 1926, the Webbers razed the second half of the old Farmer Street store. Before the end of the year, a matching 16-story building had been finished and a quarter-million dollar ventilation system — which drew air into the building, then washed, cooled and dried the air to the desired temperature — was in place . . . the first ventilation system of its kind installed in a U.S. department store. The new buildings provided two levels for the Basement Store and ten above-ground floors for merchandising, plus eleventh floor executive offices—soon known to employees as the "Golden Corridor." A twelfth floor auditorium seating 1,200 people. Buyers' offices, educational rooms, and alteration rooms on the 13th floor. An employees' cafeteria on the 14th floor that could feed 2,500 employees every noon, 400 at a time. A 15th floor occupied by receiving, marking and stock rooms. And a 16th floor for various services, including carpenters and painters.

Still, the Newcomb, Endicott store, sitting in all its aging magnificence at the north end of the Woodward Avenue block that the Webbers wanted for Hudson's, was a thorn in the flesh of the brothers. But in 1927, Newcomb, Endicott agreed to sell out to Hudson's. A year later, the Webbers erected a 17-story building with a 25-story tower on the newly purchased site. This building not only doubled the facilities of Hudson's store and enlarged the Basement Store to 160,000 square feet, but it also completed Hudson's frontage on four streets—Woodward, Farmer, Gratiot, and Grand River except for a small piece of property at the corner of Woodward and Gratiot occupied by the Sallan Building. The Webbers could not have known that it would take nearly 20 years to acquire that corner.

In the same year that the new Hudson's building was erected at the site of the former Newcomb, Endicott store, the last of the store-founder's brothers died in Buffalo, New York. With the death of 75-year-old William Hudson, who left a son—Joseph Lowthian, only Eliza Clay remained alive of the seven original Hudson brothers and sisters. The following year brought another death to the family when the Webber brothers' only sister, Louise, was widowed as her husband, 50-year-old Roscoe Jackson, died of influenza. With Jackson's death, the Hudson family's active participation in the Hudson Motor Car Company ended.

As early as 1923, Detroit's population (including Highland Park and Hamtramck—both surrounded by Detroit) had soared to 1,090,843. Booming motor car sales and a flourishing economy throughout the country encouraged the Webbers in their expansion and promotions plans. They offered a twice-yearly Grand Prize Suggestion Contest that encouraged employees ("Hudsonians") to make suggestions for better working conditions and improved methods of operating the store. First prize—a trip to New York. Second prize—$50 in gold. Third prize—$25 in gold, and $10 in gold for fourth prize.

Shiny gold pieces may have been hoarded by some, but were spent freely by others who shopped at Hudson's for rare laces from Switzerland, tapestries from Belgium, rugs from China, Irish linens, and London and Parisian ribbons. As early as 1920, when the all-American Webbers set up offices in various European and Asian countries, Hudson's store offered choice selections of imported goods "for style of workmanship that cannot be done here." The Webber brothers pointed out that many laces, organdies, and swisses were bought overseas because they had to be "woven under water for certain desirable textures."

Hudson's buyers left by train for New York where they boarded steamships and spent three months of the winter or early spring in London and traveling "on the continent," wrapped in warm streamer rugs in their train compartments. And Hudson's advertised its "Spring Dresses from Paris" in full page advertisements, without apology.

In 1927, when Harper Hospital directors launched a fund-raising program to build a new Hudson Memorial Building which would include a surgical unit providing for 750 patients, Richard and Eloise Webber made the largest single money pledge—$500,000. With this generous donation, the Webbers established their reputation as philanthropists who, beginning in 1932, would quietly set up the first of three Webber and Hudson-Webber foundations to distribute millions of dollars each year for improving the quality of life in Metropolitan Detroit.

Except for the brief Panic of 1920-21, the country's economy had been flourishing for a decade when President Herbert Hoover took office on March 4, 1929. Although only a small number of families in the United States—8.2%—had annual incomes of $5,000 or more, and a large number—59.5%—had incomes of $2,000 or less, Americans were buying automobiles, silk stockings, and bathtub gin. They lined up in front of motion-picture palaces to see Al Jolson, Janet Gaynor, and Billie Dove in "talking pictures" and to cheer their heroes, Babe Ruth and Jack Dempsey, in Pathe newsreels.

Detroiters boasted of their new city airport, their new Detriot Institute of Arts Building, and their Olympia Stadium which attracted crowds to sporting events. Hudson's Music Store, relaxing some of its taboos, sold quantities of sheet music for Hoagy Carmichael's "Star Dust," and it seemed that the city of Detroit, bursting with vitality, was, indeed, burnished with star dust.

By this time, Oscar Webber and his wife and daughers had followed the Richard Webbers into the Grosse Pointe environs, moving into a splendid new home, complete with elaborate gardens and fountains, built for them by Leonard Willeke on Lake Shore Drive in Grosse Pointe Shores. Willeke, who was hired in 1928 by the Webbers to design the eighth floor Fine Art Galleries and Antiques department, plus other ninth and tenth floor departments, for the new J.L. Hudson Building, found that designing a home for the strong-minded Oscar Webber was a difficult venture. Webber periodically demanded a series of new designs and alterations that delayed the work.

Still, Willeke's work on Oscar Webber's home led to another commission for the architect from William A. Petzold, secretary and treasurer of the J.L. Hudson Company. The design of the Petzold home, built in Grosse Pointe Park, reflected the English-style architecture of the larger Oscar Webber residence.

As far back as 1881, when 12-year-old Petzold had come to work as parcel boy at the opening of Joseph Lowthian Hudson's first Detroit store, the youthful employee had walked, deferentially, in Joseph Hudson's footsteps. Sent to business college by Hudson, the ambitious Petzold continued his education with night studies at law school until he earned a law degree. At the store, he came up through the ranks to bookkeeper, cashier, and, in 1899, to treasurer. Two years later, he became the company's secretary-treasurer, and was still treading the Hudson-Webber course at the time of J.L. Hudson's death in 1912, at which time his faithful service was rewarded with a bequest of stock in the privately owned J.L. Hudson Company.

The 79-year-old Petzold would be honored by the Webbers with a vice-presidency appointment in 1948, three years before his retirement after 70 years with the company. Petzold's length of employment and his achievements established a record, but his advancement through the ranks was typical of the rise of Hudson employees to better positions within the company and the rewarding of long term executive employees with shares of Hudson's closely held stock.

By the end of the 1920s, after all the original Hudson brothers had died, the staid and sober Webber brothers sold the last of the out-of-town Hudson branch stores, except for the Buffalo store which would be sold to another company in the early 1930s. With company sales figures totalling $67 million in 1929, the Webbers were obsessed with expansion and sales growth for their beautiful Woodward Avenue department store and with their "all eggs in one basket" tenet.

The Webbers were unworried, at this point, about the $10 million note outstanding for the expansion of their Greater Hudson Store with the acquistion of the Newcomb, Endicott site. The J.L. Hudson Company was now the third largest department store in the nation—after Macy's in New York and Marshall Field's in Chicago; annual sales had reached a peak and, until the time of the stock market crash in October, 1929, even the practical Webbers were caught up in the American public's anticipation of bigger and better things to come.

Chapter 7

Dreary Days; Troubled Times

No city in the country was hit harder by the Great Depression than was Detroit. Within a year of the October, 1929, stock market crash, 5,000 of the nation's banks collapsed and six million workers lost their jobs. By 1932, the worst year of the Depression, the toll of unemployed reach 15 million. Few people could afford to buy cars, and, as the giant automobile industry shriveled and fell to its knees, Detroit's pulse beat more slowly . . . more faintly.

The Webber brothers worried, now, about their lavish building program and their $10 million debt as Hudson's sales volume plummeted, in 1930, to $31 million—less than half its 1929 sales. Although limousines still rolled up to Hudson's Farmer Street entrance where doorman William, a black man resplendent in a brass-buttoned uniform, opened the door for ladies of wealth, the rows of Hudson elevators were no longer jammed with customers. Many women wandered about the store without ever opening their handbags. Instead, they walked the aisles, bringing their children to gaze at the model Helen Hayes Dollhouse on display, its windows hung with curtains and its miniature furnishings carefully arranged under the glow of tiny chandeliers. The dollhouse continued to symbolize the American Dream, even though, at Christmas time, most shoppers considered carefully before purchasing as much as a game of Monopoly—the craze of the early 1930s.

Behind Hudson's on Randolph Street, Sam's Cut-Rate store attracted working-class customers from Hudson's Basement Store to Sam's—touted as "the largest single retailer of work clothes in America." Sam's Cut-Rate also offered household goods, prescription drugs, and a variety of essential products at cash-and-carry low prices. Elegant furnishings and super-courteous salepeople were no longer so important to Depression-era shoppers with thin wallets.

Still, Oscar Webber drew crowds to Hudson's Basement Store in 1931 with a 16th Basement Birthday Sale that filled its 106 fitting rooms with customers trying on black and white, or navy and white, one-piece dresses with jackets. Despite the competition from Sam's, Hudson's boasted of 14,000 photographs taken in its Basement Store photography studio during February . . . 400,000 silk dresses sold there in the past year.

Refusing to bow to the oppressive economic climate, the Webbers struggled to maintain a vigorous but dignified image for their Woodward Avenue store. One innovation of 1931 was a WWJ radio broadcast describing Hudson's Thanksgiving Parade, which had grown larger each year, as it moved down Woodward. The use of horses to pull floats had ended after an accident with a runaway team in an early-year parade. At the sound of a sudden fanfare from a practicing band, the team bolted, float dragging behind, and ran into a gas station building—wrecking both float and building. Because of this incident, horse-drawn wagons were withdrawn in favor of tractors and man-power—as many as 24 people required to move one float. More tractors soon would come into use as a result of cold-weather problems—metal-rimmed wagon wheels freezing to the street surface or sticking in trolley-car tracks.

Joe Mills saw to it that Christmas at Hudson's was festive, even in those years of low volume holiday sales. In 1931, he organized Hudson Carolers—a group of Hudson-employee singers, who auditioned for membership in the Carolers. The group met for early morning rehearsals, then sang at the store every morning during the holidays. By 1933, the Hudson singers were broadcasting from radio WWJ as a part of the new Hudson Minute Parade—another of Mills' innovations.

Inside the beautifully decorated store, it was possible to forget, for a time, that the worst years of the Great Depression were still wreaking vengeance on the Automotive City. But those who came out of Hudson's Woodward Avenue door into the January cold of 1931 could see a crowd of unemployed men gathered in front of Detroit City Hall to demand action from city officials . . . could watch in horror as mounted police rode right into the crowd to disperse the protesters. Still, it took a much more appalling incident, a 1932 protest march of 300 men to the gates of the Ford Motor Company's Rouge plant, to rouse a new era of activism in Detroit when police and plant guards fired their guns into the crowd, killing four of the marchers.

At the corner in front of Hudson's store, newsboys sold Detroit papers with photos of disheartened men milling around the barred gates of automobile plants . . . photos of children standing in bread lines—as many as 400 youngsters in one line. Photographers set up their tripods on Woodward again when President Herbert Hoover made a pre-election visit to Detroit in 1932. Bitter, unemployed men and shabbily dressed women and children lined the avenue and an eerie silence greeted Hoover as the presidential car moved down the wide street, past the sullen crowd.

Hoover's loss to Franklin Delano Roosevelt in a landslide November vote aroused great excitement among union organizers and brewery and distillery owners, and kindled hope among the unemployed. But the Webber brothers, like most traditional Republican businessmen, nervously regarded Roosevelt as a radical reformer with his promises of federally funded programs to put people to work, his support for unions, his pledge to work for the repeal of Prohibition, and his Presidential Proclamation which temporarily closed all banks that had not already failed.

When Congress repealed the Eighteenth Amendment in 1933, Michigan was the first state to adopt the repeal amendment. The Webbers went on with their lives as if the repeal had not occurred, and refused to allow Hudson advertising to include descriptions of such colors as "champagne beige," "burgundy," "claret" or any other hue associated with alcohol. When, some years later, "cocktail" dresses became fashionable, the Webbers insisted that Hudson advertising should use the term "after-five" dresses.

In that same year of 1933, Detroit became the first large city in the nation to complete its NRA (National Industrial Recovery Act) Drive in late summer. Since an important section of the Act affirmed employees' rights to organize into unions and to bargain collectively with employers, a rash of protests and picketing broke out in Detroit, led by union organizers. But because unemployment was still a major problem in Detroit, with 80% of black men out of work, four more years would pass before the Motor City would be wrenched by mass sit-down strikes and fierce battles between unionists and police.

Even as the Depression prevailed through the dreary months of 1933, the Webbers never abandoned their commitment to introduce new concepts into Hudson's that would attract more customers to the store. One of the innovations of 1933 was Hudson's Bridal Registry—the first in the country. Even the Webber brothers could not have imagined how popular their Bridal Registry would become . . . how quickly other prestigious stores would adopt the idea . . . how unconventional it soon would be for a Detroit bride not to be "registered at Hudson's." The number of registrants grew each year until as many as 16,500 brides' names would fill the Detroit store's listings each year of the 1960s, making Hudson's Bridal Registry the world's largest register.

In May, 1934, J.T. Webber—the 83-year-old father of the Webber brothers and their sister Louise O'Brien, now remarried—died in his Iroquois Avenue home. Although the Depression continued, the year became one of faint promise symbolized by the country's love affair with a ringlet-haired motion-picture moppet, Shirley Temple, who sang and danced her way through "Stand Up and Cheer" and "Little Miss Marker." For the price of a 25-cent movie ticket, a customer at a theater box-office could see a "double feature" and have a chance to win a "Bank Night" lottery. Hudson's sold Shirley Temple paper dolls, huge jigsaw puzzles, and the most popular fashions in 1934 women's wear—dirndl skirts and turban-styled hats.

In grocery stores, milk sold at ten cents a quart and bread at seven cents a loaf—a family of four could buy groceries, carefully, for five dollars a week. And if there were a few dimes left over in the family budget, they could be risked on a number of get-rich-fast schemes . . . in illegal slot machines installed in beer gardens, in dime-a-chance punch-boards—equally illegal—carried around in the pockets of desperate entrepreneurs, and in chain letters with dimes sent to names at the head of the letters.

When youthful Louise Solomon was hired to work at Hudson's in 1934, she was happy to get the job and to enroll in Hudson's sales-training program. This program gave the tall, handsome Louise the opportunity to rotate through every store department in the course of a year. She moved on from her first job, putting stickers on cheese, to more interesting assignments, such as modeling wide-legged beach pajamas, and, finally, into Millinery where she soon became a buyer. Since most millinery was bought in this country, Louise, unlike many buyers, was not required to travel to Europe, but made as many as 23 train trips in one year to Chicago, to California, and to the East Coast.

Ambitious to do well, Louise was promoted again, becoming a buyer for Hudson's Crystal Room, stocked with higher priced clothing by major designers. In the Crystal Room, there was not such a quick turnover of merchandise, and buying trips to London, Paris, Zurich, and Florence, where Hudson's representatives stayed at the Ritz or other luxury hotels, became a part of Louise's busy life.

Ambition never stirred more strongly within Louise than on the day she attended a meeting of buyers presided over by Oscar Webber. When one woman boldly demanded to know why women were not promoted higher than buyer at Hudson's, Louise pressed her long, tapered fingernails into the palms of her hands as Webber explained that women took time out to have children . . . that they were too emotional. "I have yet to find a woman who is capable of a management job," he said.

Such male attitudes were typical in the 1930s and 1940s, and Louise and other ambitious female Hudson employees realized that it would not be easy to find employers as fair-minded, gentlemanly, and generous as the Webber brothers. On one point, however, Richard Webber, especially, and his brother Oscar, to a slightly lesser degree, were determined to allow no disgressing—the matter of alcoholic beverages.

When a California designer came to Hudson's to stage a show in the fashion era when "cocktail dresses" first became popular, Crystal Room buyers warned him to use the more acceptable "late-day dresses" terminology while he remained in Hudson territory. Instead, the designer chose to vent his irritation by poking fun at the Webbers' rules. "We don't call this a cocktail dress," he joked as one of the models walked down the runway. "We call it a drinking dress." The joke backfired when the designer was never permitted to return to Hudson's.

Still, the sedate Webbers saw the humor in certain situations, even those in which store employees burst the boundaries of Hudson protocol. When Receiving hired a new employee, the young woman became totally confused in a blitz of paperwork on her first day of work. Frantic at the thought of losing her job, she decided to tear up all the paper, dispose of it, and start out fresh the next day. The Webbers saw to it that the tearful employee was lectured and then given a second chance.

A stock boy in the Junior Department encountered an even more troublesome disposal problem. On the day that a mouse emerged in the department and scampered across the floor, scattering horrified clerks and shoppers, a Junior Department buyer summoned the stock boy and ordered him to catch the mouse. The boy must get rid of it, the buyer ordered, before the tiny rodent ruined Hudson's hallowed reputation.

The mouse-catching expedition was performed with swiftness and discretion. The mouse dispatching was even swifter, but much less discreet, as the stock boy quickly disposed of the dazed animal in the nearest container—one of the metal carriers placed inside a pneumatic tube bound for the eleventh floor Tube Room. A "tube girl," sitting on her high stool at the receiving end, opened the receptacle only to fall from her perch to the floor as the mouse popped out of the carrier.

Nature provided a much more troublesome, and serious, situation on July 8, 1936, when a killer heat wave moved into Michigan. Detroiters crowded into department stores to buy electric fans as

DREARY DAYS; TROUBLED TIMES

the temperature soared to 104.4 degrees later that afternoon. People filled air-conditioned motion picture theaters that night, sleeping in the seats, and pushed their way from scorched sidewalks into the cool relief of Hudson's the next day. By midnight of the second day, the relentless heat had killed 22 Detroiters. And exhausted Detroiters no longer had the energy to come downtown to Hudson's. Offices closed, and Woodward Avenue, emptied of its crowds, took on the appearance of a deserted rural highway sizzling under the sun. When, on the seventh day of the suffocating heat, the temperature again hit the 104-degree mark, relief came suddenly as a wild thunderstorm drenched Detroit, restoring normal temperatures and normal activities to a city in which 364 people had died from the blistering temperatures.

After seven days, the killer heat wave had ended; after seven years, the killer Depression still was tapering off in 1936. As early as 1934, Chrysler Corporation had introduced its "airflow" designed automobiles, setting a trend toward "streamlining" that was subsequently adopted by other automotive companies. The production of angular motor cars ended. Gradually, more Detroit workers were called back to their jobs to turn out the new model cars that inspired Americans with a lust for ownership of the sleek automobiles. And by 1936, Detroiters looked forward to a continuing pattern of economic recovery.

At Hudson's, women flocked back to the Beauty Shop to get $5.00 permanents, complete with shampoo and finger waves, then stopped in Books to buy copies of Margaret Mitchell's *Gone With the Wind*. They lingered at lunchtime in one or another of Hudson's five restaurants where they talked of "Scarlett and Rhett" and of King Edward VIII, the popular former Prince of Wales, and his well publicized love affair with an American woman—Wallis Simpson.

Although the abdication of a king, in December, 1936, to marry "the woman I love" may have thrilled romanticists preoccupied with the love lives of fictional residents of Tara and of flesh-and-blood residents of Buckingham Palace, events of major consequence were occurring in Detroit—and were reported on the front pages of December newspapers along with stories of the love-struck, abdicating monarch. The Detroit crisis began in December,

1936, and continued into 1937 as the automotive industry was crippled by a plague of sitdown strikes at General Motors factories and other plants, including the Hudson Motor Car Company.

The Hudson car company, recognized as a leader in technological advances, had prospered until the Depression ravaged the automotive industry when the company lost $2 million in 1931 and $5 1/2 million in 1932. As the economy gradually improved, the industry had to contend with armies of sitdown strikers demanding UAW recognition, better wages, and seniority rights. In March, 1937, strikers seized two Hudson plants. One month later, they marched out triumphantly when Hudson Motor Car Company began negotiating with the UAW, as General Motors previously had done. An agreement between the Hudson automobile company and strikers provided for a 40-hour week with a minimum wage of 75 cents an hour for men and 65 cents an hour for women.

Even before the sitdown strike began at the Hudson car company, union organizers for waiters, bartenders, and store clerks were fired with enthusiasm for spreading the sitdowns into Detroit stores, restaurants, hotels, and meat packing plants. Shoppers on Woodward Avenue, a block north of Hudson's store, found themselves involved in the first major takeover of a downtown store when, on a busy Saturday, February 27, a group of union organizers rushed into Woolworth's to the accompaniment of shrill whistle blasts and loud commands. "Striiike!" they shouted as cash register drawers banged shut and customers milled about in confusion, then filed out the doors—already policed by burly union agents. *Life* magazine ran picture spreads on the Detroit Woolworth strike. New York radio news commentator, H.V. Kaltenborn, came to the Motor City and then made his report to the nation.

The Webbers did not wait for the Woolworth strike to end, almost a week later, before policing Hudson's doors with some of their own male employees—muscular carpenters, painters, security people. They added to their security measures when, on March 10, union representatives took over Hudson's neighbor—the Crowley, Milner Company department store. By 1:10 that afternoon, the store was emptied of its several thousand customers and Crowley managers surrendered their keys to union organizers.

Nationwide, Detroit's reputation as a sitdown-strike city grew when guests left the city's leading hotels—Book-Cadillac, Statler, Fort Shelby, Detroit-Leland—to bands of occupying strikers. Hudson's store remained untouched by the strikers, but Woodward Avenue was nearly deserted as people stayed at home rather than risk being trapped in an eruption of violence. Housewives hoarded food when Teamsters threatened to strike. And bus and streetcar drivers also declared their readiness to strike.

Michigan's Governor Murphy announced his intention of proclaiming martial law to restore order in the streets of Detroit. And when the giant American Federation of Labor publicly announced its policy of disavowing the tactics of sitdown strikers, Detroit union organizers recognized that the sitdowns had reached a saturation point and began to consider substituting other protest techniques.

With considerable relief, shoppers returned to Woodward Avenue and to the safe, familiar tiers, departments, and aisles of Hudson's store and its 42 3/4 acres of floor space. Throughout the pre-Christmas season of 1937, Hudson's cash registers jingled almost as rythmically as they had in 1929—humming their holiday sales tally in harmony with the music of Hudson's Carolers.

For Detroit families, and out-of-town visitors, Christmas at Hudson's became as much a part of family traditions as setting up Christmas trees in their homes. Having lunch in one of Hudson's restaurants was part of the tradition—children often demanding the chicken-with-gravy sandwich listed as the "Tommy Tucker Special." Their mothers could choose among a variety of tasty entrees served in a pleasant atmosphere of crystal chandeliers, silver teapots, beautiful flower arrangements, and an all-white clientele. For the most part, Detroit's black residents complied with an unwritten restaurant-segregation rule. If blacks did approach Hudson's restaurants, they often found themselves in a waiting line that never diminished as, strangely, no more tables became available.

Inside the bronze-door entrances to Hudson's, the Webbers never relaxed their strict ban against the use of artificial flowers anywhere within the store. Vases of fresh flowers always decorated the perfume and cosmetics department, the furniture department, and other sections of the store—including the Golden Corridor and its executive offices . . . all the lavish floral bouquets wafting their fragances in tribute to Hudson's own Floral Shop.

Crowds filled Hudson's tenth floor auditorium at the end of March, 1938, when Mrs. Constance Spry, who had arranged flowers for the wedding of the Duke and Duchess of Windsor, came to give a talk. The springtime schedule for the auditorium was a busy one—featuring a demonstration of modern table settings and dining etiquette, a fourth Annual Exhibit of Registered Dogs, and gardening lectures among the many events.

In the springtime, women who owned furs delivered their coats to Hudson's 17th floor Fur Storage, where furs were guaranteed protection from moths, moisture, heat, fire, and theft in three enormous temperature-controlled vaults that would hold as many as 50,000 furs. Experts in fur-care checked the coats periodically during the summer months, with such good results that people from other cities and states sent their fur coats to Hudson's for safe storage.

Shoppers at Hudson's also felt that their safety was assured at the big Woodward Avenue store where, if a customer felt dizzy or ill, a floor walker quickly would assist the customer to Hudson's Hospital for treatment. And as soon as the customer felt a bit stronger, he or she would be delivered home by a taxi company with which Hudson's had an ongoing credit-arrangement for such emergencies. If a customer merely bumped a shin or ruined a pair of silk hose, the hospital was ready to offer a dab of iodine, a band-aid, and a new pair of hosiery.

By this time, Hudson's Hospital was recognized by the American Medical Association and the American College of Surgeons. In a single day, as many as 100 to 400 employees and customers were treated, with no charge, at the hospital. Hudson retirees also could come in for free treatment, which included the services of a dentist and a chiropodist.

Most Hudson retirees would not think of shopping anywhere but in the Woodward Avenue store which had provided them with their 20% discount cards. The feeling of "family" was so strong among employees that relatives of current employees and retirees also thought of Hudson's as a most desirable workplace . . . a second "home." A second-generation Polish clerk from Hamtramck summed up the feelings of many first and second-generation ethnic employees in the big store when she said: "We were just so proud to be working at Hudson's."

They were equally proud to return to their homes and to boast to their families and neighbors that they had seen one or another of the celebrities who periodically came to shop at Hudson's — actor Paul Lukas buying a tennis outfit in the Sports department; teen-age Judy Garland attracting a crowd in the Basement Store's Early Teen Shop where "Judy Garland Dresses" were big sellers; Jane Pickens — of the singing Pickens' Sisters; Constance Bennett of the Ziegfeld Follies.

In a pre-television, pre-Disneyland era, shopgirls found a whole new world of entertainment and enlightenment within the cosmopolitan sphere of the huge store — a total floor area of "2,373,439 square feet," Hudson's advertising department boasted in 1939 — that dominated Woodward Avenue. Forty model rooms of furnishings opened to the pubic in April, 1937. Replicas of the Crown Jewels of England went on exhibition at Hudson's that same year. And, even more exciting to the hundreds of employees who crowded the auditorium in November, 1937, was the appearance of Miss Yvonne Leroux, a nurse for the Dionne quintuplets — the famous Canadian toddlers.

Never had little girls seized the public's fancy as firmly as had the five Dionne sisters — born in 1934 to an impoverished, rural Canadian family — who were now removed from their parents and cared for by the government. News cameras filmed their daily activities. Visitors came from around the world, paying admission to view the children in their enclosed play yard. Advertising companies competed to offer premium payments for endorsements of their products. And millions of Dionne paperdolls were sold to eager little girls who were as familiar with the names of the quintuplets — Yvonne, Cecile, Emilie, Annette, Marie — as with the names of their own sisters. As yet, no one could imagine how tragedy would stalk the little girls as they grew into adulthood; how they would be alienated from their parents; how the doctor, celebrated for saving the premature infants' lives under primitive conditions, would later be villified by the same people who now lauded him.

But for now, everyone was a hero or heroine — including the

nurse and the quintuplets' tutor who also made public appearances at Hudson's. In the few years since the quintuplets' birth, the Depression gradually had faded from the American scene, but not from the memories of the working-class families who survived it. And with the German invasion of Poland in September, 1939, and the quick involvement of England and France in World War II, the footprints of the Depression would be stamped out, in 1940, by the steady tramp of workers' feet on three-shift treks into Detroit's automobile factories as the plants began the manufacture of war machines and materials. The call for more workers in Detroit echoed into Kentucky, Tennessee and Alabama where families— black and white—packed up their possessions in cardboard boxes, crowded into northbound trains, and headed for the promised land. "Dee-troit."

Chapter 8

Drumbeats in the 1940s

In 1941, for the first time in 17 years, there were no Mother Goose characters, marching bands, or Santa Claus' elves cavorting along Woodward Avenue on Thanksgiving Day. Hudson's extravaganza—its annual parade—succumbed to the unrelenting reality of shortages of materials as workers packed huge rubber animals from Hudson's parade floats for donation to the war-salvage collection.

Salvage dumps—for rubber, metal and paper products, and used cans—dotted the city. The United States was not yet at war, but Woodward Avenue, somber and quiet on Thanksgiving morning, had a mystic quality about it—as if the lively footsteps of hundreds of drum-corps and band members had vanished into the distance to make way for marchers to a slower, military drumbeat, on their way to army camps and navy bases.

It was a somber time, also, for the Webbers when Marjorie Lambert Webber, wife of Oscar and mother of one daughter, died from pneumonia. The store, decked out in colorful lights and glittering tinsel to reflect Christmas cheer, contrasted strangely that year with the sadness in Oscar Webber's personal life. But, regardless of personal tragedy in the lives of the Webbers, Santa Land had to be ready for Detroit's children. And by early December, steady streams of Detroiters, recently transplanted from the South, were bringing their youngsters for a first visit to Hudson's Santa Land.

Even native Detroit youngsters, making their annual treks to Santa's headquarters at Hudson's, gazed in wonder at the red-cheeked, white-bearded man from the North Pole who seemed to have an inexaustible supply of good humor as he gathered an equally inexhaustible line of children, one at a time, into his lap. The children did not guess that a quantity of Santas were on duty throughout the day, one relieving another at intervals when summoned by a signal from a tired St. Nick as he stepped on a button that flashed a light.

This plan ensured the retention of each Santa's good-humor quotient as children were funneled into one of several pathways to the performing Santas' throne-like stations—five of them at peak hours. Each pathway was concealed from the others and each led to a "real Santa" clone—one a little stouter, one a bit taller, but each measuring up to Hudson's stiff requirements. And then there were the captivating elves—dwarfs, in real life—hired to scurry about the toy workshop and entertain the children.

On December 7, a gray and cloudy Sunday, Detroit telephone exchanges lit up with calls in late afternoon after a startling news bulletin on the radio. . . . "The White House has announced that the Japanese have attacked Pearl Harbor . . ." Detroit's profile changed immediately as army guards were posted at the entrance to the Detroit-Windsor Tunnel and the Ambassador Bridge because of possible sabotage. Public buildings sported air-raid warning sirens and their wails could be heard across the city when air-raid drills were held.

Still, these protective measures continued to be only mock actions against enemies who never spanned the great oceans to invade or bomb the North American continent. And while Europe suffered devastation and hunger, the United States put up with lesser adversities—the rationing of gasoline, tires, sugar and meat; rent controls; frozen wages, and restrictions preventing workers from changing jobs without permission of the War Labor Board.

After the Pearl Harbor attack, Detroit's automotive assembly lines grated to a halt as all available machinery and workers were utilized for production of war materials. Growing numbers of women joined the work force in Ford Motor Company's converted River Rouge plant, now producing tanks; in Chrysler's new tank arsenal; in Ford's new Willow Run factory where giant B-24 bombers were under construction.

The dwarfs from Hudson's Santa Land took jobs in the Ford bomber plant, where the undersized workers could squeeze into cramped fuselage spaces to perform essential tasks. And Hudson's shipped two of its gigantic air-conditioning units to California for temperature-control use in an aircraft factory. Since Hudson's air-conditioning plant was the world's largest, the remaining machinery continued cooling the store at approximately the same level as in previous years until, at the war's end, the government would return the machines to the third basement of the Woodward Avenue store.

The worst consequences of the war hit Detroit and the entire country with publication of U.S. casualty lists from the Bataan peninsula from which, after three months of bloody battles with the Japanese, U.S. troops withdrew to Corregidor. On May 6, 1942, Corregidor also fell to the enemy. Until this time, many Americans had believed firmly in the invincibility of their country, and were convinced that this war, like World War I, would be ended quickly once U.S. troops had "gone over" to join the fighting. Newsreels showing the fall of Corregidor and the horrors of the "Bataan Death March" destroyed any such illusions.

Hudson's store lost many of its employees to the armed forces and to higher-paying factory jobs in the early war years. The Webbers hired new people to replace those who left, and more new employees for the upsurge in business generated by "factory workers, with wads of cash, coming in to buy furs coats," long-time Hudson employee Mary Mellor recalls. She remembers that clerks could hardly work fast enough to wait on wall-to-wall customers at Christmas time when buyers abandoned their elevated status and helped clerks to wrap merchandise.

Mellor's 41 years of Hudson employment began in those war years—March, 1942—when she came to work in a huge department on the sixth floor, Women's Ready-to-Wear, at a time when clerks were paid 55 cents an hour, plus commissions in some departments.

Annual raises amounted to two dollars a week. Factory work paid much more, but Mellor did not want shift work and she liked the glamour of Hudson's . . . the excitement of going up to the Music department, now on the 13th floor, and seeing Jimmy Dorsey there . . . the "down-home" contentment of making lifelong friends among co-workers in the self-contained world of Hudson's.

Louise Solomon, a buyer in Better Millinery in those early war years, still recalls an incident involving an unusual and expensive hat designed by Lilly Daché during a period when New York's Broadway was blacked out. Detroit, too, experienced a practice blackout on May 3, 1942, when all lights in the city were extinguished for an hour. At this time, the large Daché hat was displayed prominently at Hudson's, each of its flowers nestling around a tiny light bulb with a covered wire leading to a small battery. One of the many female factory workers who shopped at Hudson's, and were popularly referred to by the term "Rosie the Riveter," wanted to try on the flashing-flower hat as soon as she saw it. Undeterred by the price tag, she bought the designer creation. Her only concern was with the batteries—where she could go to get them recharged.

Early in 1943, Hudson employees talked somberly among themselves when they heard news of the sudden death of the only son of their president, Richard H. Webber, on February 27. The twenty-year-old naval aviation cadet, Joseph Hudson Webber, had been killed in the crash of an airplane near Corpus Christi, Texas, just two weeks before he would have received his wings. The young cadet's body was brought to the Richard Webbers' Grosse Pointe home for the funeral service. His $100,000 estate was willed to the children of his two sisters—Jean Webber Sutphin of Cincinnati and Mary Webber Parker of Grosse Pointe.

As a blustery March moved into spring and early summer heat, Hudson's store offered a refreshing coolness to its customers, many of whom were defense plant workers living in cramped, airless semi-apartments partitioned off within larger quarters that had been single-family flats. Each of these flats now housed two or three families from the steady flow of 300,000 white people who had moved into Detroit in the past 15 months. New government-financed housing projects for war workers had long waiting lists of white applicants. Black families fared much worse as 50,000 more

"Negroes" arrived in Detroit between March 1942 and June 1943 and crowded into east-side slums already stuffed to capacity.

The desperate housing shortage intensified a festering black-white hatred stemming from the strikebreaker roles that blacks had played during a number of strikes against automobile companies—especially the April, 1941, UAW strike at Ford's sprawling Rouge plant. In an August 7, 1942 article citing the labor unrest in Detroit, *Life* magazine stated that "Detroit can either blow up Hitler or it can blow up the U.S."

Detroit, already straining its muscles to meet the enormous demands of an insatiable war production effort, had little surplus fervor to tackle the problems of a critical housing shortage and worsening race relations. But the city was forced to confront these issues with the outbreak of a riot on a hot Sunday night, June 20, 1943.

In sultry weather, it was not unusual for black families to leave their east-side ghetto known, somewhat extravagantly, as "Paradise Valley." Vacating their sweltering homes, they headed for Belle Isle—nature's 985-acre scenic island paradise in the Detroit River. But, this Sunday in June, 1943, took on an ugly contour when a series of fist fights between blacks and white youths spread into a mob scene involving 5,000 people. As riot police forced people off the island, trouble-makers began spreading false horror stories through lower east-side neighborhoods, inciting blacks to surge through the streets, smashing windows and looting stores.

Most white people still knew nothing of the mob scenes as they left for work on Monday morning, many of them driving into black neighborhoods where they were pulled from their cars and attacked. When one white man was killed, the news brought crowds of whites into the Woodward Avenue area to hunt for blacks on streetcars, in automobiles, and on the sidewalks where the blacks were punched and beaten. Forced into action by this war within a war, Governor Kelly ordered the closing of bars, theaters, and other public gathering places, and set up a stiff curfew that emptied downtown Detroit of its angry mobs and left Woodward and its neighboring streets to the rumble of jeeps, armored personnel carriers, and a tank as military police patrolled the area.

Ten days after the rioting had begun, the extra troops departed from Detroit and the city was left to deal with its scars: 34 people killed, 675 injured, $2 million lost in destroyed and looted properties. And racial hatreds had intensified. Blacks and whites, who worked side-by-side in factories committed to the production of war materials, were more wary of each other. The housing shortage worsened month by month. But the successful invasion and conquering of Sicily by the Allies in that same summer of 1943 brought fresh hope to all Americans that the war in Europe might be won, soon. In November, 1943, Hudson's Thanksgiving Day parade marched, again, down Woodward Avenue, bringing a psychological uplift to thousands of cheering spectators.

Eliza Clay, the last of the Joseph Lowthian Hudson brothers and sisters, died in March, 1944. Three months later, the Allies landed in Normandy and by the end of the summer, U.S. and French troops freed Paris from Nazi occupation. The good news sparked a happy spirit of optimism among Detroiters, many of whom had signed pledges at work to set aside part of their earnings for the purchase of U.S. Series E Savings Bonds. Nowhere was patriotism more evident than at Hudson's, where the Webbers hired 15 full time people to process bond orders. More bonds were sold at Hudson's than at any other store — amounting to $52 million, at purchase value, by the war's end.

Oscar Webber served the government as Deputy Chief of the Detroit Ordnance District of the War Department in the early years, assuming the responsibility for procuring great quantities of tanks, guns, ammunition, and motor vehicles from the Detroit area for the army. When he left this demanding job — a $5 billion annual operation — "for personal reasons," he then accepted the chairmanship of the Michigan Retailers War Savings Committee. But in April, 1944, he again agreed to take the Detroit Ordnance District Deputy Chief appointment, on a part time basis.

Even in those busy war years, Hudson's never abandoned the public-service programs to which it always had been committed. In 1941, the sixtieth anniversary of the date when Joseph Lowthian Hudson had opened his first Detroit store, Hudson's published a booklet presenting a cross-section of Detroit history through the past 60 years.

DRUMBEATS IN THE 1940s

The hefty 91-page booklet was distributed to schools and libraries. Only four years previously, Hudson's had published a 149-page booklet in celebration of Michigan's Centennial Year. This 1937 booklet gave the history of communities in every part of the state and was distributed to anyone who requested a copy.

When Eugenia Kresik came to work at Hudson's in August, 1940, she was assigned to Hosiery near the bottom of the escalator. The department was a busy one, even when, during the war years, stores frequently ran out of their limited provisions of women's hose, and women resorted to painting their legs with leg-makeup instead of wearing stockings. Hudson's reserved supplies of hosiery for its female clerks, who were not allowed to paint their legs nor to wear pants, which were recently brought into vogue by women workers in defense plants. The big Woodward store issued stamps to its female employees to ensure that each Hudsonian could receive her share of the precious hose.

Germany's surrender to the Allies on May 8, 1945, ended the war in Europe and promised a speedy end to the silk, rayon, nylon, gasoline, and other shortages that plagued the country. Although Detroit Mayor Edward Jeffries appealed to workers to stay at their jobs because weapons still were needed in the war against the Japanese, Hudson Motor Car Company released its employees early in the day. When other auto plants did the same, thousands of workers headed downtown to join crowds celebrating in Cadillac Square. People blowing whistles and waving flags spread out into the streets, bringing bumper-to-bumper traffic to a halt.

Two months later, Detroit's automobile plants began their reconversion to turn out new cars. And, on August 14, Detroiters went wild in the streets on V-J Day as Japan surrendered.

In the same year the war ended, the Webbers bought the old Sallan Building which housed a jewelry store at the corner of Woodward and Gratiot and which, until now, had clung to the substantial edifice that towered over Woodward Avenue—the J.L. Hudson store. The Webbers then demolished the Sallan Building and erected a 12-story addition to their department store which expanded Hudson's to a full square block in 1946. The impressiveness of the huge brick building was hardly diminished by its divergent shades of red, a result of construction in stages—often as little as 100 feet of frontage or addition of two floors—beginning in 1911. Now, with the Sallan Building replacement, the Webber brothers completed their construction program by adding two more stories to the Grand River end of Hudson's and enlarging the mezzanine floors in both the Woodward Avenue and Farmer Street buildings.

From May 29 to June 9, 1946, the entire block of Hudson's Woodward Avenue windows, etched with the monogram JLH, formed a panorama of automotive and Detroit history. The display paid tribute to a double celebration of the city's Automotive Golden Jubilee and Detroit's Sesquicentennial observance of the 1796 date when the U.S. first took actual possession of the Michigan city. Many of the store's 14 windows facing Woodward Avenue featured the early experiments of Henry Ford, related to the Hudson-Webbers through Edsel Ford's marriage to Eleanor Clay. Another window pictured various automotive pioneers and featured a large photograph of Joseph Lowthian Hudson behind the steering wheel of the first Hudson car.

By this time, eager customers were besieging automobile dealerships, adding their names to long lists of Detroiters waiting to purchase new cars as they came off the assembly lines. World War II veterans returned to prosperous times, many of them taking jobs in Detroit's automobile plants. Now that the war had ended, some women workers left their rigorous jobs for lighter work at less pay, or to stay at home with their families. But a great number of women workers did not want to surrender their new independence and the fat pay checks that enabled them to shop freely at Hudson's; to buy new wardrobes when the "New Look"—long, full skirts with hip pads—came into vogue in 1947. And as long as the demand continued for automobiles—along with other products, including housing, that had been scarce during the war years—good-paying jobs continued to be available, both for women and for war veterans.

During World War II, 1,446 Hudsonians had served in the armed forces. In 1947, the Webbers ordered a handsome bronze tablet inscribed with the names of these employees, gold stars marking the names of those who had died. The memorial tablet was placed in a conspicious first-floor location on the escalator wall near the store's Grand River entrance.

Before throngs of shoppers came through the store's entrances in the mornings, employees washed Hudson's lengthy span of show-windows, hosed down the sidewalks, and polished the brass doors as Detroit city employees cleared the streets of litter. At Hudson's Delivery garage on Beaubien, seven employees armed with long hose-brushes, had washed the previous day's mud and grime from Hudson's fleet of nearly 300 delivery vehicles during the night. Seventeen mechanics kept the trucks in mint condition, while two painters worked steadily at re-finishing one truck each day. The mechanics also made replacement parts for the eight electric "trucks" still used for transporting merchandise and necessary materials into and out of the store's freight elevators. The noiseless "electrics" remained in use because of fire-restrictions banning gas engines from freight elevators.

Hudson's drivers, delivering increasing numbers of packages each year to a record ten million in 1953, still were seen as Good Samaritans by women struggling to start stalled cars or trying to locate lost dogs. One delivery man, Joe Krul, was cited by Hudson's for saving a child from drowning in a water-filled excavation and for rescuing a woman from a house crushed by an out-of-control airplane. But Hudson's delivery men were not immune to personal mishaps—in the course of making their deliveries, some had been slugged and robbed, and one had his face pushed through the window of his truck.

Hudson's mail-order and telephone-shopping services accounted for a large percentage of the deliveries. Although the installation of private telephones, which had stagnated during the war years, had not yet caught up with the enormous backlog of requests for phone service, Hudson's store now encompassed 1,370 office and floor phones and 109 pay stations. Four Michigan Bell employees worked full time at the store to service the 15th floor main switchboard, with 30 positions and 52 operators, and the 17th floor central order board, with 132 floor positions which handled more than 9,000 of the store's average 22,000 daily incoming calls. Some of the operators were hired because of their ability to speak Polish,

Italian, and other languages and to deal with foreign-speaking callers.

Many former local customers of Hudson's, who had moved to other parts of the country, retained their charge cards as they persisted in mailing or phoning their orders to the big Woodward Avenue store. No matter how confused or outlandish any caller's request might be, Hudson's operators were required to respond courteously and helpfully unless they were willing to risk losing their jobs.

In a June, 1950, issue of the *Hudsonian* magazine, one operator was quoted: "You can tell the time of day, the season, the weather, and even if there is a big game in Ann Arbor, just from the number and kinds of calls." The largest number of calls came in on Mondays; the least on Saturdays.

The increasing number of incoming phone calls stemmed from the popularity of Hudson's unique Personal Shopping Service. As mail and phone orders arrived at the store, Hudson's shoppers actually moved through the store, selecting merchandise to fill customers' requests. And it was not unknown for a shopper personally to drop off a rush order at a customer's residence.

Like regular deliveries by Hudson's trucks, such special rush-order deliveries were free. And the store even made use of a special messenger service, often provided for "complainers," which was handled by another company under contract to Hudson's. The store's distinctive reputation was nourished by the growing number of services available to its customers. Silver engraving. Handbag, zipper, jewelry, camera, umbrella, and shoe repair. Tickets for Tiger baseball games or theater entertainment. An "Ask Mr. Foster" travel service. Interior decorating counsel. A huge pharmacy. A Hudson's custom-made fur coat if a customer wished to select her own pelts. An auditorium often used by groups such as the Southeast Michigan Gladiolus Society for its displays. Medical care—frequently for children brought into Hudson's Hospital after getting their rubber boots caught in the escalator.

The emphasis on special services continued after 59-year-old Oscar Webber, the most commanding of the Webber brothers, became company president in November, 1948. Richard H. Webber, at age 69, then progressed to chairman of the board of directors—a newly created post. Since the death of Richard's young son, Joseph Hudson Webber, the only remaining younger-generation male Webber was James Benson Webber, Jr.—the son of the Webber twin known as Jerry. At this point, James Jr., who had come into the store in 1936 after attending Trinity College and Harvard School of Business, succeeded his Uncle Oscar as vice president and general manager. James Jr., with one arm paralyzed by infantile paralysis, was now heir-apparent to the J.L. Hudson dynasty. The twin Webbers, Tom and Jerry, remained in their offices as vice-presidents in charge of merchandising.

Ever since Eugenia Kresik had been hired in 1940, she had exemplified the ideal Hudson's clerk—neat, polite but not timid, meticulous with details, and dedicated to observing every guideline for salespeople set forth in her Hudson's manual. The manual contained many restrictions, including rules that clerks should not wear ribbons, clips, or ornaments in their hair. Clad in her Hudson's "uniform," navy or black skirt and white blouse with sleeves at elbows or longer, Miss Kresik, of Hosiery, compiled an enviable sales record. She accomplished this by applying newsletter suggestions. "May I suggest that you buy two pairs—and get the wear of three?"

Her sales success paid off when Mr. Seibert, of the Bureau of Adjustments, interviewed her for a job in that twelfth floor department. Eugenia refused to be overwhelmed by the formidable Mr. Seibert—a tall, slender, elderly man with a collar as unrelentingly stiff as his personality—and made up her mind to make friends with him if she was approved for the job.

Eugenia got the job, and, before long, she did make friends with Seibert. But first, there was a period of training for the new Adjustments employee . . . and introduction to all parts of the store beginning with fourth basement Delivery, continuing with third basement Stock, and up each level to floor 21.

In the Bureau of Adjustments, there were no desks—just tables which were too high for comfort. Eugenia, eminently practical, found a Detroit City Directory and used it for a booster seat. Later, the adjustors were given individual desks, and, still later, partitions were provided for semi-privacy.

Customers would go, first, to the individual department with their claims. If the clerk could not satisfy the customer, the department manager was summoned. If a problem still existed, the customer was sent up to Adjustments, Hudson's higher court. The adjustor would fill out a form and check back with the original department while the customer waited. Then the adjustor would decide whether to rule "a positive or a negative," depending on a number of factors—whether the faulty merchandise was damaged by the customer . . . whether the warranty had expired.

Adjustments was a busy department where, despite Hudson's generous policy of refunds and supervisors' insistence that Adjustment employees "must be tactful, even when ruling a negative," it was not unusual for customers' tempers to flare. Tact did not placate the customer who tried, unsuccessfully, to return a silk suit with perspiration stains under the arms. When, as occasionally happened, such a customer became abusive to Adjustment employees, department workers could call Special Problems—a division that included store detectives dressed in civilian clothes.

A great deal of tact was necessary in dealing with complainers who persistently telephoned Adjustments to insist that something was wrong with deliveries they had received. One Grosse Pointe customer phoned the department so often that all the adjustors tried to avoid taking her calls. Eugenia finally took a drive out to Grosse Pointe on a Sunday to see in what grand mansion this self-important lady lived. Eugenia was surprised when she located the address—a very old and shabby frame house clinging to remnants of its former glory.

Mrs. Ernest Kanzler, the former Josephine Clay and niece of the original Joseph L. Hudson, was another Grosse Pointe resident who sometimes requested personal services from Hudson's Bureau of Adjustments. She called, on one occasion, to say that stacks of wedding gifts had been delivered to her home just previous to her son's wedding and to request Adjustments to send out workers to pack the gifts into barrels for storage.

Bureau of Adjustments workers were proud that their decisions carried a great deal of clout throughout the store. But they knew that Hudson bloodlines and family ties ran deep, and that, in any case, a "positive" was the only practical decision. The decision received priority attention, and packers were soon on their way to the Kanzler manor.

Later, Bea Speal, whose mother had worked at Hudson's, got work in the Bureau of Adjustments during the Christmas season. Assigned to taking complaints about Christmas card orders, Bea received a phone call from an irate customer who had ordered five boxes of cards with gold-lined envelopes. After addressing the first three boxes of cards, she opened the last two—saved for special friends. When the customer discovered that these envelopes were not gold-lined, she poured her angry complaints into Bea's ear. Knowing that Hudson's would go to any amount of trouble to rectify an error on the part of the store or a supplier, Bea soothed the customer, then worked with her supervisor to order a special delivery of the cards flown in from Chicago. A Hudson's employee met the plane, and personally rushed the cards to the customer's door.

Hudson's self-styled "portable museum"—an exhibit of 100 paintings featuring contemporary Michigan scenes and housed in a 22-foot trailer complete with complementary lighting and accessories—made its first, 8,700-mile tour of 17 Michigan cities in 1948. The following year, the trailer was transported a greater distance, to Marquette and other Upper Peninsula cities.

But of all the strategies exercised by Hudson's to foster good public relations, none drew more customers than the store's long established policies of prompt, no-charge deliveries and generous refunds. At the end of the 1940s, refunds amounted to 13% of Hudson's sales—a sizeable amount, but sales figures, too, were constantly rising. Looking forward to a new decade of increasing revenue, the Webbers decided to renovate the store's tower, reaching 25 stories above Woodward Avenue, with porcelain-faced copper letters and some 1300 feet of neon tubing. The glowing neon illuminated the nine-foot-high name of the store on all four sides of the towers, flashing it over the city at night.

HUDSON'S   HUDSON'S   HUDSON'S   HUDSON'S

Chapter 9

Reaching an Apex

The Great Depression of the 1930s had faded into history during World War II and the prosperous post-war years. Expectations for continued prosperity were magnified in 1950 when Detroit's armament industry went into increased production of weapons for the Korean War and of equipment for free-world allies under the U.S. government's military aid programs.

Detroit's black population had doubled between 1940 and 1950, with 140,000 blacks crammed into the Paradise Valley ghetto and more than twice that number spilling over into other Detroit neighborhoods. During the same decade, as new suburban housing became available after World War II, more than 400,000 whites moved into the suburbs from which housewives returned, regularly, to shop in the city's flourishing downtown stores.

The Korean War did not bring about shortages like those of World War II years, and Detroit-area shoppers poured into the city's hub early in the mornings, catching sight of their reflections in the Avenue's display windows and adjusting their hats as they waited for the magic moment when Hudson's store opened for business. Then, reaching daintily gloved hands toward the revolving doors, now swishing with non-stop efficiency, they pushed their way into scented first-floor aisles of cosmetics, powders, hosiery, and costume jewelry nestled, like precious gems, on swirls of dark blue velvet.

Shoppers moved at a leisurely pace, their indecisiveness suffered willingly enough by attentive, pleasant-mannered clerks who smiled politely even when a demanding customer ultimately wandered away without making a purchase. For the shopper, there was no pressure. No demands. Only aisle after aisle, floor after floor—reached on one of Hudson's 51 passenger elevators—of explorations in an immaculate and beautiful fantasy land where no one had to be burdened with packages; parcels and coats could be checked.

Although employees ate in their own cafeteria, paying only 38 cents for the day's Special which included beverage and ice cream, shoppers were perfectly content to pay more to eat Hudson's beef and kidney pie, Scotch barley broth, Old English pudding, or to choose from a list of appetizing entrees in one of the store's public restaurants. An escalator, running between the second basement and the twelfth level, then carried shoppers to a spacious ladies' room with gleaming marble floors and a pink, plush sitting room for penning cards or letters at individual desks.

In 1951, Detroit geared up to celebrate its 250th anniversary in July. On Flag Day, June 14, Hudson's prefaced the July festivities with a traditional unfurling of the World's Largest Flag—a new and bigger "Stars and Stripes" with which the Webbers had replaced the original banner so that Hudson's would retain the "World's Largest" title for its flag.

The 1500-pound flag, rolled, folded, and kept at the warehouse, was stored in a huge box equipped with casters so that men from the warehouse could push the box down Woodward Avenue and hoist the flag from the box onto the marquee. Some 60 men, handling hoisting tackle, raised the rolled flag to a catwalk that ran along the bottom of the ninth-floor windows where carpenters and display-department men secured the top of the flag and began to unfurl it to the accompaniment of music by the Detroit Police Band. The unfurled flag, with its four-inch border of heavy canvas and 6,240 feet of one-inch rope, reached from the ninth floor to the bottom of the second floor windows.

Joseph Lowthian Hudson, founder of The J. L. Hudson Company was known as Detroit's "Merchant Prince." (Courtesy of Dayton Hudson Corporation)

A Word for Ourselves.

WE aim to make our store popular, by keeping always a full stock of the most desirable goods obtainable, selling them at low prices, and dealing fairly and squarely with our customers.

We will in no case allow our salesmen to misrepresent goods. We shall endeavor to make our patrons feel at home with us, and have engaged gentlemanly salesmen, who will extend the same courtesy to all who may come either to buy or simply to look at our goods and get our prices.

Our large experience as buyers gives us an advantage in the market, by which our patrons are sure to be benefited.

We have adopted the "Strictly One Price" system, and mark all our goods in plain figures.

And lastly, we respectfully ask the public to call and see us before purchasing goods in our line, and let us show them our goods and prices.

J. L. HUDSON, Clothier,

Detroit Opera House Building,

Stores formerly occupied by Newcomb, Endicott & Co.

The "Advertising Credo" circulated by Joseph L. Hudson in 1881 promoted a "strictly one-price" policy in an era when bargaining was a routine practice. (Burton Historical Collection)

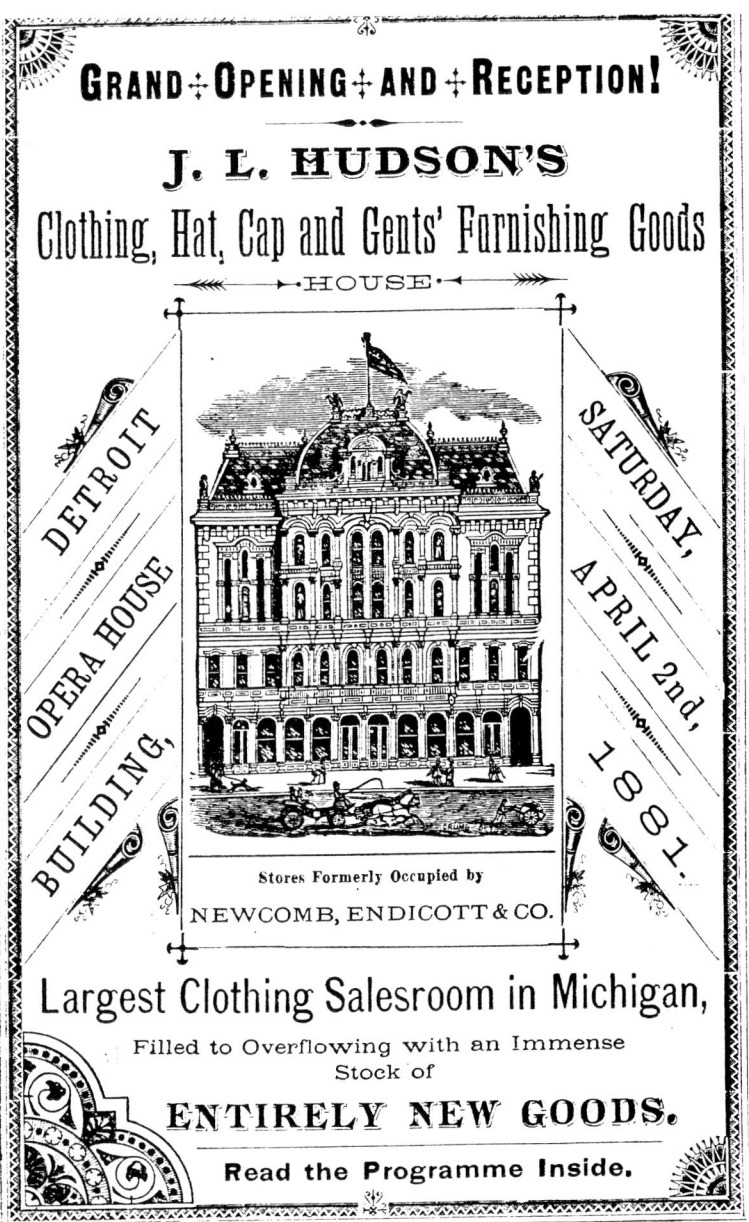

A "Programme" for the concerts and reception to mark the 1881 Grand Opening of Joseph L. Hudson's first store in Detroit. (Burton Historical Collection)

The ornate Detroit Opera House in which Hudson's first Detroit store was located. (Courtesy of Dayton Hudson Corporation)

An early fleet of J. L. Hudson's delivery trucks, with drivers, lined up in front of the Woodward Avenue store. (Courtesy of Dayton Hudson Corporation)

A corner view of Downtown Hudson's in pre-World War II days when the narrow corner building still owned by Sallan's Jewelry flaunted a competitor's sign for men's clothes at Gray's, at Woodward and State. (*The Detroit News*)

Downtown Hudson's tower, reaching high above Woodward Avenue, flashed the name HUDSON'S over the city at night in nine-foot high letters. (Courtesy of Dayton Hudson Corporation)

A more modern fleet of Hudson's panel delivery trucks parked at the company's warehouse where, in the early 1950s, nearly 300 Hudson's delivery trucks were washed each night. (Courtesy of Dayton Hudson Corporation)

In 1934, a science-fiction float was a big attraction in the J. L. Hudson Thanksgiving parade. (*The Detroit News*)

Lucky children relished an opportunity to talk with the "real" Santa in his chariot at the annual Hudson's parade. (*The Detroit News*)

A side-street view of Downtown Hudson's in 1942, when Annis Furs was a competitor with Hudson's fur department. (*The Detroit News*)

In 1953, the Webber brothers—(left to right) Oscar, Richard, and twins Joseph and James—celebrated a combined 205 years of service to The J. L. Hudson Company. (Courtesy of Dayton Hudson Corporation)

This was a typical scene, after a two-year hiatus during World War II, of throngs of Detroiters hailing Santa as he left his sleigh to ascend the steps leading to a platform where he received a key to the city. (Burton Historical Collection)

Police officers kept traffic and crowds of shoppers under control at the Hudson's–Kern's Woodward Avenue intersection in the department stores' "glory years." (*The Detroit News*)

Downtown Hudson's was in its heyday when it staged a scene from yesteryear on Woodward Avenue with an old-time J. L. Hudson Company delivery wagon and a team of horses. (Courtesy of Dayton Hudson Corporation)

The 1500 pound "World's Largest Flag" frequently was on display across the facade of Downtown Hudson's. (Courtesy of Dayton Hudson Corporation)

A typical, busy shopping day, amid Downtown Hudson's attractive first-floor displays. (*The Detroit News*)

REACHING AN APEX

Wind and rain were major problems threatening the flag display. On a windy day, the sides of the flag had to be totally secured. And if it rained, employee-attendants to the "World's Largest" had to move in double-time to roll it up and remove it from the store's facade. If the flag got wet, it had to be stretched out to dry on the warehouse floor to prevent mildew.

A one-day flag display incurred substantial expense in man-hours and in subsequent restoration and storing processes—but the World's Largest Flag was a Hudson's tradition, and such traditions were not easily surrendered. When, in the late 1950s, Alaska and Hawaii would become states, six seamstresses would work at ripping out the flag's field and, in three weeks' time, stitching a new field with 50 stars—each six feet from point to point—onto the body of the flag.

At Hudson's, planning and researching for Detroit's 250th anniversary had begun a year earlier, culminating in a three-dimensional display of dioramas in its Woodward Avenue chain of windows during the July celebration. Miniature details, in carefully reduced scale, depicted historical events in the life of the city, extending from Cadillac's receipt of a charter from King Louis XIV of France through a projection of the Detroit of Tomorrow. The dioramas, later presented to the Detroit Historical Museum, were replaced with another series in Hudson's 14 Woodward windows in observance of Detroit History Week on July 18. The second display featured fashions of different eras, beginning with the French period of 1701.

Hudson's Historama, exhibited on the store's twelfth floor, attracted more than 125,000 people to see the collection of historical items—some loaned by Edison Institute and others donated by individuals for the occasion. But the highlight of the celebration—a six-hour parade with an official float designed and built by Hudson's, which carried the festival empress and her court—attracted enormous crowds to the downtown area. As the celebration ended, Hudson's combined its own end-of-the-decade birthday observance with the larger civic event in a public-relations coup typical of the Automotive City emporium. The store published and distributed 5,000 copies of a booklet, "Detroit's 250th Anniversary, Hudson's

70th Year," featuring photographs of the anniversary celebration and recording its highlights.

In many stores, night crews took care of all cleaning chores. But at Hudson's, 119 housekeepers also worked eight hours a day to give what the Webbers referred to as a "guests-are-coming" touch to every department in the store. The uniformed women were trained to work, as unobtrusively as possible, at general "tidying up" and keeping china, silver, and furniture clean and gleaming while making note of spots needing paint or repairs to be done by the night crew.

Housekeepers stationed in the washrooms plied mops, brushes, sponges, and scented deodorizers throughout their assigned marble, porcelain, and chrome territories, only to circle back and begin again in their dedication to dry floors, dripless sinks, spotless mirrors, and faucets that gleamed as brightly as trays in the Sterling silver display. At night, maintenance crews reported for duty to take care of heavier cleaning, to make repairs, and to correct any problems that might have threatened Hudson's reputation for immaculate perfection.

During the 1950s, theft of merchandise became a bigger problem at Hudson's. One woman, who had stolen a girdle and feared being caught, got rid of the stolen item by flushing it down a toilet. Subsequently, three maintenance men, wearing headlamps, had to go down into the sump in the fifth basement to find out why the sump pump was not working properly. They soon found that the pump was strangling on a rubberized girdle that was partly sucked in each time the machine was activated.

A more difficult problem arose when three plumbers were called to the fourth floor restrooms where long rows of women's toilet stalls were ankle-deep in soapsuds. In both the children's and mothers' washrooms, suds bubbled out of the floor drains and basins. Armed with shovels and canvas pushcarts, maintenance workers scooped up the suds and deposited them in carts until the area was cleared. The maids, six of them on duty at all times, were questioned, but the soapsuds mystery remained unsolved.

When, some three weeks later, the restrooms again were awash in soapsuds, a suds sample was taken and sent to a testing laboratory. The final analysis was that someone who was allergic to the soap supplied by Hudson's had been given a pill with which to wash. To avoid any more bubbly floods, each maid was provided with a two-ounce bottle of a chemical which she was instructed to pour down a drain when there was any sign of soapsuds.

Lewis ("Buck") Huff came to work in Maintenance for Hudson's in 1950. He often saw Richard Webber walking through the store on his regular morning reconnaissance, pen and notepaper in hand as he carried on the early-day ritual established years earlier by his Uncle Joseph L. Hudson.

Huff recalls a summons from "Mr. R.H." on one occasion to repair a leaking radiator valve in the chairman's eleventh floor office. When the maintenance man finished repairing the valve, he called the chairman's attention to the battered condition of an imitation walnut wastebasket at the side of his desk. "Can you fix it? Or get me a new one?" Webber asked. The employee walked down the "Golden Corridor" to the Contract department and picked up a heavy wastebasket, made of walnut. He tore off the $39 price tag and took it into "Mr. R.H.'s" office, saying "I think this one fits your office perfectly."

"I didn't know we had these," Webber said, thanking Huff as appreciatively as if the maintenance man had presented his boss with a hand-made gift.

Huff was summoned up to the eleventh floor executive offices on a different mission after Richard Webber's newly engaged secretary, Denise, told her boss she had dropped her diamond ring down the drain while washing her hands in a restroom basin. Huff dismantled the trap under the basin indicated by the secretary, but there was no ring. "I'm sure I didn't go father down," Denise insisted, looking forlornly at the line of basins. "Maybe it was the next one," Huff suggested, then took apart the traps of basins on either side of the first one—with no luck.

By this time, "Mr. R.H." came into the washroom to inquire about the ring. "I want the diamond found. Take off all the basins and check the traps," he ordered.

This, too, was done. But Huff could not find the ring. Two days later, the maintenance man was again called up to the "Golden Corridor" where a gold framed portrait of the store's unsmiling founder surveyed his executive-descendants. This time, a happy Denise held up her fur coat and pointed to the lining. There was the sparkling diamond, its Tiffany mounting attached to the inside of her coat for the past two days.

Although Richard Hudson checked the store each morning, he was not there to observe night-shift employees who worked behind the scenes so that Hudson's picture-perfect image was never marred by revelations of the more unlovely plumbing or patching processes necessary to improve the health, vitality, and appearance of "The Grand Lady of Woodward." Detroiters who passed the partly darkened Hudson's store on Woodward, Farmer, Gratiot, or Grand River at night could not have guessed that high jinks and practical jokes often prevailed inside the nearly deserted emporium.

Many of the practical jokes were at the expense of the night watchman, jangling a ring of keys at his side, who sometimes found keyholes filled with putty. The jokesters rarely ran out of pranks—turning off the lights in a corridor as the watchman approached, then taking a bicycle and covering the rider with a white sheet as he pedaled the bike down the hallway . . . sticking a cigar in the mouth of a mannequin inside the watchman's empty number 4 elevator before pressing a button for the 20th floor where the watchman would open the door.

Some of the night workers broke the monotony of midnight hours with a more dangerous diversion involving one of three chutes that spiraled through the core of the building. A trash chute, emptying into an incinerator, fascinated two teen-age boys who worked in tenth-floor China. The boys occasionally ignited handfuls of excelsior and tossed the burning packing-crate materials down with the trash. Maintenance men had to go into the chute with pitchforks, then, to put out the fires until store detectives were able to locate the young culprits.

The paper chute emptied onto a platform from which the paper was loaded into two huge balers, each operated by an orderly. Money from sale of the baled waste paper helped pay the salaries of more than 50 orderlies working for Hudson's Housekeeping department.

The third chute, for packages, ran from floor 13 to a fourth basement sliding board that emptied onto a conveyor. From here, packages were stacked in carryalls, and then transferred to trucks for delivery. A messy mistake occurred when a bus boy from one of the store's restaurants dumped a pail of garbage down this chute. Five pounds of garbage, mixed with packages, promptly spewed out on the conveyor.

Thrill-seeking night workers found a new, and dangerous, use for the package chute. They waxed the backs of small rugs and rode them, like sleds, in fast descents down the chute to the fourth basement. The package chute escapades continued, periodically, for years, until a Hudson employee, intending to throw light bulbs down the trash disposal, accidentally fell into the chute and was killed.

Each year, Hudson's staged an anniversary dinner to honor employees with 25 years, or more, of service. In 1953, 267 veteran employees decided to make use of this annual affair to honor the four Webber brothers on the 67th birthday anniversary of the twins, known as Tom and Jerry. Hudsonians looked fondly on the twin Webbers as "regular guys" who, 50 years earlier, while working as errand boys in Men's Clothing, had played pitcher and catcher positions on the old Hudson baseball team.

Through the years, the twins continued their friendly companionship with employees—bowling in Hudson leagues and going hunting and fishing, often up to their properties near Hale, Michigan, with store employees. Neither twin desired any publicity or acclaim; they were content to have their eldest brother, Richard, and youngest brother, Oscar, receive all public recognition. Even on the night of the birthday party, the twins chose not to sit at the head table. Instead, they sat at separate tables with employees, and watched as each guest received a diamond-studded pin.

Jerry Webber's son, James Benson Webber, Jr., served as toastmaster at the dinner. Clearly at ease in his role as successor to his Uncle Oscar as Hudson's future president, young "Mr. Jim" performed at the dinner party without a shred of the self-conscious diffidence that plagued his father and his Uncle Tom. When it was time for the testimonials in honor of the twin Webbers, their faces reddened with embarrassment at the unwanted attention. They would not stand to receive the golden memorial books presented to them. It was known, however, that the twins did not intend to retire, but planned to continue as vice presidents in charge of merchandising.

The twins finally consented to stand up and be photographed with their two brothers. When the photo appeared in a newspaper the next day, it marked the first time the four brothers had been pictured together. Although "Mr. Tom" and "Mr. Jerry" were not identical twins, there was a definite likeness between the two—a likeness mirrored in the faces and physiques of "Mr. Richard" and "Mr. Oscar." All four blue-eyed men wore glasses. Each was bald, or balding, and just a bit on the short side of medium height. Although their personalities were different, this distinction had not prevented them from attaining a 50-year record of family business leadership, unmarred by the discord that might have erupted if each of the brothers were as ambitious and authoritative as was Oscar Webber.

In 1950, Oscar had announced that plans were in the making to expand the Hudson dynasty by building giant shopping malls, centering around modern J.L. Hudson stores, in the northeast and northwest suburbs of Detroit. Since increasing numbers of people were moving into the suburbs in a flourishing era of prosperity, the plans for satellite J.L. Hudson stores seemed to be as practical as they were innovative.

By 1953, when the Korean War ended, Downtown Hudson's employed 12,000 people, 650 of them working in the store's nine offices. The store's sales figures for the same year soared to $153 million. Of total sales, more than $30 million were tallied in the four-acre, 60-department Basement Store. But there was a negative factor among the positive statistics for 1953—an inventory shortage that rose to $1,657,000 and prompted a reminder from Marvin Heidt, Manager of Special Services, that salespeople could earn rewards of $5 to $25 for reporting shoplifters or people using stolen charge plates. The $1,657,000 shortage—in the largely tranquil era of the early 1950s when Downtown Hudson's was the company's only store—was a shocking revelation to the Webbers, who had no prescience of the disturbing societal changes that lay ahead, rocketing the company's shortages into multi-million-dollar figures.

Carol Crothers had worked for Hudson's Special Services for 27 years and was accustomed to approaching shoplifters with a polite

"I'm afraid you've made a slight mistake — Would you mind coming to our office for a moment?" But even the experienced Mrs. Crothers was disheartened by Hudson's 1953 statistics indicating that one percent of the store's own employees had been apprehended for theft. This, in Carol Crothers' opinion, was intolerable disloyalty to an exceptionally benevolent employer whose Webber Foundation provided help for workers with health or mental disabilities, and for those confronted with family or economic problems.

Because most employees did view Hudson's with respectful deference and appreciation, union leaders never had been successful in organizing Hudson's salespeople. "We voted the union down three times," veteran employee Mary Mellor would boast years later. Only warehouse employees and delivery men finally voted to join the union in the late 1950s. During one of the periods when Delivery workers were on strike, Louise Solomon — who, in the wake of the 1960's era focusing on recognition of minorities and women, would become a divisional merchandise manager and the second woman to be a part of Hudson's management — remembers personally delivering a wedding dress to a customer's home. But she was warned by supervisors not to make any more deliveries because of the danger involved in strike-breaking activities.

However, the earlier 1950s still were peaceful times of great expansion for Hudson's. The company's huge warehouse covered 22 acres of floor space in 1953, its aisles and storage places kept clean with daily sweeping by a giant machine. And by the end of 1954, a new adjoining building was added to the warehouse, increasing facilities by an additional 25 acres.

In 1954, the Hudson Credit Union was established for employees who could invest as little as 25 cents at a time to purchase $5 shares in their saving and lending association. But the most important of Hudson's innovations in that year was the opening of Northland — the $25 million, 161-acre mall built and financed by the J.L. Hudson Company to serve 400,000 residents of Detroit's northwest suburbs. Northland's 22 acres of shops, restaurants and clubrooms for use by civic groups, along with its covered courts, halls and walks, were presided over by a magnificent three-story Hudson's store accessible to 70 acres of parking.

Sales at Hudson's Northland store amounted to an incredible $42 million in the first year of its existence. The amount, nearly double the sales figure expected by the Webbers, stimulated their eagerness to complete Eastland Center—another $25 million mall in the northeast suburb of Harper Woods. Many problems had arisen to delay the Eastland project—attempts by Harper Woods to raise taxes on the Eastland site and disagreements about constructing an Edsel Ford Expressway route through Harper Woods which would funnel shoppers close to Eastland's entrance.

"We still have hopes of building Eastland Center," Oscar Webber said at one point. "But the people—I mean the officials of Harper Woods—don't seem to welcome us."

The implied threat worked. Harper Woods officials became more cooperative, and on April 5, 1955, James B. Webber, Jr., announced that Hudson's would begin construction of Eastland Center. The 73-store Eastland opened for business in July, 1957, and the Webbers settled back to relish the booming sales they expected. They did not yet realize the full extent of the independent lives that Eastland and Northland would assume. Like two strong-willed, even ungrateful, offspring, the suburban twins would eventually wreak havoc on the Grand Matriarch of Woodward, seizing its legacy as their own. But for now, the infant twin centers, like precocious children, brought only pride and glory to the J.L. Hudson empire.

But Eastland was not yet under construction, and Downtown Hudson's was still thriving, as was Detroit's automobile industry, when American Motors absorbed the Hudson Motor Car Company in 1954. The last Hudson automobiles—overgrown vehicles loaded with chrome and burdened with high fins—would be built in 1957 when American Motors began gearing its production to smaller, compact Ramblers.

Marguerite Clark, born in France and employed in Hudson's Art Supplies in the early 1950s, was one of the bilingual clerks who became accustomed to answering summons from other departments whenever a foreign visitor or immigrant customer needed assistance. To Marguerite, the work at Hudson's was pleasant—and the 20% discount on merchandise was a delightful fringe benefit. She was only mildly surprised to learn that a co-worker was a Grosse Pointe dentist's wife who also enjoyed the work and the employee discount.

Cash registers, at that time, did not add, and costs of purchased items had to be tallied by clerks who also figured discounts and sales taxes. "Lay-aways" required more accounting. When the aisles cleared of shoppers at closing time, clerks had to take care of their returned goods and had to clear registers before they could leave—usually an hour after closing.

When Marguerite came home late from work, her husband would say: "If I loved my job the way you do, I'd be so happy." Happiness to Marguerite, was earning a silver pin for not making mistakes at her register for a required length of time—and working toward five such pins, at which time a gold one was presented. Marguerite's lively chatter about Hudson's induced her young daughter to get temporary work at the store. Mrs. Clark's memories of that brief time include the night when her daughter personally delivered a shower cap to a customer's home, after the customer had forgotten the package at her counter.

Such unique and personal favors did not seem unusual to Hudson employees, who were influenced by Hudson's fetish for service to customers and to the city of Detroit. In 1952, Hudson's had presented the city with a large bronze tablet with a description of the site where the local unit of the YMCA was founded during the original J.L. Hudson's lifetime. This tablet was the 33rd historical bronze marker—each placed at an important site in Detroit's history—given to the city by Hudson's.

In 1959, the local televising of Hudson's Thanksgiving Day parade was done by two Detroit stations. Ardis Kenealy of "Romper Room" narrated WWJ-TV's regular, annual telecast, competing, this year, with celebrity Shari Lewis and her Lamb Chop puppet narrating for WXYZ-TV. A part of the latter telecast was carried nationally on the ABC network.

The following year, popular Detroit television weatherman Sonny Eliot and his wife, Annette, began their 21-year-stint as master and mistress of ceremonies for the WWJ telecast. In the same year, CBS made arrangements with store executives to nationally televise a segment of the parade—the start of a long-term tradition.

When Hudson's learned, shortly before the parade, that ABC network people also were coming to televise the parade nationally, Oscar Webber was perturbed by ABC's plans to sell commercial spots for its televised portion of the extravaganza. Hudson's never had "commercialized" its parade, Webber pointed out to his legal people, and he wanted this precedent continued.

The legal people conferred, agreeing that since the line of march moved along Detroit's public streets, they could not bar other networks' cameras from filming the parade. But the day before the event, they ordered Hudson's print shop employees to make signs imprinted with copyright notices attributed to "The J.L. Hudson Company."

Carpenters and mechanics, spurred by the excitement of national television coverage, arrived at the warehouse at 1:30 a.m. on Thanksgiving Day—beginning a mad scramble to assemble floats which had been built in sections to accommodate the eleven-foot-high door of the warehouse. Workers pushed each float outside, then attached two more sections on top. A few floats, operated on bicycle wheels, had artificial feet attached to each wheel—one at the top and another at the bottom. But people actually provided propulsion for the bicycle-wheel floats by cranking handles to move the wheels from inside the vehicles.

The float marshal knew that timing had never before been so important to a successful parade. It was his responsibility to make sure that each float moved in front of CBS cameras at a specified time. At the last-minute arrival of copyright signs, workers hurriedly used stapling guns and hammers and nails to attach a sign to each float. At the same time, each float master was told to warn his riders and the marchers who came behind that they must smile or wave only to CBS cameras—not in the direction of the other network's cameras. The marchers wearing "heads" had no such concerns. Their smiles remained in place, and their concentration always focused on staying upright.

For the next 25 years, CBS returned to Detroit each year to televise Hudson's parade. Its cameras kindly overlooked such mishaps as the occasion when the Santa float accidentally bumped a police car as the parade ended in front of Downtown Hudson's. The impact ruptured the *papier mache* float and propelled the second, hidden Santa from beneath the seat. As he rolled to the street, he held his tasseled cap and curly beard in his hands — ready to perform his emergency role. Fortunately, since he had been niping from a whiskey bottle while keeping warm in his underseat niche, he was not required to fill the role of understudy.

More often, parade participants sneaked away to drink in sidestreets bars, as they waited, through the cold, dark, early-morning hours, for the starting signal. The problem was that an intoxicated tractor driver or a clown occasionally missed the starting signal for the line of march . . . sometimes missed the entire parade, in which case offenders received a two-day layoff slip.

Missing the parade rarely was intentional because participants were paid time and a half, based on their individual wage scale. Strong, muscular, male employees vied to carry "big heads," which commanded eight hours of pay, since balancing a 12 or 13-foot high "big head," imported from Italy, was no easy feat. "Medium heads" and "small heads" rated six and four hours' pay, respectively.

In the 1954 parade, "Buck" Huff, assigned a snowman costume, had worn a nine-foot-tall, fur-felt "medium head" that settled down over his head and shoulders and loomed into the air. He found the small hole provided for vision inadequate when, each time he exhaled, condensation formed on his spectacles. Fortunately, he'd been told to closely follow a heavy-set woman whose ample figure provided a guidepost for the foggy-eyed snowman. In his struggle to stay on course and to resist a strong cross-wind that wobbled the "head," and threatened to upend the snowman at Grand Circus Park, "Buck" could not search out and wave to his young son and daughter, watching from the crowd. But the children recognized him, nonetheless, by his feet — clad in his favorite hunting boots for tramping the woods of northern Michigan. Huff's larger problem was to avoid tramping through manure deposited on the street by parade horses.

Some 1300 Hudsonians had taken part in this 28th annual Thanksgiving Day parade of 21 floats and 12 bands in 1954. Myrtel Shannon, of seventh floor Shoes, reigned over a perennial favorite—the Old Woman in a Shoe float. Wearing a bonnet and flowing cape, and obviously proud that her participation in the Thanksgiving Day cavalcade dated back to the parade's first year in 1925, Myrtel waved vigorously from her high perch at the top of a huge shoe. Her memories of Hudson's extended back to the days when water was distributed within the store from large crocks, and when shoe laces and polishes were wheeled around on a kind of tea-wagon for selection by customers.

Although television brought the parade into homes across the nation in 1959, crowds of Detroiters continued to line downtown streets along the parade route. Even earlier in the 1950s, Hudson's had bowed to the public's newly acquired devotion to television stars by arranging for William Boyd—known as "Hopalong Cassidy"—to appear at the store's twelfth floor auditorium. The response to Hudson's invitation to "come and meet 'Hopalong'" overwhelmed the big store on Woodward as kids with parents and kids without parents poured through the revolving doors, made two complete circles around the twelfth floor, filled the steps down to the eleventh floor where the waiting line again circled around twice, then down the stairs to the tenth floor. And youngsters still were coming into the store at the first level. For a time, maintenance people conferred with the Webbers, considering whether there was too much weight on the floors and whether the entrance doors should be temporarily closed—until the incoming flow began to subside.

On another occasion, Fess Parker, the actor who played the role of Daniel Boone, appeared at the store. Parker was so tall that, as he ducked down—moving into and out of the revolving doors, maintenance people wondered if they should have pulled the cable and folded the doors . . . a procedure they followed when a wheelchair was brought into the store, where there were no special facilities for handicapped people at that time. Once inside the store, however, blind people or those confined to wheelchairs received personal attention from floor walkers or Special Services employees who recruited maids, orderlies, or even clerks to push wheelchairs or to take blind customers to elevators or into other departments.

The unannounced arrival of the ermine-robed Prophet Jones for a shopping spree at Hudson's attracted as much attention from other shoppers as did the well publicized arrival of national television stars. Black cult leader Jones, with bodyguards and attendants, would sweep into the store and frequently head for Women's Millinery where the Prophet would select several expensive hats for his mother. When he finished his selections, one of his attendants would reach into a briefcase and get a fistful of cash to pay for the purchase.

In September, 1953, a mammoth telephone switchboard had gone into operation at Hudson's to handle the increasing number of telephone orders. As a part of the phone order department remodeling, workers installed mirrors — one mirror in front of each operator to reflect the operator's face as a reminder of Hudson's insistence on phones being answered by a "voice with a smile."

Exceeded in size only by the switchboards in use at the Pentagon and the Bell system itself, the huge Hudson board had its own exchange — CApitol. Hudson operators now could handle as many as 40,000 calls a day, many of them from teen-agers whose buying power — prompted by prosperous times plus television programming geared to teens — began to blossom in the 1950s. The teens came to, or phoned, Hudson's to order white buck shoes and saddle shoes, colognes, cosmetics, and cashmere cardigan sweaters — which girls wore backwards.

These early 1950s' peak years of business at Hudson's had a downside for the Webbers when, in 1954, Josephine Clay Kanzler drowned after falling into her own pool at the Kanzlers' Hobe Sound, Florida, home. At the tragic death of Josephine, whose weakness for alcohol was as deep-seated as was her Webber cousins' distaste for liquor, the Webbers rallied to support Eleanor Clay Ford in the loss of her only sister. Both Richard and Oscar Webber — the two brothers most rigidly bound to the teetotaler precepts of their Uncle Joseph L. Hudson — realized that they could not similarly restrict the social drinking of the twin Webbers nor of young Jim Webber, heir apparent to the Hudson dynasty.

But the Webbers' plan for James B. Webber, Jr. — who was also a trustee of the Ford Foundation and a director of Ford Motor Company — were disrupted abruptly in August, 1956, when the 44-year-old Hudson executive unexpectedly died in his sleep of an acute heart attack while vacationing at Turtle Lake Club near Alpena, Michigan. James Jr.'s survivors included his widow, two daughters, and a son. His father, 70-year-old Jerry Webber, and his father's twin, Tom, retired from Hudson's that same year.

Henry Ford II served as a pallbearer at the funeral when the Hudson-Webber family members gathered, again, in an expression of family solidarity. Years later, Henry Ford II would express his personal feelings about his Hudson background to biographer Robert Lacey by saying he was not a Ford, but a Hudson—like his mother.

At Jim Webber's untimely death, the heir-apparent mandate quickly was passed to young Joseph L. Hudson, Jr. The 25-year-old Joseph was a grandson of deceased William Hudson, youngest brother of the original retailer, Joseph Lowthian Hudson. For many years, William Hudson had managed the Hudson store in Buffalo, and his son, Joseph L. Hudson, Sr., now was treasurer of a Buffalo department store—Adam, Meldrum and Anderson Co., Inc. Growing up in a department store family, Joseph, Jr., had gone off to Yale after high school graduation, but had come to Detroit to work on the receiving docks and in the Basement Store at Hudson's during summer vacations from the university.

At Yale, he earned a letter as goalie for the hockey team, and graduated in 1953 with a degree in economics. When he returned to Detroit after graduation, to work in Personnel as an executive trainee, the Webber brothers were pleased that the slim, six-foot-tall Ivy Leaguer would bring back the name *Joseph Lowthian Hudson* to the country's second largest department store—surpassed only by New York's giant Macy's at this point.

Unlike the store's founder, young Joseph Hudson was not a bachelor. His blond wife, Jean, had the classic good looks and quiet, well-bred demeanor that complemented the friendly personality of her handsome husband who preferred to be known, simply, as "Joe" Hudson. But a year later, the young Hudson went into the U.S. Army for two years. When he was sent to Germany to serve as an artillery officer, his wife and baby son, Joseph L. Hudson IV, went with him. By the time of their return to Detroit in 1956, they had a second child—a daughter named Jean.

Assigned to Eugenia Kresik for training in affairs of the Bureau of Adjustments, the genial and polite heir to the Hudson empire "chased packages through various departments," Eugenia recalls. This procedure took the authority figure, Eugenia, and her willing pupil, Joe Hudson, on tracing expeditions from the fourth floor basement to the 21st floor. By February, 1957, young Hudson became a company vice president and member of the board of directors. And in October, 1957, he advanced to vice president and succeeded Oscar Webber as general manager, while Oscar continued as president of the company.

By June, 1956, the early 1950s' prosperity was fading as Detroit became a city with 138,000 jobless people. Sales at Downtown Hudson's had declined since 1953 but the company's refund policy, which now amounted to some $25 million a year, remained as generous as in earlier years. Because of Hudson's commitment to its popular Bridal Registry, Detroiters did not hesitate to return Hudson boxes containing gifts, for exchange, that had not been purchased from The J.L. Hudson Company. Still, the store's policy—offering liberal exchanges to young brides who might otherwise have been disillusioned—remained unchanged. And Hudson's continued its practice of providing layettes for any women who went into labor while shopping in the store, and of refunding money for layettes and nursery furniture, bought at Hudson's, if the customer's baby died.

"We could be accused of being ridiculously liberal," Oscar Webber was quoted in *The Oakland Press*. "However, we think it has been the cheapest form of advertising we ever used."

By 1958, former assistant general manager Frank Colombo had taken over the duties of Hudson's general manager. Under Colombo's management and despite Hudson's beefed-up Special Services and rewards to employee-informers, inventory shortages continued increasing each year. In March, 1958, three Men's Wear employees caught a shoplifter stealing $794 worth of merchandise. When detectives went to the shoplifter's car, they found a cache of additional stolen goods taken from other stores, and discovered that the thief was wanted in three states for robbery and breaking out of jail. Still, the $794 theft was only a minor part of Hudson's inventory shortage that amounted to an alarming average of $8,740 each day in 1958.

HUDSON'S: HUB OF AMERICA'S HEARTLAND

In 1959, the first major crack appeared in the facade of Detroit's glossy and prosperous downtown shopping nucleus when the 62-year-old Kern's Woodward Avenue department store, a block south of Hudson's, went out of business, a victim of its own proud elegance—its refusal to bow to the burgeoning of America's more casual lifestyle. A victim, also, to the persistent, biting effects of inventory shortages and to the surge of shoppers to suburban malls. The final throes of Kern's sales of marked-down merchandise echoed along the Woodward Avenue corridor with a dreadful finality to that flourishing earlier era when wealthy women were chauffered downtown in limousines that circled from Kern's to Crowley's to Hudson's private entrance.

Hudson's diligently disassociated itself from any signs of fading vitality with a vigorous program of renovation—floor by floor, year by year. Renovation of the 13th floor dining room was completed by May, 1959, in time for the sixth anniversary dinner celebrating the careers of three employees who had worked for 45 years at the store. Another four employees, of forty years' experience, were feted at the banquet along with more than 260 who had worked for more than 25 years. And, in its campaign to promote its downtown store as a symbol of a vital Detroit, Hudson's pursued an energetic program of daily newspaper advertising.

The store's traditions were treated as tenderly as in past years. By November, cooks in the 13th floor kitchen were busily preparing some 3,000 pounds of plum pudding and 4,250 pounds of fruit cake—both dark cake and the light Scotch Dundee requested by long-time customers. But traditions and innovations coexisted comfortably at Hudson's where, in 1958, the Detroit emporium became one of the first department stores to offer its charge customers a convenient car rental plan. The customer could present only a driver's license and a Hudson charge plate to any Avis car rental, and, with no deposit, could drive away—driver and car covered by insurance. Billing for the service would appear on the customer's regular Hudson statement.

A spectacular Hudson's-sponsored Fourth of July fireworks display lit up the skies over the Detroit River between downtown Detroit and downtown Windsor, Canada, in 1959, dazzling spectators on both sides of the river with its brilliance. The magnificent fireworks pageantry would become another annual Hudson's tradition on each Independence Day, growing year by year and leading to a three-day combination Detroit-Windsor International Freedom Day Festival.

When the turbulent 1960s arrived, Hudson's still was leading the way in protecting the glamorous image of downtown Detroit and keeping Woodward Avenue pulsing in rhythm with the flow of motor traffic and pedestrians throughout the hub of the Motor City. Still, occupants of the most luxurious offices in the Golden Corridor were planning to build more suburban Hudson stores as new and better expressways took shoppers further away from downtown Detroit into the glossy malls of Suburbia.

Chapter 10

"The Ever Whirling Wheels of Change"

Very early in the restless 1960s, Hudson's underwent a series of changes beginning with the death of one of the four Webber brothers. One of the twins, James Benson (Jerry) Webber, died in 1960, leaving his wife and a daughter—Mrs. Wm. C. Tost. In April, 1961, several management shifts elevated 29-year-old Joseph L. Hudson to president of the J.L. Hudson Company as Oscar Webber became chairman of the board. The eldest Webber, Richard, took the title of honorary chairman.

The new, young and vital company president assumed the Webber scepter with a disarming friendliness that charmed employees as he moved through the store, greeting clerks by name without discernible glances at their name tags. Like his founding ancestor, young Joseph Lowthian dressed well—wearing a fresh suit each day selected from the racks of Hudson's Men's Wear. He also wore a hat whenever he came to, or left, the store, and ruled that all Hudson executives must wear hats. How else could they expect to sell hats to a public openly admiring of President John F. Kennedy, who had set aside his high silk hat at his inauguration because of the strong wind, and had gone hatless thereafter.

Hudson's Millinery had its own problems with the growing trend to hatlessness for women—a trend exacerbated by the popularity of lacquered beehive and bouffant hairdos in the middle and late 1960s. The store's leased-out Beauty Salon benefitted from the exaggerated hair styles, but Millinery buyers had to choose carefully when ordering expensive designer hats to entice women customers into buying designer creations to match their costumes.

When buyers arranged for Joan Crawford, representing a millinery association, to make a personal appearance at the store, a crush of people created a major traffic problem inside the store and outside on Woodward Avenue. Crawford's longshoreman language, off-stage, astounded some of the buyers, who were ordered by the Hollywood star to supply her with 100-proof vodka. But on-stage, the movie star was all glamour and elegance in her designer costumes and large hats.

The Millinery department also offered custom designing of hats to suit individual tastes. Department clerks dealt patiently with customers who bought several hats at a time, then returned all but one for refunds—usually after wearing each of the hats—which would contribute to a total $30 million in 1964 returns as young Joe Hudson continued the liberal exchange and refund policies of the pleasant mannered Webbers.

Despite the reputation of the Webbers for polite gentility, clerks Genevieve Dzialak and Marguerite Clark were intimidated when, on one payday, they went up to the quiet, thickly carpeted eleventh floor to collect their pay envelopes. As they waited outside the pay office, they sat down on a plush sofa. They were still sitting there, resting, when they saw two men approach from the elevator. Realizing that both men were Webbers, the women guiltily sprang to their feet. "That's okay. Sit down," one of the brothers urged, waving at the sofa.

Clerks found these easy and pleasant manners reflected in the Webbers' first cousin, once-removed, Joe Hudson—who rode the same elevators as the workers and who drove his own car to Hudson's branch stores. And they soon learned there was more to the man than charm; within the first few years of his appointment as president, he made several changes.

In May, 1961, the store announced a new method of paying workers because of many deductions that added to the complexity

"THE EVER WHIRLING WHEELS OF CHANGE"

of payroll computations. Stacks of yard-wide old ledger books, with faded, hand-posted pages, now were stored on the 24th floor — a part of Hudson's history as the company moved into the computer age, beginning with the paymaster's office which issued checks instead of distributing pay envelopes containing cash.

A month later, Hudson's proudly accepted a gold cup presented by the Committee of French Good Taste, made up of 25 business and cultural leaders of France. The trophy, the committee said, symbolized "the good taste which the J.L. Hudson Company has exercised in its merchandise presentation and takes recognition of the honesty of its tradition and the prestige it enjoys internationally in its field."

The leadership that Hudson's exercised in the fields of business and culture did not extend into the turbulent area of politics. But in February, 1962, Joe Hudson — known for his puritanical leanings — encouraged his employees to support two bills under consideration in the state Legislature for regulation of the sale of general merchandise on Sundays.

During the past decade, debate concerning stores that opened for business on Sundays had become an explosive issue. Catholic and Protestant churches, alike, pressed their congregations to sign individual pledges not to patronize the offending stores. Women picketed businesses that violated long-standing "blue laws" prohibiting the sale of merchandise on the Sabbath.

Like Hudson's, Kresge Stores had resisted following the leadership of other large businesses that opened on Sundays in the late 1950s. And now, in response to Joe Hudson's statement that he believed it was unwise to keep downtown stores open on Sundays, and that he was "working with church leaders to reverse this trend," 7,500 Hudson employees wrote letters to their representatives, supporting the proposed restrictive legislation.

When Kresge Stores finally surrendered to the pressure of competition in 1966 and opened their doors to Sunday customers, Mrs. S.S. Kresge protested by selling her personal stock in the company. Fifteen years later, her son would give away most of his Kmart stock when that discount chain began selling beer and wine.

By 1968, the fight against Sunday openings for stores had almost collapsed, although Hudson's still remained closed. But during the holiday season of 1968, the company opened its telephone shopping service each Sunday, receiving an average 1700 orders.

Ever since downtown sales had begun to slide when Hudson's first suburban mall pulled hordes of shoppers away from the heart of the city in 1954, Detroit merchants had concerned themselves with luring customers back to Woodward Avenue. As early as May, 1954, the association of downtown merchants hit upon the idea of sponsoring "Downtown Detroit Days" — three days of enticing customers with reduced bus fares, discounted merchandise, and a variety of freebies, including 1,000 movie tickets and certificates for weekends at some of the city's posh hotels, presented to lucky shoppers. When stores reported a minimum 25% increase in sales during the promotion, merchants decided to make the three "Downtown Detroit Days" an annual affair, which continued to expand each year.

While bucking the growing 1960s' trend toward Sundays sales, Hudson's relied on a variety of innovations to draw customers. The Books department was expanded to include a huge display of paperback titles on the Mezzanine, qualifying Hudson's to boast that no outlet in the world carried more than the Woodward store's 9,000 titles.

In the summer of 1962, the store featured nostalgic and colorful settings relating to turn-of-the-century retailing, minus any unpleasant reminders of child labor, 14-hour working days, or unsanitary washrooms. In the aisles and the auditorium, and even on the sidewalks outside the store, there were old-fashioned ice cream parlors, flower carts, popcorn wagons, pseudo Keystone Cops, hurdy-gurdy men, costumed barbershop quartets, German bands, and a photo studio with old-time props.

Joe Hudson's unique ideas for promoting Downtown Hudson's attracted media attention in November, 1963, when he opened the J.L. Hudson Art Gallery on the seventh floor between Better Dresses and Millinery. For the opening, maintenance workers laid a thick red carpet from the elevator doors to the Art Gallery entrance where works by Jacques Lipchitz, Picasso, and Enrico Donati would be on display under the watchful eyes of the gallery's director, former New York art dealer Albert Landry. And where champagne would be served for the first time within the walls of the venerable J.L. Hudson store as visitors came to the evening reception at the Gallery.

Avoiding the evening reception, and the champagne, Richard Webber came to visit the Gallery in the afternoon. But his more outgoing wife, and even his brother Oscar, made evening appearances at what was reported as the "first serious art gallery in a U.S. department store." Times were changing in the 1960s, and even the staid Webbers reluctantly recognized that the way to do business in the 1960s was not necessarily the way "Uncle Joseph" had done it. And so, under the great-nephew's presidency, the alcohol taboo was broken—and very soon, Hudson's first floor pantry stocked fine wines to accompany its delicatessen foods.

By this time, the young Joseph L. Hudsons were the parents of four children. And the 32-year-old company president was able to handle his many business and civic responsibilities, including serving as general chairman of Detroit's 1965 Torch Drive, while retaining a reservoir of vigor for his favorite sports of tennis and squash. An elevator trip to the 24th floor took young Hudson up to the squash court—or to the sun room or exercise room, with a rowing machine—at lunchtime. One early afternoon as the store executive played squash with a Kresge vice president, Buck Huff's beeper sounded. Maintenance was needed on the 24th floor where water pressure had failed, he was told. There, Huff found Hudson in the shower, all soaped and unable to rinse.

The problem was not unsolvable—a tank just above the 24th floor provided water pressure for the exercise room showers, with water pumped up to floor 26, then down. But, for the moment, Huff had to carry pails of warm water, climb a stepladder, and pour the contents of the pails down on the soapy, but cheerful, Hudson. The two men decided to call the incident "How to Meet the Company President."

In his intense loyalty to Hudson's, Huff expressed annoyance each time he heard, or read, the familiar references to the store's "25 floors." "Twenty-eight floors," he insisted, always remembering the many times he serviced the huge sprinklers housed on floors 26 to 28.

To Huff, the top three floors were as much as part of his life as a penthouse might be to its occupant. Equally important was the fourth basement—its maze of conveyors and mechanical equipment to route packages to delivery, and its engine rooms for air conditioners. The fifth basement and its sump pumps. Even the Detroit Edison Company steam tunnel, 80 feet underground, running from Gratiot to Grand River and passing through Hudson's at the third basement level. In the company of Detroit Edison people, Huff sometimes entered a street-level manhole into the huge tunnel, which supplied steam to all buildings in the downtown area, and walked from the bowels of the City-County Building to Grand Circus Park, experiencing the same feeling of intimate knowledge that a physician might have when performing exploratory surgery.

In its first year, the J.L. Hudson Art Gallery proved successful. At an end-of-year birthday press-party, director Landry was euphoric—refusing to accept the premise that there was anything crass about an art gallery incorporated into a department store as he acknowledged that 90% of sales of paintings were made to Hudson's charge account customers. Customers could take 90 days to pay for the art works, some of which ran into five or six figures and were written up on the same sales slips used to record sales of bath mats or dish towels, the director pointed out.

Joe Hudson told a *New York Times* reporter that the gallery was founded to expose Detroiters to "the finest art available," in response to what he called a "cultural explosion." But there was a strange underside to the "cultural explosion" in 1963—an Andy Warhol-inspired rise of pop-art and junk sculpture and a general erosion of standards in literature and morality. Even at Hudson's, it became more difficult to screen out this erosion as best-selling books, plays, and entertainment became more sexually explicit and the counterculture's influence on fashion became more popular.

In the midst of a changing society ridden with anxieties, citizens were not consoled by President Kennedy's emphasis on the personal, as well as national, responsibilities of citizens to prepare fallout shelters as protection against Russian atomic bombs. The safeness, and saneness, of a familiar Hudson's—where erotic books and anti-establishment vests and leather goods were not on display—appeared to be assured by the issuing of a 1963 dress code for Hudson employees, scarcely relieved from its former austerity.

Women employees' dresses, suits, and skirts had to be solid colors—dark blue, grey, black, or medium to dark green or brown. Sleeves at least halfway between shoulders and elbows. No patterns permitted in trimmings or scarves. Sweaters worn only under suit coats. No figure-revealing clothing. Only "businesslike" shoes of dark, solid colors. No hair ornaments could be worn except by salespeople in departments where such ornaments were sold. For men, conservative business suits, dress shirts, ties, dark shoes—always polished, and dark hose.

Along with young Hudson's respect for tradition and customs, there was still another side to his personality—a strong concern for social problems. As early as 1961, when he had taken over as company president, he had expressed his concerns with the use of narcotics by Detroiters and with the problem of chronic unemployment, especially among blacks, reaching back to the middle 1950s. "We must find new ways of creating jobs," he insisted.

Shortly before Hudson had become president, young Diane Ross—a student at Cass Technical High School—began working as a bus girl in Hudson's Basement Cafeteria. The skinny, intense teen-ager had already enrolled in modeling classes at Hudson's, which may have been the reason she was the first black bus girl hired by the department store, according to Connie Burman's biography, *Diana Ross: Supreme Lady*. While Diane studied dress design and sewing at Cass and dreamed of becoming a fashion designer or model, she also sang in the choir at Olivet Baptist Church and with a singing group of three, sometimes four, girls called the *Primettes*. They sang at dances, parties, and civic affairs—blending rock and gospel—and finally began to work for Berry Gordy at Motown Records, clapping and cooing, "oohing" and "do-wahing" background for the *Shirelles*, Marvin Gaye, and the *Vandellas*.

By this time, Diane had quit her job at Hudson's, although she was making very little money at Motown. And by 1964, Diane was known as Diana, the *Primettes* had become the *Supremes*, and the trio recorded its first blockbuster record—"Where Did Our Love Go." The three Supremes moved their families out of Brewster housing project and bought fine homes for them in northwest Detroit. When Diana returned to Hudson's, she often came with

Berry Gordy's sister, Esther, as the two bought expensive hats of assorted styles and colors.

Some years later, Ross's clothes would be custom made by designer Bob Mackie. And if she decided to visit a department store, a Diana Ross shopping tour could command special openings at night to accommodate the renowned singer.

On a Sunday afternoon in June, 1963, 125,000 Detroit blacks, singing "We Shall Overcome," marched down Woodward Avenue to Cobo Hall in what was called a "Walk to Freedom." Detroit's young mayor, Jerome P. Cavanagh, and labor leader Walter Reuther were present at Cobo Hall as Dr. Martin Luther King, Jr., addressed the crowd, loudspeakers carrying his message to those outside. "We want all of our rights," Dr. King told them. "We want them here, and we want them now."

Reporters' accounts of Dr. King's marches, of Freedom Rides and about the furor over desegregation of southern schools filled the front pages of newspapers. A new term, "polarization" of the races, came into vogue as anxiety-plagued Americans tried to cope with problems of racism. Even those who chose to ignore the problems of a troubled America were shocked into facing reality when, on November 22, 1963, the country's charismatic President John F. Kennedy—a man with magnetic appeal to both blacks and whites—was assassinated in Dallas, Texas.

Pearly Lashley, an elevator starter at Hudson's, stood near the perfume counter on the main floor on November 22 when she saw people gathering, outside, in groups on the sidewalk. Some of them were weeping, she noticed as she turned to see that many of the first-floor clerks were dabbing at their eyes. When an elevator operator told Pearly that the president had been shot, "I just stood there holding my stomach," Pearly recalled later for a *Detroit News* reporter. "Nobody got any work done that day and it didn't simmer down the next day either."

As the tragic news raced through the store, a very disturbed Eugenia Kresik came down to the main floor from Adjustments. She saw dazed clerks and customers standing in clusters, crying, while others ran aimlessly up and down the aisles—to and from the elevators.

"THE EVER WHIRLING WHEELS OF CHANGE"

The country was changed irrevocably by the assassination and subsequent charges of a variety of sinister conspiracies. Recovery of the nation's confidence was further eroded by Vietnam War protest disturbances and the 1968 assassinations of both Martin Luther King, Jr., and Robert Kennedy.

During these same years, downtown Detroit struggled to retain its status as a major shopping metropolis against the odds of white flight from the city to the suburbs, induced by rising crime and the forced busing of schoolchildren. Hudson's fought valiantly to keep its "Queen of Woodward" image by installing a Magic IBM Gift Selector that processed 57,000 requests during the 1962 holiday season. By changing its Farmer Street entrance to accommodate wheelchairs and baby carriages with installation of an "air door" — a set of swinging doors and a high velocity "curtain of air" — in place of revolving doors. By boasting of surpassing its "Million Dollar Day" goal twice in December, 1962, with its biggest sales volume since 1955. By advertising a Spring Sale competition in 1963 in which its Downtown Men's Store did more business than its men's departments in Hudson's branch stores. By continuing to sponsor the Detroit-Windsor International Freedom Festival — a week long celebration featuring a fireworks display, preceded by military and police band concerts, visible for miles along the international border and touted as the largest in the country. By converting its Credit Department from manual systems to electronic data processing in 1965, after credit sales rose to 64.4% of Hudson's business in 1963. And by adapting to the women's budding revolution with the employment of two male telephone operators to help respond to customers' calls.

At Christmas time, Downtown Hudson's still held an irresistible attraction for suburbanites who flocked to the Woodward Avenue emporium where store windows were transformed into a wonderland of animated dolls and woodland animals — presenting "The Little Lost Reindeer," with musical accompaniment, in 1964. Just outside of Hudson's main doors, instrumentalists in a Salvation Army brass ensemble would be alternately blowing on their hands to warm them and blowing into their trombones and trumpets to peal Christmas carols into the frosty air. Each time the brass players ducked into Hudson's vestibule to get warm, a Salvation Army volunteer clanged a large bell to call attention to the Army's red kettle for donations while, at noon, carols rang out from Hudson's public address system, punctuated by whistle blasts from the traffic cop. At intervals, mounted police — on duty to control the Christmas crowds on Woodward — rode their horses into Hudson's huge, third-basement freight elevator to get warm.

The facade of Hudson's on Woodward, above the span of display windows, glowed with the brilliance of its enormous "Tree of Lights" shaped in three tiers with 5,000 outdoor white bulbs and many more thousands of Italian lights — 120 feet wide at its base and reaching nine stories high. Inside the store, a dozen huge Christmas trees glittered on the main floor. Shoppers and their children boarded one of 38 elevators swishing up to the 13th floor dining room, transformed into a Candy Cane Room where clowns entertained while nearly 400 people, with reservations, ate breakfast. From the Candy Cane Room, visitors moved to join a line of people going to the twelfth floor's 1/2 acre devoted to a "Fantasy Forest" complete with shimmering trees, cottony snow, and furry, animated animals. There, they were greeted by a young girl, called "Christmas Carol," and several Santa's helpers who directed children to the "real" Santa Claus.

And still there was more, including a Children's Only Shop where each child was interviewed with his or her parents, before entering the child-sized low door. While parents waited in chairs outside the doorway, or went on to shop in the eighth floor Gallery Boutique or seventh floor Xmas Gifterama, teen-age counselors helped the children to shop from a colorful display of merchandise on low shelves, regardless of possible breakage, priced between 50 cents and $3.00. An average of 30,000 children each holiday season bought and paid for their gifts — with the help of staff people, wrote gift cards at miniature desks, then stopped for refreshments at a milk and cookies bar before delivery to their parents.

Speranzo Pagnucco, of Dearborn, was among throngs of suburban visitors to Downtown Hudson's Toyland in 1964. When, among the hundreds of dolls from every nation, she saw a three-foot-high doll, blond and blue-eyed and typically American, she bought the doll as a Christmas present for her five-year-old daughter, Pola. As the daughter matured and, eventually, married and moved away from home, the lonely and widowed mother, who had come to the Detroit area from Venice, Italy, would resist storing the lovely doll away in a closet. Instead, she dressed it in little-girl clothing that her own daughter had worn, and set the life-like doll in the large picture window of her living room, looking out on the street. If the sun was bright, she put sunglasses on the doll's face, and, regardless of bright or dull weather, she frequently changed the doll's dress and brushed the blond hair smoothly into place.

Before long, the doll-child in the window attracted groups of neighborhood children who sneaked into the neatly kept yard to get closer looks at the blond mannequin. People in cars drove around and around the block to stare at the figure in the window. A persistent and untrue rumor — that the doll symbolized a small child of the Pagnuccos who was killed by a car in the driveway of the family's Dearborn home — endowed the child-sized mannequin with a poignancy that would continue to attract curious sight-seers two decades later.

Like many other new employees recruited by family members to go to work at Hudson's, Gladys (Mrs. Lewis) Huff began working only part time — helping with costumes for the Thanksgiving Day parade at Hudson's warehouse for two months in the fall of 1964. For the next three years, Gladys — a skilled seamstress — came back each fall for parade preparations. Within a few years, Gladys was so involved with the parade that she began working six-month stints, going up on a lift to work on "Dumbo, the Flying Elephant" — making ears from pillowcases with pink lining. And soon she was working full time, partly in clerical work as she kept an inventory of costumes, filled out time-cards for Hudsonian parade participants, and helped select bands.

High-school bands had to have at least 90 members to be considered as one of a dozen or more bands selected to march in the parade, after directors had applied to Hudson's and sent photographs of their bands in action. Although Hudson's made a contribution to each band director, transportation expenses — earned in advance by washing cars or selling candy — were the responsibility of individual bands who, on arrival in Detroit, were housed in schools or in hotels offering reduced rates.

Gladys also looked over an artist's drawings of new floats, selected by a committee from letters submitted by elementary school children who described the kinds of floats they would like to see in the parade. The child suggesting the prize-winning float was presented with a saving bond.

By the early 1970s, Gladys was named "Fort Street's Dragon Lady" in a *Detroit News* article recounting her three months of handiwork on the 80-foot body of a 100-foot-long, fuzzy green monster-float named "Dragon A'long." Working from the artist's color sketch, the petite Gladys cut 17-foot-long decorative strips from eight-foot-wide cardboard patterns, sewing them together, then climbing a ladder and appliqueing the strips to the dragon's body.

The "Studio" section of the warehouse basement was equipped with an industrial sewing machine—fine for stitching canvas and webbing, which was done by Chester Sinila and other male employees. Gladys found it easier to work on her own portable sewing machine that she brought from home to make hoop skirts for bumble-bee costumes.

It became Gladys' responsibility to choose parade participants by height and weight for costumes, and by experience for certain floats and duties. Long before Thanksgiving, phone calls would come in to the "Studio." "Hold me a spot, Gladys," the caller would say, specifying which costume or "head" or float he or she preferred.

On parade day, Gladys showed up early to supervise the seven a.m. costuming, as did Joe Hudson—sharing coffee and doughnuts with his employees and greeting everyone with a genial "good morning." When the costuming procedure was finished and the paraders' buses left for the lineup, a bus took Gladys and other parade supervisors to the waiting line-of-march where they would walk the length of 18 floats and hundred of marchers, checking to make sure everything was in proper order and that any emergencies were taken care of. When the parade ended, Gladys was ready to begin another three months of work—sorting, mending, and storing away the costumes—before beginning new projects for the next year's Thanksgiving march down Woodward Avenue.

Each year's parade was a magic time for Gladys, but equally

magic was the opportunity to meet the celebrities who came to Detroit to be a part of Hudson's annual extravaganza. Bess Myerson—the former Miss America. Both Arthur Godfrey and Lassie, one year. Gladys had admired Godfrey on television, but found him autocratic in person. Lassie, accompanied by a small dog-companion, was housed in the presidential suite at the Book Cadillac Hotel, and Godfrey, assigned to the next floor, complained loudly about being upstaged by a dog.

The Beverly Hillbillies came one Thanksgiving—a day of cold, drizzly rain. And another year, Goldie Hawn arrived late at the airport in a downpour of rain, removed her purple pumps and gave them to Buck Huff to carry, and was assigned to a police lieutenant for a bodyguard. When Goldie was lifted up to the float, she had to wear the lieutenant's raincoat and hat to protect her from the weather. Still, she hung onto her smile and good humor.

The Good Times couple were equally pleasant. But when Greg Morris and June Lockhart, from Mission Impossible, came for the parade, Gladys Huff was annoyed by Lockhart's demand for "a hot cup of tea" in the midst of bustling preparations to put the parade together.

By the middle 1960s, Hudson's fast-service restaurants on the store's lower floors included a "scramble" or buffet-type mezzanine restaurant in place of its former elegant Tea Room. The quick-service areas, including a Basement Store (now known as the Budget Store) Snack Bar and a sandwich cart in the Beauty Salon, were now handling a million more customers than was the store's plush 13th floor Riverview Room, which had a seating capacity equal to that of the combined quick-service accommodations. The store quickly made changes to conform with customer preferences—converting its 13th floor Pine Rooms to a limited-menu restaurant for quick service and expanding its fourth-floor Snack Bar . . . stocking its Pantry Shop with delicatessen items and frozen foods made in Hudson's bakery. Products from the store's 16th floor Candy Kitchen still were popular items on first floor, glass fronted counters—especially fudge, with 2,800 pounds of it made each day by Candy Kitchen cooks.

The days of leisurely luncheons at tables covered with fresh linen cloths set with silver and fragile china were moving into Hudson's history, along with the store's traditional dedication to conservative styles favored by Grosse Pointe matrons and Junior Leaguers. Catering to teens with money or charge cards stuffed in the pockets of their jeans became a survival priority at Hudson's as the store began sponsoring youth activities . . . Teen Take Over Day; Action Age-Seventeen Day; Teen Stop and Shop Pop Day. To enhance its "with-it" image, the store also sponsored a Youth Council—a group of high school seniors who met with store fashion coordinators to discuss local acceptance of fashion innovations.

The change in focus became apparent at Hudson's very quickly as its College-Career Shop was renamed and outfitted as The Purple Clothespin, and with the installation of juke boxes in the Young Junior Shop. Boutiques, stocked with an array of mod and kooky merchandise, sprang up within the confines of Hudson's, and even the Miss Hudson Shop, featuring more expensive clothing for affluent young women, stocked such novelties as fun fur coats.

Although Oscar Webber had moved boldly with major investments in Northland and Eastland Centers, the Webbers and Joe Hudson were more cautious with suburban expansion plans in the late 1950s and early 1960s. They had set up a Hudson's Lincoln Park Budget Store branch in 1959, followed by two more Budget Stores in Madison Heights and Pontiac in 1962—at which time Hudson's employees numbered 13,000 people. Nine thousand of these employees worked at the Downtown store, where hundreds more were employed during the Christmas shopping season.

Eighty-five percent of the company's executive positions, at this point, were held by former management trainees—almost all of whom had begun their careers in Hudson's Merchandising network, a massive operation dealing with 28,000 vendors in 10,000 cities. In this respect, Hudson procedures of up-through-the-ranks advancement had changed only in degree from the policies established by the company's founder. And with the expansion of Hudson's into suburban shopping malls in the 1950s and 1960s, the Webbers and young Joe Hudson were getting away from the "all eggs in one basket" tenet and returning to business practices engaged in by the original Joseph Lowthian Hudson who had built additional stores in other cities.

Encouraged by mounting revenues from Northland and Eas-

"THE EVER WHIRLING WHEELS OF CHANGE"

tland Centers, the great-nephew, Joe Hudson, then planned another huge Hudson complex. Westland Center opened in 1964 and helped push the company to a profit peak of $12 million in 1965. Its success spurred Joe Hudson to complete plans for two more suburban shopping malls — Oakland Mall, to open in 1968, and Southland Center, in 1970.

On November 30, 1966, a college student walked along Downtown Hudson's Mezzanine, on his way to his part-time evening job — operating a computer in Central Auditing on the 18th floor. At the same time, one floor above the Mezzanine, a young black man removed a $185 quarter-length suede coat from a rack in Men's Clothing, and tried it on. Still wearing the coat, he made a sudden dash toward the escalator. But clerk William Frederick and store detective Bonnie Lobb were at the thief's heels, seizing him and forcing him off the escalator at the Mezzanine level. Shoppers watched as the clerk and the security officer pulled the struggling young man toward the security elevator when, twisting violently, he wrenched free of Lobb's grasp, knocked the woman down, pulled a knife, and plunged it into the clerk's chest.

The clerk crumpled to the floor as the man in the suede coat raced toward the closest escalator, upward-bound from the first floor. With the college-student employee and a salesman from Coins and Stamps in pursuit, the thief leaped onto the escalator, holding the bloodied knife in his hand. Swiftly, he ran down as the steps moved upward, plowing through shoppers coming up from the first floor and knocking down three elderly women — one of them on a cane. The downward progress of the pursuers on the up-escalator was sufficiently impeded by the bowled-over women that the man in the suede coat was able to run out the Farmer Street exit and disappear into the night.

Thirty-year-old William Frederick, a ten-year employee of Hudson's and the father of two small children, was pronounced dead of stab wounds — three in the stomach and one in the chest — at 8:04 p.m. in Receiving Hospital. Four witnesses to the murder spent most of the night at the police station, Homicide Division, trying to identify the murderer through four lineups of suspects rounded up by police officers. But the guilty man was not found until Hudson's offered a $10,000 reward for his capture, at which time the father of Detroiter Donald Larry turned in his son and collected the money.

Judge Colombo heard the case, during which he chastised Larry for grinning when details of the salesman's death were given. Then he sentenced the defendant to a prison term of 14 1/2 to 15 years — the longest possible sentence for felony manslaughter at that time. But Larry would be out of prison in eight years, and, in 1984, would be found guilty of killing another man, by stabbing and shooting the victim, because, Larry said, "I didn't like him."

Accounts of the vicious murder chilled store employees and left its scar on Hudson's — but it was not the only scar. The following year, one of Hudson's phone-order operators was walking down the stairs at closing time when a man grabbed her on the landing near the 19th floor and beat her on the head with one of her own shoes. Someone eventually heard her screams, but the woman had been raped by the time security people arrived and found the operator struggling to her feet, blood running from her head, and her assailant's bloody handprints on the wall.

The woman was taken to the hospital, and security forces were alerted to stop the rapist before he could escape from the store, but they were unable to find the man. The next day, they discovered evidence indicating that the unknown rapist had spent the night hiding in the store after washing up in a blood-stained sink on the 16th floor, and still undetected, had left the building the next morning. When there was no mention of the attack in the newspapers, employees felt that Hudson's suppressed the story because of the bad effect it might have on upcoming Downtown Detroit Days.

Doors to the stairwells were kept locked, after that, to prevent any more such attacks. But Hudson's would bleed from other, unanticipated scars when a man came down the escalator from the first to the second basement, walked up to a cubbyhole office where his wife worked at a desk, pulled a pistol from his pocket, and shot the woman before running up the escalator and out on Farmer Street.

Other chilling incidents began to take their toll of employees' nerves. One such incident occurred after the warning bell rang, signaling employees to finish the day's transactions. As clerks began to hurry toward the elevators and out of the building, a laggard female employee was seized by a rapist in the Furniture department and tossed onto a bed where the woman's screams attracted help before the assault was completed.

A different kind of tragedy took place when a distraught woman chose a window, just outside the 20th floor purchaser's office, from which to jump to her death—hitting the marquee and then grazing a truck driver as the body ricocheted to Farmer Street. In the wake of the woman's suicide, Hudson's windows, above the shopping floors, were secured and the grand Matriarch of Woodward began to take on a different, more guarded personality. But the personality change was only in its beginning stages.

Just as the 1966 shooting of the president seared the country with a time-division referred to as "before Kennedy's assassination" and "after Kennedy's assassination," so, too, Detroit was lanced by a time-split acknowledged as "before the '67 riot" and "after the '67 riot." Two Webber brothers died shortly before the riot, but not before founding a Harper-Webber Medical Center Fund to benefit the hospital with which the family had been closely associated for so many years. Ninety-year-old Richard died in February, 1967. The death of the youngest Webber brother, 78-year-old Oscar, occurred in Harper Hospital the following May. With their deaths, only the twin, Joseph L. Webber—known as Tom, remained alive until March, 1970, when he, too, died at age 84.

Detroit's 1967 riot exploded in the very early hours of a hot Sunday, July 23, when police raided a sleazy "blind pig" in a black neighborhood on Twelfth Street. An hour later, hundreds of people crowded the glass-littered street where burglar alarms rang as looters seized liquor and groceries and cigarettes from stores with smashed windows.

Police, ordered by city officials not to use force, were stoned by mobs, as were black politicians and ministers who tried to calm the rioters. The response to their pleas was the explosive sound of Molotov cocktails setting fire to stores as arson and looting spread to Grand River Avenue, to Mack, and to upper Woodward. Showers of sparks ignited roofs of homes on nearby residential blocks, and fire fighters, summoned by home owners, had to retreat from a barrage of missiles—rocks, bricks, bottles—while police watched from patrol cars without taking action.

For twelve hours, radio and television newscasters made no mention of the rioting at the request of Mayor Cavanagh, who hoped to keep the trouble from spreading by suppressing news reports of the rampaging mobs.

In 1964, Buck Huff had transferred from the store to a new job as maintenance supervisor at Hudson's warehouse. Before seven a.m. on Sunday, July 23, 1967, he drove to work from his suburban home, gradually realizing that something was terribly wrong as he approached the "number 3" sorting and delivery warehouse at Madison and Beaubien and saw clusters of people on the streets, running from one place to another.

Deciding to drive around the three-block warehouse complex to find out what was going on, Buck headed his car west on Madison, switching on his radio in time to catch an announcement asking all Detroit policemen to report for work immediately. Turning north on Brush, Huff could see people sleeping in the street as he crossed Adams and drove up to Elizabeth where he saw a number of men draining gasoline into bottles from the side-tanks of some of the 70 Hudson trucks parked in a Stroh's lot that Hudson's rented from the brewery company. Huff realized that the men were using the gasoline for Molotov cocktails, and that each side-tank held some 50 gallons of fuel—a generous supply.

With the help of a passing policeman, Huff went into the warehouse and phoned six delivery supervisors. The men came quickly to the warehouse, followed by a company vice president, who was assigned to opening and closing the truck-entry door. Each of the other seven men would take a truck key from a first-floor keyboard, then hurry over to the parking lot where, since some of the tractors were still hitched to trailers, he would have to release the tractor, drive it to the warehouse, then drive the truck into the basement and go back for another set of keys to repeat the process. The dangerous part for the men was walking back to the parking lot, making their way through crowds drinking from whiskey bottles and others robbing stores and restaurants.

Before noon, Joe Hudson and the company's corporate attorney also arrived at the warehouse and parked their cars in the building before going on to the main store where they set up "Operation Headquarters." The warehouse men set up a similar operation, patrolling the building in pairs as they kept on the lookout for Molotov cocktails that might be hurled, or bricks that might smash warehouse windows.

By Sunday night, the men were tired but too jittery to sleep as they kept in touch with the main store, learning that Detroit's police commissioner had confiscated all the guns and ammunition from Hudson's second-floor gun shop. And by Monday night, although there were 617 fire alarms that day, only two gasoline-bombs had been thrown at the warehouse, with little damage. The rioting had spread to other parts of the city by this time, and crowds were more eager to loot and torch pawn shops, jewelry stores, and appliance outlets — from which they seized every available televison set — than to attack guarded and fortified buildings such as Hudson's warehouse.

At three a.m. on Tuesday, federal troops in full battle dress arrived at the center of the riot area in answer to Governor Romney's request for help. And on Tuesday morning, when warehouse-cafeteria food supplies were depleted, Huff called the main store to asks for razors and food. An army half-track promptly came to the warehouse to pick up Huff. Arriving at Hudson's 13th floor restaurant, Huff saw that the place was filled with uniformed army officers and Hudson officials.

Accompanied by a security man armed with a handgun, Huff took five boxes of food, a box of underwear, a pair of field glasses, and an assortment of razors, toothbrushes, and toothpaste back with him to the warehouse. From the rooftops of one or the other of the warehouse buildings, the men could see a crowd of people on Adams Street, where neighbors were barbecuing roasts taken from looted stores. Just north of Grand Circus Park, a large fire burned, smoke spiraling into the hazy cloud that hung low over the city. Most frightening of all, the men could see people with long-guns shooting at firemen who were trying to fight the flames.

Headlines in newspapers around the world carried the same report. "Detroit is Burning." American soldiers, fighting in the jungles and rice paddies of Vietnam and already sickened by news reports of hippie war-protesters disrupting college campuses and taunting police, now learned of the destructive rioting in the streets of Detroit and wondered to what kind of country they would return. *If* they returned.

Hudson employee Louise Solomon had received a telephone call late on Sunday, July 23, instructing her not to report to work the next day. On Wednesday, she reported to work but was sent home because of sniper fire from the roofs of buildings. Snipers were bold enough, that same day, to attack the police command post at Herman Kiefer Hospital.

Even on Thursday as the rioting faded and people returned to work, sporadic sniper fire still erupted. Five thousand people, burned out of their homes, were in need of shelter. Food supplies were so scarce that grocery store owners—those who had escaped the worst of the arson and looting—charged as much as one dollar for a quart of milk. Prisons and jails spilled over with arrested rioters who also were detained in police garages and other public buildings.

More than 2,000 police had worked to bring the riot under control, along with 6,800 National Guardsmen and 3,300 U.S. Army troops. The riot's toll amounted to 43 killed, more than 657 injured, and an estimated $50 million in property damage. Yet, for many Detroiters, the riot was "one big party," as some of the 12th Street residents admitted, with stolen merchandise stored in old garages where color television sets were selling for ten or fifteen dollars.

The argument would persist for years as to whether the uprising was a "race riot." City officials insisted it was not a racial outbreak, but rather a mutiny of disadvantaged blacks and whites against a power structure indifferent to the needs of the inner-city poor. Regardless of the kind of uprising, Detroit's national image was scarred.

The minor scars marring the appearance of downtown Woodward Avenue, protected by a phalanx of police and soldiers, would be quickly healed. But the people and owners of businesses—who lived and worked a block behind Woodward's hub, or on upper Woodward, and in countless other areas—would continue to suffer from housing shortages, and from the loss of corner grocery stores and other convenient services.

"THE EVER WHIRLING WHEELS OF CHANGE"

As early as Thursday of the week of the riot, both Governor Romney and Mayor Cavanagh phoned Downtown Hudson's to tell Joseph L. Hudson, Jr., that they needed response and leadership from businessmen in forming a committee that would enlist the help of community organizations in solving Detroit's problems. Would Joe Hudson head the committee, they wanted to know.

Hudson would—and did. He met that weekend with 27 other Detroit movers and shakers, including Hudson's second cousin Henry Ford II, General Motors Chairman James M. Roche, Detroit Edison Chairman Walter L. Cisler, financier Max Fisher and Superintendent Arthur Johnson of Detroit Public Schools. They came up with a name—the New Detroit Committee—and invited young black activists to meet with the committee members to help "pick up the pieces of a proud city, which has become the scene of a national tragedy," as Mayor Cavanagh stated. Vice President Hubert Humphrey met privately with the mayor, the governor, and Joe Hudson to discuss the rebuilding of devastated neighborhoods.

The corporate-elite members of the committee learned, immediately, that the meetings would be more confrontational than cooperative; that they would continue to be more divisive than unifying unless New Detroit officials would quickly make a number of concessions. One militant black, quoted in *The Detroit News*, warned Roche of General Motors that "We regard GM as a great cow out to pasture that you bring in to milk. That's what we intend to do, milk GM."

Nonetheless, the committee members reported regularly to Wayne State University for their sessions, at which black militants—some of them wearing dashikis and sandals that contrasted strangely with the committee members' pin-striped suits and wing-tipped shoes—spouted black-power edicts to their captive audience. And by November, Joe Hudson announced his company's plans to hire 500 blacks at Hudson's—250 of them hard-core unemployed, and 250 potential high school dropouts. Hudson appointed Norman Johnson as Director for the Community Training Program at the store to guide and advise the new employees.

Henry Ford, always impatient with "talky" meetings, soon stopped attending New Detroit assemblies, but retained a personal dedication to the goals of New Detroit and began recruiting blacks into Ford Motor Company's senior management. Through his newly created Economic Development Corporation, Ford also supplied capital for new, inner-city businesses. And other power-broker members of New Detroit adopted similar programs.

But after one year of chairing New Detroit, Joe Hudson was not reluctant to turn over his post to Max Fisher. Hudson's year of heading the committee turned out to be one of controversy, despite the chairman's untiring efforts to improve race relations in Detroit. He had not realized that many white people, angered by their conception that Joe Hudson was coddling and rewarding rioters, would cancel their charge cards and would even picket Hudson's stores. Nor had he realized that his efforts to placate militant blacks would antagonize more moderate blacks who accused the militants of being "racial racketeers . . . who try to blackmail businessmen." Expressing outrage that Hudson had "supported the militant-separatists" in their attempted leadership takeover of Detroit's "Negro-community," Baptist pastor Ray A. Allen also threatened a moderate-black boycott of Hudson stores.

The militants were equally unsatisfied. Albert Cleage, the minister who had brought the radical "Rap" Brown to speak at his Detroit church shortly before the riot, was now demanding money from New Detroit for investment in the ghetto even while he stated that he would not accept "white leadership and dictation." Hudson, the militants claimed, could not possibly understand the problems of the "disenfranchised black man."

Representative John Conyers, Detroit Democrat, also tongue-lashed Joe Hudson's efforts. "For one thing," Conyers said, "Joe Hudson could close his gun shop. It's not the Negroes who are standing in line to buy guns."

"New Detroit can't claim a miracle, " Joe Hudson admitted in his typically understated fashion.

Hudson's efforts were not unappreciated, however, by the NAACP. In 1968, New Detroit's past chairman was presented with a life membership in that organization of moderate blacks. Two years later, he would be honored as the first Detroit recipient of the National B'nai B'rith Humanitarian Award. Presented with the award at a $100-a-plate dinner at the Hilton Hotel, Hudson was praised for "his vision and leadership in the civic, social, and economic life of our nation and his keen sense of community responsibility for serving the needs of people everywhere."

The J.L. Hudson Company's total profits in 1967 amounted to $9.8 million, a more than $2 million decrease from 1965. The company attributed another sharp drop of $1 million in 1968 profits (even while sales rose that year from $358 million to $372 million, including revenues from Hudson's two real estate subsidiaries — one known as Shopping Centers, Inc.) to fallout from the previous year's riot, a nine-month Detroit newspaper strike in 1967-68, and the start-up expense of opening new Hudson's stores.

But the 1960's era of changes brought its greatest transformation to Hudson's in March, 1969. At that time, the J.L. Hudson Company and its eleven stores merged with Dayton Corporation of Minneapolis — which already operated 68 department stores (none of them as large as Downtown Hudson's, with its 2.1 million square feet of space, and none of them as profitable as Hudson's Northland store,) discount stores, specialty stores, and shopping centers. Dayton's sales, however, had jumped from $375.3 million for 1967 to $441.8 million in 1968. The 1969 merger elevated Dayton Hudson to a position as ninth largest non-food retailing chain in the country.

The 67-year-old Minneapolis company, formed by George D. Dayton in 1902, had flourished over the years and had continued to flourish after the founder's death under management by his grandsons — Donald and Wallace (both retired before 1969 from Dayton,) and Bruce, Kenneth, and Douglas Dayton. Now, the chief executives of both companies quickly supplied explanations for the 1969 merger, pointing out many similarities and parallels between Dayton's and Hudson's.

Bruce Dayton spoke of the present merger as "a long developing process" that had led to serious discussions in November, 1968. "In this age, family-owned businesses have a tough time meeting competition," he pointed out, while Joe Hudson claimed the merger had less to do with profits than with "compatibility" plus "progress and long-term growth." Both Dayton and Hudson reassured Detroiters that although Dayton would be the parent company, Hudson's would retain its autonomy.

Previous to the merger, 220 J.L. Hudson Company shareholders — including Hudson family members, the two foundations for Hudson and Webber, and 70 store executives — held all Hudson stock, which had never been listed on any exchange. With the merger, Hudson's stock was converted into $148 million in Dayton Hudson shares — amounting to approximately 28% of total Dayton stock — that could be publicly traded. Joseph L. Hudson Jr., owned some $1 1/2 million of the stock, but the unmarried Robert Hudson Tannahill — only son of Robert B. Tannahill and Anna Hudson — was the largest shareholder among the Hudson-Webber-Tannahill-Ford clan.

In that same year of the Dayton Hudson merger, the 76-year-old Tannahill died, lauded in lengthy obituaries as "the connoisseur of collectors" among admirers of modern art. He had served on the Arts Commission for the Detroit Institute of Arts for 37 years, along with his cousin, Eleanor (Mrs. Edsel) Ford — and, in recent years, with Joseph L. Hudson, Jr. At his death, Tannahill left his valuable art collection along with a large fund for acquisitions, to the Detroit Institute of Arts, carrying on the traditions of the Hudson family in its generous contributions to the city.

And regardless of changes, disappointments, and, even, a company merger, Joseph L. Hudson planned to continue the traditions established by his great-uncle, founder of the J.L. Hudson Company. This would include turning back a generous five percent of the company's annual profits to the Institute of Arts, the Detroit Symphony Orchestra, the Harper-Webber Medical Center, and other projects for the improvement and enhancement of the city of Detroit.

Chapter 11

The Decline

The Dayton Hudson business merger was sweetened for Hudson employees in 1970 when the company offered Hudson workers an optional stock savings plan. For every dollar invested by an employee, Hudson's contributed fifty cents to the plan. More than 370 Hudsonians immediately invested in Dayton Hudson stocks. The number of investor-employees rose to more than 5,500 in 1971, when 600,000 Dayton-Hudson common shares were priced at $35.50 a share.

In that same year, Hudson's also offered its workers a long-term disability plan through insurance paid for by the company. Hudson's now claimed that its employee-benefit package surpassed that of any department store in the country . . . that its concern for employees reached back to 1910 when the founding Joseph L. Hudson built a summer resort where the store's female clerks could spend two vacation weeks free of charge . . . that all Hudson employees had received paid vacations by 1918 — a year when few other industries had such benefits. Current benefits entitled employees of four years and seven months' employment by any January first to receive three paid vacation weeks annually; at 25 years of service, vacation time increased to an annual four weeks plus an extra four weeks every five years, beginning at the 25-year mark.

Hudson's also prided itself on its charter membership in Blue Cross—a hospital-medical plan continued after employee retirement; it offered life insurance with premiums paid by the store, and provided sick-absence pay which started on the third day of illness or on the first day for a hospitalized worker. No employee with at least five years of service could be fired unless Joe Hudson personally approved the dismissal.

But Joe Hudson faced a major problem when accounting statements showed that sales volume at Downtown Hudson's dropped below $100 million for 1970. Rapidly escalating operating and maintenance expenses for the Woodward emporium's 2 million square feet of space burdened the aging store. Increased costs for workers' benefits, amounting to 82 cents for every hour of work paid by the company in 1971, added to the burden. And a growing problem of theft at Downtown Hudson's contributed to a total $12 million in shortages at all Hudson stores in 1972.

Retraction became the byword as Hudson's cut back staffing and reduced retail space. The retractions included a reduction of the generous 20% employee discount on certain merchandise that had to be competitively priced in order for Hudson's to survive.

But the store chose not to abandon its Shoppers' Comparison plan or its assurance to customers that Hudson's would meet the best price offered at other stores. As a result, when appliances went on sale at any of the rapidly growing discount stores, Hudson's lost money by honoring its promise—and no special discounts were given to employees on the already discounted appliances.

Employees grumbled when their discounts were reduced to 15% or 10% on these items, and protested even more strongly when no discount was allowed. And as Kmart stores proliferated and advertised sale prices on a variety of merchandise, Hudson's resorted to removing identical items from its shelves, replacing them when their competitor's sale ended—to avoid having to match rock-bottom Kmart prices.

Even while New Detroit gushed about "the rebirth of a downtown Detroit," residents continued to move out of the city in the wake of the 1967 riots—decreasing Detroit's population by a

THE DECLINE

quarter-million people during the 1970s. In its struggle for survival, Downtown Hudson's resigned itself to a personality change that was quite suitable for young Hudson anchors—with their emphasis on futuristic, specialty boutiques flaunting bold colors—but became a painful process for the hulking Woodward Avenue store as it tried to update its sagging image with advertising reflecting the lastest in modish fashions for trendy teens. The store boasted of its "early" advertising of "hot pants." Of its mini-skirts and "go-go" boots. Of its men's "body" shirts. And, soon, of its faded, recycled denims.

Groups of teen-age girls ran into Downtown Hudson's between buses, crowding the "Aisles of Beauty" to sniff expensive perfumes and to spray sample fragrances on their wrists. To test sample lipsticks on the backs of their hands. And to admire themselves in small mirrors as they riffled through costume jewelry and fastened gold hoop earrings in their pierced ears.

The arrival of Mary Quant and her Quant-ities from London's Carnaby Street attracted a crowd of teens and young women and created a ruckus at Downtown Hudson's. The crowd collected to admire the originator of the mini-skirt and her abbreviated fashions. The ruckus occurred behind the scenes when Quant's models divested themselves of their skimpy costumes between fashion shows, did a lot of drinking, and slept backstage, partially or totally nude, on the floor—according to Jack Ray, Special Events Director at Hudson's, in an interview with a *Detroit News* reporter.

Millie Aimar, an H.R. Block employee, came to work at Downtown Hudson's in 1971 to offer income tax services to customers. Seated at a large desk in an open area near the fourth floor rest rooms, H. R. Block employees had an excellent view of one of the store's busiest areas as they worked for three months annually, preceding income tax filing date. As a teen model at Hudson's years earlier, the blonde, blue-eyed Millie had fallen in love with the big Woodward Avenue store. Now, she was both intrigued by the panorama of people passing her desk and disappointed at the changes in Hudson's once elegant image.

Certain street people came, regularly, up to the fourth floor rest rooms. Stella, the bag lady. And a rowdy black man, long hair falling to his shoulders, who mumbled incoherently as he passed the H.R. Block desk. More intimidating were the drug addicts, obviously going into the rest rooms for "a fix." But most appalling, to Millie, was the sight of a newborn baby, abandoned in the rest rooms . . . an infant, store detectives soon learned, who had been born to a 14-year-old girl in one of Hudson's toilet stalls and left there by its child-mother.

Maturing flower-children and hippies from the 1960s also trailed their marijuana-fogged orbits past the tax computation desks and on to the rest rooms. One Hudson clerk recalls seeing one of the city's most notorious bearded and beaded hippies visiting Downtown Hudson's in the summertime with his long-haired, long-skirted wife at his side and the couple's naked baby daughter in his arms. As the man and his wife stepped onto the escalator, he set the small child down—whereupon she promptly urinated on the moving stairs.

Beginning in September, 1970, Hudson's relaxed its hard-nosed policy prohibiting Sunday sales in its suburban stores. "We find it impossible to ignore any longer the trend toward Sunday opening," a store representative stated. "Our customers' needs are changing, and we must change, too." But there was little activity in downtown Detroit to justify Sunday openings for the big Woodward store where customary genuflecting to tradition was giving way to catering to modernism and social concerns of the seventies.

Male and female buyers possessed management status at Hudson's, but when buyer Louise Solomon became divisional manager for the posh Woodward Shops in early 1971, newspapers touted her as the "first woman to crack the exclusively male grip" on this type of key management job. A Hudson spokesman tempered this by explaining that Madelyn Coe's job of fashion director was "on a comparable level."

In this same year, the store introduced black Santas to Hudson's Toyland after Thanksgiving. As children and their parents joined a line snaking through Santa's workshop, attendants informed black parents that a black Santa was available. Reaching the head of the line, the parents indicated their choice to Santa's helpers, who led them into the presence of a black, or white, St. Nick. Although only 25% of black parents chose a Santa of their own race that first day, the ratio increased as the holiday season progressed and people became accustomed to the idea.

And, in 1971, Hudson's developed a program on drug abuse and made it part of their 27-year-old Hudsonian Assistance and Counseling Program, under the Hudson Webber Foundation. Terming drug addiction a "disease," the program director denied that drug abuse was a major and widespread problem among Hudson workers. But the director pointed out that among the company's 17,000 employees, some workers had to be affected by drug abuse. He added that most of the drug addiction problems (70 to 80%) brought to the counseling center involved members of Hudson workers' families — not the employees themselves.

Despite Hudson's problem-solving innovations, there seemed to be a significant omen in the appearance of Eloise (Mrs. Richard H.) Webber, Eleanor (Mrs. Edsel B.) Ford, and Jean (Mrs. Joseph L.) Hudson at the Detroit Public Library in April, 1971. There, as Downtown Hudson's observed its 90th anniversary, the trio presented Hudson papers and memorabilia to the library's Burton Historical Collection. One year later, Hudson clerks and Detroiters were startled by the store's announcement that Hudson's would have a new president — the first from outside the Hudson family.

Edwin G. Roberts came to his new position at the J.L. Hudson Company from Minneapolis, after a year's service as president of Dayton Hudson Jewelers. But Roberts had previously lived in Detroit where he worked in management positions at other Detroit stores. Joe Hudson, now wearing his sideburns and hair longer, publicly welcomed Ed Roberts back to the Motor City, pointing out that since Hudson's had opened three new stores within the past two years as a part of its expansion program, the dual role of chief executive officer and president had become too demanding for one man. Joe Hudson would now retain the role of chairman and chief executive, working closely with President Edwin Roberts.

At the end of the year, President Roberts' confidence was shaken when Hudson's annual inventory revealed the $12 million shortage for 1972. Conferring with Joe Hudson and the newly appointed director of shortage control, Ludger Beauvais, Roberts set a tough goal for 1973 — reduction of Hudson's inventory shortage by at least $2 1/2 million.

Roberts also upgraded the store's security reward program, stationed shortage representatives in each division, and distributed inventory shortage prevention check lists to each employee. He obtained significant results—a reduction of some $1 1/2 million in 1973 shortages. But this amount still fell short of Roberts' goal. Undaunted, he announced a new goal for 1974—to bring shortages down to $8 million or less. However, a mid-year inventory in 1974 proved disappointing when shortages rose higher than those of the 1973 mid-year inventory.

Roberts made a decision to upgrade Hudson's nine Budget Stores in 1973, beginning with a new name—Hudson's Rainbow—and new image, including widened aisles and white walls boldly splashed with magenta, green, and blue. Budget priced merchandise gave way to an emphasis on "fashion-minded good values" keyed to a youth (20 to 25-year-old) market.

In 1974, the Roberts-Hudson management team came up with an innovation, at Hudson's Northland, that eventually sparked another messy controversy. The introduction of Valet Parking service at the Northland store, the company's largest branch Hudson's, began innocuously enough with attendants, dressed in uniforms to help repress increasing security problems, taking customers' cars near a sign advertising valet parking for $1.25. But later, with crime and reports of crime increasing, Hudson's would begin issuing cards for free valet service to "preferred" customers in an attempt to check their retreat from Northland. Enraged by what many blacks perceived as preferential treatment to a white clientele, black leaders would call for a boycott of Hudson's in 1980. Joe Hudson, still respected by most blacks for inherent fairness, would meet with boycott leaders and defuse the impending boycott at that point by promising free valet service cards to any customer, on request.

Inventory shortages continued to be a problem that plagued the Hudson company in the 1970s—largely at the Downtown store where a number of employees had devised different ways to get merchandise out of the store over the years. A cook's helper, weighing 110 pounds, reported to work at night, but left the store at the end of his shift, weighing 160 pounds. Another employee got away with $52,000 worth of television sets stolen from the warehouse before police—dressed as Hudson truck drivers—finally made an arrest.

A thief who repeatedly hid in the store at night, would put on a new suit and hide assorted items in his pockets, then walk out the next morning with his loot. He soon became greedy enough to risk filling suitcases with merchandise during the night. He would set the suitcases out on the marquee, then watch for an opportunity to drop his baggage—ripping off the store for an estimated $40,000 worth of merchandise before he was caught. At that point, Downtown Hudson's brought in search dogs—Bouviers, which would not attack—to patrol the store at night. In the mornings, the dogs were taken out to patrol around the warehouse.

Louise Solomon recalls that after wigs became popular items in the late 1960s, in-store thieves stole cartons of them. Hudson's resorted to camouflaging wig cartons by marking them with names of other items. Louise also recalls staying late at the store to catch up with paper work on many nights, then joining hands with other buyers to walk through the darkened store to an exit. But after repeated forays by overnight thieves, Hudson's ruled on a time limitation for buyers and supervisors to leave the building after business hours, for their own safety.

Even in daytime hours, in-house theft mounted as some Adjustments employees signed their own refund vouchers for items that were never purchased—triggering a new requirement for countersigning of vouchers. And clerks, waiting on friends, often slipped extra unpurchased items into shopping bags.

The store could only estimate the increasing amounts of merchandise stolen by professional shoplifters, wearing belts with hooks or coats with concealed pockets. Security people who stopped a suspected thief—who might have already passed a stolen item to an accomplice—opened the way for a lawsuit against the store if no stolen goods were found on a suspect.

Store detectives were more likely to arrest narcotic addicts, stealing openly because of their desperate need for drugs, who grabbed valuable merchandise and tried to escape from the building. Like other stores, Hudson's installed closed-circuit television cameras, attached tiny transmitter-tags to merchandise to trip an alarm when the tags were not removed before the items were taken from the store, and affixed chains to expensive clothing and furs.

Still, huge shortages—led by stolen credit card losses—took their toll of Downtown Hudson's in a 1970s' decline that revealed itself in many ways. Alterations on women's clothing were no longer provided gratis, but were charged to customers. Hudson's strict dress code no longer prevailed among employees, and at least one young Hudson's clerk horrified her more circumspect co-workers by wearing a navel-exposing outfit to work.

As early as 1970, delivery man Ed Roszak recalls that drivers had to begin loading their own trucks instead of having them loaded by night workers. When, after the 1967 riot, thieves began stealing the contents of Hudson trucks while truck drivers made their deliveries, the drivers could no longer leave their vehicles open. In the 1970s, Hudson's installed safes in their delivery trucks after a series of robberies occurred. Following an incident in which a thief held a gun at one driver's head, forcing him to unlock his safe, drivers' keys were removed, and safes could be unlocked only at the station.

The life of a Hudson driver, who was not permitted to use repellents on the increasing number of vicious dogs used to guard Detroit homes, rapidly became more difficult. Although the store resorted to prohibiting c.o.d. deliveries to eliminate the need for carrying money in the trucks, package drivers had to deliver heavier and bulkier merchandise, including bales of peat moss and televison sets—items that previously had been carried in larger furniture trucks. Exchanges, returns, cancellations, and even repossessions—often accompanied by threats—became a larger and time-wasting part of the lives of Hudson drivers. Supervisors frequently rode with delivery people, timing them as a part of Hudson's ongoing studies of the routes in attempts to improve efficiency.

But the drivers, feeling they were discriminated against because they were unionized, viewed the efficiency studies as a part of Hudson's plan to get more than its money's worth from delivery people. Some of the drivers retaliated by turning their energies to defeating the time-clocks installed in their trucks to record truck movement. On occasion, some of the men parked their trucks very close together as they went into a bar for a few drinks. One man would go out and start his truck and shake it from side to side to make the other trucks move, since the slightest movement set off the time clocks so they would register—even when the motor was not running. If, by some chance, a time clock did not register, the driver could use a magnet to move the clock ahead. Regardless of the drivers' resentment of the efficiency studies, the men respected Joe Hudson who frequently stopped in at the warehouse and talked with them.

But the days of unquestioned loyalty to Hudson's—affirmed by the prideful boast of a former driver who told of delivering paint, two gallons in each hand—were fading fast when Hudson's substations were discontinued and the store's staff of 120 drivers was cut back to 30 in the middle 1970s. Drivers with ten years of service received a separation allowance, or could transfer into furniture delivery. And free package delivery was phased out as the store used UPS and Parcel Post for sending small packages.

After more than 20 years as a Hudsonian, Marguerite Clark was called into the office and told to retire, against her wishes, in 1976. Although she knew that most employees simply accepted retirement or retired voluntarily as they reached, or neared, the age of 65, Marguerite went to the state unemployment office and insisted that she was forced into retirement. Hudson's fought against the decision to grant unemployment benefits to Marguerite, but to no avail.

Still, the spunky Marguerite retained fond memories of her many years as a Hudson employee, as did most retired Hudsonians. Betty Mahoney, who had left Downtown Hudson's in 1967 after 30 years of employment, recalls being the youngest woman advanced to Floor Service and says that "Hudson's was my life." Her attachment to the store was so overwhelming that she found herself unable to return to visit Downtown Hudson's after her retirement. Gladys Huff, who left Hudson's in 1977, could not bear to watch the Thanksgiving Day parade on television after that date because of her sentimental memories of her own preparations, year after year at the warehouse "studio," for Hudson's November extravaganza.

Sophie Kopera, hired for the Christmas season in 1966, wanted a permanent job at Downtown Hudson's, but remained "on call" for a while, then became a "contingent," and stayed in that category for years. As more retirees left the store, greater numbers of part-time employees worked there. Since part-timers did not share in Hudson's benefit package, many of them felt that Hudson's was taking unfair advantage of workers who wanted full time jobs.

But Downtown Hudson's had to contend with a more important problem—the struggle to stay alive in a city which no longer attracted suburban customers fearful for their safety in Detroit, where 801 homicides earned the Motor City the name "Murder Capital" in 1974. Declining sales at the big Woodward store amounted to only $70 million in 1976—only 14% of sales for all Hudson's stores—and would decline further to $55 million in 1977 . . . a drop of more than $100 million from its 1953 peak of $156 million in sales. Allowing for inflation, the real loss amounted to an 80% decrease in transactions at Downtown Hudson's, Joe Hudson admitted in a statement given to the National Advisory Council on Historic Preservation.

As early as 1974, when Downtown Hudson's closed its Art Gallery, it had become apparent that the big store was in failing health. Employees complained to supervisory personnel that certain areas in the store were dirty, including a twelfth floor locker room where a broken mirror reflected scurrying cockroaches and piles of cigarette butts. The store immediately hired an exterminator to spray the room for bugs, then ordered the area cleaned once a day. But before the end of each cleaning day, cigarette butts again littered the floor, along with cafeteria trays overflowing with chicken bones and half filled coffee cups.

In 1976, when the cost of refurbishing the "Largest Flag in the World" rose to more than $30,000, the aging Woodward store ended another tradition by donating its famous Old Glory to the Smithsonian Institute, which later gave the huge flag to the Great American Flag Foundation in Houston, Texas. But Hudson's received help in the early 1970s from Stroh's Brewery in preserving another of its traditions as the brewery company assumed joint sponsorship, with Hudson's, in presenting the annual July fireworks display from barges on the Detroit River.

The gigantic fireworks production of July, 1976, was marred for some of the hundreds of thousands of Detroiters and suburbanites who crowded into the heart of the city. Young thugs roamed the streets, trying to elude police officers as they robbed, mugged, and terrorized fireworks spectators. The next day's newspapers reported that police had arrested 30 "hoodlums," and that future sponsorship of the fireworks display was at risk.

Stroh's immediately denied that the brewery company would stop sponsoring the International Freedom Festival event. So, too, did Joseph L. Hudson, Jr., explaining that the Hudson company held a "deep commitment" to Detroit and would continue to co-sponsor the fireworks.

When Hudson's neighbor, the Crowley-Milner department store, left Detroit's hub in 1977, it followed several other large department stores that had closed their doors. And by 1979, Himelhoch Brothers and Company would depart from the city's hub after 104 years of doing business. Hudson's swallowed this bitter medicine while its management people worked, behind the scenes, to save the life of a Downtown Hudson's that was struggling to survive Woodward decay until the $372 million, ultra-modern superstructure — the new, self-contained Renaissance Center on Jefferson Avenue at the river — could pump new vitality into the heart of the dying city.

Although Joe Hudson continued to believe that Hudson's was charged with a solid commitment to a vital Detroit, the retraction program, implemented at the Downtown store in 1970, was expanded in succeeding years. Management people were pressed to reduce operating expenses so that the Woodward Avenue store could stay in business. They shut down elevators and drastically curtailed selling space in the Farmer Street section by eliminating retailing from one upper floor each year during the 1970s. Later, they cut back sales departments in the remainder of the store from floors 10 through 13 and confined merchandising to floors one through nine. And they removed the second basement from retail use, which helped cut total occupancy of the building to 60% of available space.

Hudson management also cut back its maintenance staff, issuing orders to stop washing windows and to do only necessary preventive maintenance on the store's antiquated electrical and mechanical equipment. But of all the cutbacks, none jarred Detroiters more than the depressing sight of Hudson workers covering ("boarding up," reporters described it) a flank of the big store's Farmer Street display windows with heavy panels in 1977. "People weren't coming downtown to window shop any more," Joe Hudson explained later. "And the elimination of display windows provided more room for merchandise and selling space on our lower floors."

President Edwin Roberts had taken a lot of flack as he presided over the swift, and inevitable, decline of Downtown Hudson's—an aging, oversized building at the heart of a city with a failing pulse, skipping beats to the uneven rhythm of an exodus that claimed a half million residents in the past 25 years. Roberts' resignation to join the May Stores of California in 1978 brought a changing of the guard to the royal house of Hudson. Theodore A. Bintz, Jr., who had joined Hudson's as a research analyst in 1955, now stepped into the president's office—and into the core of major problems plaguing occupants of the Golden Corridor.

One year earlier, Hudson's management had given up a search for potential tenants to share occupancy of its oversized building—to ease Hudson's burden of excess space and high occupancy costs. None of the largest private or public companies using great expanses of Detroit office accomodations expressed any interest in leasing quarters in Downtown Hudson's, where only half the building was in use by 1978 and even less space was needed by the store. And still, the physical and mechanical anatomy of the Matriarch of Woodward consumed as much heat and air conditioning as were utilized when the entire store operated at full capacity. Joe Hudson reported that the water bill for Downtown Hudson's equalled the combined bills for all 15 of Hudson's branch stores. He projected that the Downtown store's utility bills for 1979 would exceed $2 million.

By the time Theodore Bintz took over as Hudson's president, plans were already in place to raze the Woodward store and to build a new Downtown Hudson's as part of a Cadillac Square shopping center. Hudson's management was enthusiastic about its proposed new building, slated to be the largest retail store in the Cadillac Square Center, and was equally enthusiastic about Detroit's proposal for the installation of a "People Mover" to facilitate transportation in the downtown area.

Encouraged by the proximity of a new $59 million Joe Louis Arena, already in progress, and by proposals for the construction of a major downtown apartment complex—the Millender Center, Joe Hudson lauded "the second renaissance of Detroit" as he assured employees of Downtown Hudson's that they would not lose their jobs. The new Hudson store would include all departments now in operation, he promised. Among Downtown Hudson's employees was his son, Joseph L. Hudson IV, who was now a Buyer for men's clothing.

When the *Hudsonian* magazine published the plans for a new Downtown Hudson's, employees at the big store on Woodward eagerly read about the future work place—its four merchandise floors covering 320,000 square feet plus two floors for corporate offices. Joe Hudson promised that some of Hudson's historical memorabilia would be preserved in the new store, which would anchor a huge center containing two other major department stores, four parking decks, and a number of skywalks and pedestrian concourses connecting nearby shops and office buildings. But Hudson warned that unless plans for the Cadillac Square Center were definitely moving forward by 1980, with two other major stores pledged to participate, Hudson's would raze its Woodward Avenue building at that time, ending its commitment to Downtown Detroit.

A group of people, calling themselves "People for Downtown Hudson's," vigorously protested the plan to raze the historic building. But Joe Hudson pointed out that he had conferred with Alfred Taubman & Company, developers of shopping centers, in analyzing the possibility of renovating and making use of the existing Hudson building. The analysis revealed that it would cost $50 million more to renovate the store than to tear it down and build a new one.

"Off-again, On-again" would have been an apt phrase to describe plans for Cadillac Square Center in the late 1970s. Even with cooperation from Hudson's and the support of Mayor Coleman Young, no other major department store would commit itself to "Detroit's Second Renaissance" by financing a downtown store. And while Downtown Hudson's languished, total sales for all Hudson stores climbed to a healthy $664 million in 1978—encouraging

Hudson's to open a new store in Lansing the following year and to plan for new stores in Kalamazoo and South Bend, Indiana, in 1980.

Within Dayton Hudson Corporation's department store group—including Dayton stores in Minnesota and the Dakotas, Diamond's stores in Arizona, and John A. Brown stores in Oklahoma—Hudson's was recognized as "the largest and most important division" by Dayton Hudson's chairman and chief executive officer. And the "People for Downtown Hudson's" group clung to its determination to preserve the towering red brick building on Woodward Avenue as an important part of Hudson's—and Detroit's—heritage. No matter that its 70 elevators, 5,000 drafty windows, and its antiquated physical plant made it an "energy guzzler," in Joe Hudson's own words. "Save the Big One," became the plea of the preservationists who prevailed upon panelists from the U.S. Advisory Council on Historic Preservations to hold a two-day meeting on the matter in 1979.

Joe Hudson could sympathize with the "People for Downtown Hudson's" group and its nostalgic interest in preserving a landmark now characterized by *The Detroit News* as a "warmly familiar but uneconomic, unattractive building that really is a collection of different structures erected at different times." But the fact remained that renovation costs would be $91 million, compared to the city's estimate of $40 million to raze the building and construct a new Hudson's. Just as troublesome was the fact that preservationists' attempts to place the Hudson building on the National Register of Historic Places could delay or destroy the construction of the proposed $219 million downtown mall. Federal funds for the new mall would be at risk if construction of the mall would imperil an "historic" building.

The great-nephew of the store's founder still envisioned a new and modern Hudson's as a part of a Cadillac Square Center, even though no other major retailer had made any pledges to the proposed downtown mall by the end of 1979. "I can tell you," Joe Hudson was quoted in December of that year, "I am more optimistic than I was six months or a year ago."

But Detroit area residents became much less optimistic when, in 1979, Hudson's turned over the sponsorship of its annual Thanksgiving Day parade to Detroit Renaissance—a group of major business executives. In recent years, it had become necessary to police the parade more vigorously because of unruly youths throwing rocks from rooftops of buildings along the line of march. Although there had been mishaps in previous years—in 1960, a nine-year-old boy had been injured when several children were pushed under the Santa Claus float as a crowd of spectators suddenly surged forward—the earlier misfortunes had been accidents, not deliberate disruptions. An even more pressing reason for Hudson withdrawal from sole sponsorship of the parade was the expense. Although the store had discontinued paying parade participants in 1978, annual costs for the affair amounted to nearly $600,000.

Still, as Hudson's turned over its parade to Detroit Renaissance, the store agreed to remain a major contributor to the extravaganza which had been so closely identified with the J.L. Hudson Company for more than 50 years—even though, in its characteristically restrained style, the company had refrained from displaying its name at any point in the procession. And with this changeover of parade sponsorship, another important Hudson's tradition expired.

In the same year, 1979, Dayton Hudson Corporation sold four major shopping centers that had been built by the J.L. Hudson Company—Eastland, Northland, Westland and Southland. Even after the sale to Real Estate Investment Management Inc. of Atlanta, Hudson's kingpin stores continued to preside, as anchors, over each of the four giant shopping centers.

Chapter 12

The Exodus—After 102 Years

Sophisticated technology of the 1980s spawned many advances in electrical surveillance equipment. Department stores installed the expensive equipment in desperate attempts to cope with shoplifters, employee-theft, and robberies. Security measures included tiny cameras hidden behind the thickly lashed eyes of impassive mannequins placed in strategic locations, and simpler devices such as observation areas from which shoppers could be watched while using fitting rooms.

When, in 1980, a man suspected of shoplifting walked into a fitting room in a Hudson's branch store, a security guard summoned police as he spied on the man in the fitting room from a concealed, overhead peephole. Although the suspect—who turned out to be an undercover police officer—never was taken to court by Hudson's, the man filed invasion of privacy charges against Dayton Hudson Corporation, suing for more than $10,000. After the judge threw the case out of court, the plaintiff refused to drop the charges, taking his case to the Michigan Court of Appeals. The higher court upheld the first judge's decision with a statement that "one who enters a fitting room in a retail establishment is only entitled to the modicum of privacy it appears to afford"—according to a summary of the ruling.

Some stores, concerned by the threat of court suits and anxious not to offend honest customers discontinued the surveillance of dressing rooms. Others, including Hudson's—where shoppers now moved freely into and out of fitting rooms without benefit of attending salespeople, as a cost-saving measure—put signs in dressing rooms, warning that the rooms were "under surveillance."

Credit card fraud remained a major source of loss for Hudson's, regardless of precautions taken over the years. One of the more flagrant frauds occurred between 1979 and 1981 when a series of suburban customers phoned in complaints to Hudson's at being charged for merchandise they never ordered or received. Hudson's security chief finally tracked down two addresses for a corner house in Detroit, with a door on each of the intersecting streets, from which orders were telephoned to Downtown Hudson's and three suburban branch stores.

Two police officers, dressed as delivery men, finally brought several packages to the Detroit house—at one door and then the other—where the same man signed for all the packages . . . a ploy that had worked so well that he had acquired some $1,000 worth of merchandise from Downtown Hudson's in the past month. Since the suburban customers had not lost their credit cards, they could not explain how the Detroit man obtained their card numbers. Police surmised that the man received help from an accomplice employed at Hudson's who supplied the numbers.

Although Hudson's profits declined 19% in 1980 on sales of $641.5 million in the company's 18 stores, which included a suburban Kalamazoo store that opened in the latter part of the year, a 19th store was scheduled to open in Fort Wayne, Indiana, in July, 1981. The Fort Wayne store's opening would coincide with a year-long celebration of Hudson's 100th anniversary featuring an historical exhibition to which Hudson employees and retirees were contributing all kinds of commemorative memorabilia.

The collection made up part of a traveling historical exhibit slated for display at each of Hudson's stores at some time during the anniversary year. In a grand finale to the tour, Hudson's Histor-

THE EXODUS—AFTER 102 YEARS

ical Exhibit would arrive at the Downtown store for "permanent" display.

But even the most dedicated employees at Downtown Hudson's questioned the permanent placement of any exhibit at a store whose future was undetermined. A lagging economy and a stubborn resistance from other department stores to any commitment to downtown Detroit's proposed $238 million project, now referred to as Cadillac Mall, continued to jeopardize the founding of Detroit's "Second Renaissance." And if the obsolete "Matriarch of Woodward," with air-conditioning-system parts that dated back to the 1920s, was no longer vigorous enough to escape the wrecker's ball, how could the exhibit—or store employees—remain a part of Downtown Detroit?

The store's lack of vigor betrayed itself in frayed carpeting, soiled walls, and in an eighth-floor monument to past elegance—a Furniture department where handsome Queen Anne dining sets, crushed velvet sofas, and heavy mahogany bedroom suites still were arranged into "rooms" with attractive accessories. But visitors rarely strolled among the model settings to admire the furnishings. And in 1980, when the emptiness enveloping the furniture displays seemed only to emphasize that there was no one living there, Downtown Hudson's closed its Furniture department.

Only parts of the store remained alive and active. At noon, the store temporarily bustled with the arrival of downtown business people purchasing cosmetics, gifts, candy, and clothing. But as business customers rushed out to return to their desks, the store became the domain of a different kind of clientele. The lonely elderly from nearby senior citizens' homes—passing time with a snack at a Hudson's lunch counter and, possibly, with purchase of small items. Street people and those from the Salvation Army center—seeking a kind of social life within the fading glory of the store. Young ADC mothers—bringing their children in from the heat of Detroit's sidewalks in the summertime or from the cold of drafty apartments in the winter.

Much of the store's activity centered around the fourth floor, where a small corner section now housed Toys—a department which once had occupied most of the twelfth floor. Now, noisy children ran heedlessly through Toys displays until they were hauled, by their bored mothers, off to Hudson's nearby rest rooms—the one part of the store where there was always activity.

In November, 1980, when Cadillac Mall planning wavered into confusion as a lingering economic recession triggered layoffs in the automotive industry, Dayton Hudson dispatched its troubleshooter, P. Gerald Mills, to Detroit. Mills, who previously headed Dayton's department stores in Minneapolis, now took over the presidency of Hudson's from Theodore Bintz who became vice-chairman in charge of merchandising.

Although many of Hudson's executives had bailed out of the company during the past year, Detroit's business community was startled when P. Gerald Mills also replaced Joseph L. Hudson, Jr., as chief executive officer. "I didn't initiate it," Hudson commented to reporters who asked why his executive post was turned over to Mills, "but I fully support it."

Still retaining his post as company chairman, Hudson now was required to report to Mills—president and chief executive officer—on all business matters. And Detroit's business leaders shuddered at the thought that Dayton Hudson's commitment to downtown Detroit might evaporate with Joe Hudson's fading power at the J.L. Hudson Company. This fear was only partly assuaged when Mills quickly conferred with Detroit's Mayor Young and then announced his intention to upgrade and revitalize the existing Downtown Hudson's.

The revitalization of Downtown Hudson's definitely did not indicate the demise of the Cadillac Mall project, the Detroit mayor reassured newspaper reporters. On the contrary, it indicated "prospects for the mall are even more positive," he insisted.

In May, 1981, at the same time that Jack Coe, manager of Downtown Hudson's, jubilantly announced that "The old lady's still got life in her" and made plans to open unused sections and to expand the Woodward Shop by 2,000 feet, Dayton Hudson Corporation held its board of directors' election. Joseph L. Hudson, Jr., who had served as a corporation director since the two companies had merged, was not nominated for re-election. Two months later, former Hudson's president Theodore Bintz resigned his office of vice chairman to "pursue outside interests."

President Gerald Mills' pronouncement that "we do not have a timetable for the Downtown store" was ambiguous enough to dismay Detroit business people and the 740 sales employees still working at Downtown Hudson's—a small number compared to the 12,000 people employed there in 1953. But store manager Jack Coe remained upbeat—saying that the company's goal was to change the image of Downtown Hudson's from that of a clearance depository for unwanted merchandise from suburban stores to that of a "fashion center." The Downtown store's closed Furniture department on the eighth floor would be reopened for special promotions, including books and classical records, Coe added, promising that Downtown Hudson's would be "better stocked this holiday than last."

Although Hudson's overall sales rose two or three percent in 1981 under the leadership of President Mills, competition from other retailers forced Hudson's to cut its prices in order to promote sales. Profit margins eroded while operating expenses continued to rise. In an effort to cut expenses, Hudson's fired 280 managers of its stores in February, 1982. In March, the nameplate of fifty-year-old Joseph L. Hudson, Jr., suddenly was removed from his Golden Corridor door as he retired as chairman of the J.L. Hudson Company.

In the year prior to retirement, after 32 years with the company, Joe Hudson had sold 18,471 shares of his Dayton Hudson stock at $56 a share, retaining more than 14,000 shares. Now, with announcement of his retirement on March first, community leaders in Detroit expressed shock at the loss of the J.L. Hudson Company's "father image" after 101 years, and at the total takeover by Mills—viewed by many as an "outsider" whose allegiance was less to Downtown Hudson's than to Dayton Hudson Corporation. But regardless of what might, of necessity, happen to Downtown Hudson's, the rapidly expanding Dayton Hudson Corporation was actively re-enforcing its commitment to long established goals—to treasure traditions and to emphasize community involvement by taking ever-growing leadership roles in the area served by each of the corporation's department stores.

Newspaper reporters who tried to question Joe Hudson about the details of his separation from the company founded by his great-uncle could not trap him into an admission of whether he or

Dayton Hudson had launched the retirement issue. Instead, he spoke of "new horizons" . . . of doing more consulting and adding more corporate directorships to a list which already included Michigan Bell Telephone Company and National Bank of Detroit. He would stay in Detroit, he stated, where he had active civic ties to many organizations—Detroit Renaissance, New Detroit Inc., the United Foundation, and Detroit Arts Commission.

His younger brother, Gilbert, who had become an assistant divisional merchandising manager at Hudson's after his graduation from Yale, was now serving as president of the Hudson-Webber Foundation. Soon after retirement from the department store, Joe Hudson joined his brother in directing the foundation, becoming its chairman.

In March, 1982, documents from an unknown source arrived at the *Detroit Free Press*. According to the documents, Dayton Hudson planned to close the big Woodward store—and soon. This posed a problem for the newspaper. Hudson's was the paper's biggest advertiser, and the J.L. Hudson Company was not yet ready to publicize its plan to shut the doors of its landmark building—not at a time when the future of downtown Detroit centered around a vital Hudson's store. Still, news was news, and the *Free Press* decided to print the story, regardless of shock value and fallout.

In July, Hudson's officially announced that the store would close, but failed to provide a closing date. When curious customers questioned clerks about the date, some clerks admitted that they had been told not to talk about the closing—especially to the media. An unidentified clerk told a reporter that employees had been on a "month-to-month notice for closing for a long time."

President and Chief Executive Mills went on record as saying that since the shelving of the Cadillac Mall project in 1980, and the subsequent down-trend in store sales as the economy failed to improve, there was no alternative but to announce the closing of Downtown Hudson's. Downtown Detroit would have to be a "viable retail environment before we can be a part of it," Mills concluded.

By the end of the year, Hudson's Farmer Street bakery closed, as did the Beauty Salon and the O'Conner Photo Studio. Piece by piece, the store disintegrated even while faithful retirees continued

THE EXODUS—AFTER 102 YEARS

to come to the Riverview Restaurant—now reduced to one-third its "salad days" size—to order chicken pot pies or club sandwiches.

And soon, Detroiters were shocked, again, by December announcements from both Hudson's and Detroit Renaissance that, because of the expense of co-hosting the nationally televised Thanksgiving Day parade, they no longer would sponsor the annual march down Woodward Avenue. The death of another tradition—at a time when Downtown Hudson's was preparing to close in 1983 as decay spread through the city's hub—roused Paula Blanchard, wife of Michigan's Governor James J. Blanchard, into action.

Logging hundreds of phone calls, meetings, and letters to Michigan business leaders, the governor's wife attracted the help of advertising man Thomas Adams, who joined in a fund-raising campaign to which dozens of Michigan businesses—including Hudson's—contributed. Recruiting individuals to donate $1,000 each to wear clown costumes and perform in the parade in a "Distinguished Clown Corps," Blanchard and Adams boasted that expenses for the 1983 parade would be cut to $380,000 with the help of volunteers and by using equipment from previous years donated by Hudson's.

In its public relations campaign to promote Michigan, the parade foundation planned to have a new float with a "Say Yes to Michigan" logo and featuring a cornucopia of the state's farm products. The parade would move down Woodward from the Ford Freeway overpass, past an array of weed-filled empty lots and deserted buildings, to end at Grand Circus Park, north of a nearly deserted Downtown Hudson's from which the store's last sales employees would have retired or shifted to branch stores long before November, 1983.

Remaining, on five upper floors of the huge building, would be 1,100 corporate employees who would now enter the store at door number one through a freshly painted and carpeted lobby and would move into an elevator equipped with stereo. Such amenities, including a new cafeteria and a pleasant sit-down restaurant, were targeted at offsetting more unattractive features of the changed workplace—rows of sheathed and blinded street-level windows relieved only by corner window displays in the entire block occupied by the towering Hudson's headquarters.

On Monday, January 3, 1983—more than ten months before the first reorganized Thanksgiving parade marched down Woodward Avenue, hundreds of people thronged the sidewalk in front of Hudson's store, waiting for the bronze doors to swoosh into steady revolutions at 9:30 a.m. for the first day of a close-out sale. The crowd of shoppers provided a brief time-machine view of Downtown Hudson's in the 1950s. And as the shoppers surged through the revolving doors into the store, the time-machine view shifted back another 70 years to the 1882 price-slashing sale at Hudson's first Detroit store when women grabbed at sales merchandise and frantically searched for certain sizes, scattering piles of marked-down bargains. Now, at Hudson's last-gasp 1983 closeout, frazzled clerks tried to ring up sales as other customers besieged them, demanding help to decipher final prices on sales tickets defaced with a series of mark-downs.

Shoppers returned, day after day, as clerks repeatedly marked down assorted merchandise and dumped much of it into odd-lot bins. By Monday, January 17, many people had come—some not to shop but to reminisce about the days when Hudson's was a kind of self-contained metropolis with an array of classy restaurants, music recitals and exhibits, and hustle and bustle on every floor. But it was difficult to reminisce in the failing store which had become a haven for dwindling supplies of merchandise in helter-skelter arrangements on the lower floors. And still, no definite closing date had been announced.

President Mills had said, in response to reporters' questions, that one day the store simply would close and not reopen the next day. Shoppers got the feeling that January 17 might be the day this would happen when they observed managers handing out white envelopes to clerks. The envelopes contained invitations to a Wednesday afternoon company buffet. "I still see customers," President Mills responded when a reporter asked if this would be the closing day. But as employees left work, Woodward Avenue doors were padlocked. The store would not open for business on Tuesday, January 18.

In the post-Christmas week before the closing, most sales

THE EXODUS—AFTER 102 YEARS

employees had been offered retirement or transfers to branch stores. Mary Mellor would have preferred a transfer to the Northland store, but this required working some evening hours, and she was afraid to return to her Detroit home, by bus, after dark. Instead, she accepted retirement and, as a long time Hudson employee, one year's severance pay—which Mellor termed "wonderful."

If many Downtown Hudson's employees entertained any resentment toward the company for the abrupt closing of the store or for the modest pensions they received, Mary Mellor was not one of them. "Hudson's was just wonderful," she says, now, of the company. "They treated employees royally—while we worked for them and in retirement. I can't say enough fine things about them," she adds, in appreciation for the medical benefits and the Hudson's discount card she retains as a retiree.

Clara Giss, a conscientious employee who prided herself on never having taken a day off from work since hiring into Hudson's in 1955, considered herself fortunate because her job in Hudson's corporate buying offices was not terminated when the store closed. Giss loved her work and the family-like atmosphere at Downtown Hudson's, and tried not to worry if she would have her job next year—or the year after that.

In early April, 1983, Downtown Hudson's opened on a Monday to conduct a public store-fixture liquidation sale on the first floor. Hudson employees received a 20% discount on any purchase of fixtures that the company could not use in other stores—wood and glass display fixtures, office furniture, restaurant equipment, stock shelving, display items, and a few pieces of silver-plated J.L. Hudson sugar bowls and finger bowls. None of the brass drinking fountains, shaped like bronzed cobra heads rising from great glittering bowls, would be sold, a company representative said. The drinking fountains would remain in the building.

Paul Johnson, owner of a jewelry store in Sun City, Arizona, came for the sale, intending to buy a couple of elegant showcases from Hudson's Jewelry department. When he learned that the whole department could be bought—from carpeting to lead crystal chandeliers and handsome wall paneling, he decided to buy everything. No matter that the Hudson accessories filled two moving vans, or that, on arrival in Sun City, Johnson had to rip off the roof and a wall of his store so that he could build a new wing to accommodate his treasures. He had what he wanted—a Hudson imprint for the jewelry store.

With plans for the Cadillac Mall still shelved, the Hudson company hoped to sell its Woodward Avenue building. And while the search for a buyer continued, another search began—for a new Detroit location with some 250,000 to 350,000 square feet of work space for Hudson's corporate headquarters.

Detroit's Central Business District Association's concern for the future of downtown Detroit peaked as the 1983 Christmas season approached. In the absence of Hudson's "Tree of Lights" and its phalanx of brilliantly lit display windows, the association of business people supplied a galaxy of Christmas lights to supplement those provided by the city. The association's goal—to attract people to a glittering downtown Detroit—appeared to be accomplished when some store managers, including those of Meyer's Treasure Chest and Colonial Merchandise, boasted of sales increased from those of the previous year. And Santa Claus still reigned at downtown Woodward Avenue—now ensconced in less spacious quarters at Kresge's.

Despite the bravado of those who spoke of flourishing holiday sales, Woodward Avenue remained uncrowded that pre-Christmas season. In front of a mute and shuttered Hudson's, a desultory group of people usually could be seen—facing away from the towering building as they waited for a bus. A salesman at H&H Apparel, on Woodward, admitted to a *Detroit News* reporter that "without Hudson's, people don't bother walking this way."

Comfortable with her office job at Hudson's, Clara Giss disliked the retirement she felt was forced on her in May, 1984, when the administrative offices at Hudson stores merged with those of the parent firm's Dayton department stores, forming the Dayton Hudson Department Store Company—now the largest traditional department store company in the country. Hudson's merchandising and marketing sectors were centralized in Minneapolis, and Giss was offered an opportunity to relocate and work at the Minneapolis offices.

Some 250 employees went to Minneapolis, including the founder's namesake, Joseph L. Hudson IV, who would stay with Dayton less than four years before taking a job as buyer for a catalogue clothing firm with nine Midwestern outlets. It had cost Dayton $15 million for moving expenses and for severance pay to those who chose not to move. Clara Giss refused relocation because her husband was ill. And she would not accept any of the clerking jobs available in Hudson's branch stores because she did not want that kind of work. Instead, she applied for unemployement insurance benefits which Hudson's protested on the basis of Giss refusing to take other jobs offered by the company.

Giss held no grudge against her employer of 29 years, even though her unemployment benefits temporarily were delayed. But, like most other retired, long-term former Hudson employees, she continued to be vexed by what she interpreted as attitudinal changes on the part of many younger or less experienced Hudson employees when she shopped at Hudson's branch stores, her lifetime discount card always tucked into a convenient placket in her handbag. Retired employee Marguerite Clark was convinced that Hudson's clerks did not like to wait on retirees from the Hudson Company, because when Clark saw uninterested and bored clerks talking among themselves while customers waited for service, she was not loath to remind the clerks that "we never stood around talking in front of customers when I worked for Hudson's."

In the same month of the merger, a public announcement startled Detroiters with news of the proposed purchase of Downtown Hudson's by a group of suburbanites who formed Continental Development Corporation of Troy. Continental planned to spend $40 million to convert the Hudson building into 620,000 square feet of offices and parking for 1800 cars.

"It's a creative, adaptive use of a grand old building that didn't deserve the threat of the wrecker's ball," a Hudson consultant was quoted in *The Detroit News*. "This building will continue to stand as a landmark on the horizon of downtown Detroit for many years to come."

In November, 1984, six months after the administrative operations' merger of Hudson's 20 stores and Dayton's 16 department stores, Richard Cascio—vice president of J.L. Hudson Company's stores since 1979—became executive vice president and general manager of Region I of the Dayton Hudson Department Store Company. Four months earlier, Stephen E. Watson had been transferred from Minneapolis to the Detroit area to take the position of regional president of Hudson's as P. Gerald Mills became chairman of Dayton Hudson Department Stores.

Known as aggressive men of vision with determination to respond quickly to changing customer desires, Cascio and Watson settled into their eleventh floor Golden Corridor offices at Hudson's, where 400 regional office employees — wondering what change would come next — still held their jobs. Regional president Watson only recently had assured Detroiters that Dayton Hudson had no intention of changing the name of Hudson's stores or losing the image of "103 years of history" behind the Hudson name. But the 1980s had been years of constant changes and talk of even more changes, and office employees were wary of what might happen next.

The $650,000 Michigan Thanksgiving Day parade of 1984, planned to be bigger and better than earlier Hudson parades, included 22 bands, 25 floats, and 1,000 marchers, and attracted a crowd of more than 500,000 spectators on a subfreezing morning. While the crowd waited, unseasoned and over-zealous parade directors and participants milled about in confusion as the lineup began. Propelled into action by the clock, the Detroit Police Mounted Patrol clip-clopped, with flawless precision, at the head of the parade. Behind the patrol, some 200 handicapped Boy Scouts and disabled people moved along — many on crutches or in wheelchairs. Back of this group, floats and marchers staggered into uneven lines, with great gaps between sections. Timing fiascoes were so blatant that the Santa Claus float was pushed from its dramatic end spot into the middle of the parade — as camouflage for a huge separation of units.

"Improvements" had to be guaranteed for the 1985 parade, CBS insisted, if Detroit expected national coverage for next year. Parade promoters blamed their problems on the excessive length of the parade, which made it unmanageable, and on too many groups of marchers, some of whom had been drinking just previous to parade time. For next year, they would cut the length by 25%, they promised, and increase their staff to eliminate the timing problems. The increased staffing, plus expenses for new floats and new costumes for the 1985 parade, would bring the cost to an estimated $750,000.

A spate of ugly public relations problems vexed the promoters as they arranged the next year's lineup. "Parade officials bar handicapped," a newspaper caption charged. Although parade directors protested that each year's lineup had to be changed to make room for innovations, and that one-fourth of the lineup had to be cut, they were stung by a quote, in the newspaper article, made by a leader of the disabled group. "We apparently are not wanted and this has been very disappointing to the young people." But the bad pre-publicity and the anxiety of preparing for a disciplined parade that could meet standards set by the earlier Hudson's spectacle were erased when CBS was quite satisfied with the 1985 march down Woodward.

Four hundred corporate headquarters' employees still worked on upper floors at Downtown Hudson's when Michigan's Thanksgiving Parade Foundation achieved better results in 1985. The only snag in predicting equal success for future parades was the need for more money. Costs for the 1987 parade would approach $1 million, Carlene Bonner, executive director for the foundation, estimated. Bonner hoped to raise part of the money by renting out costumes and equipment—1,000 costumes, 390 *papier mache* heads, and a variety of huge balloons—for other parades. The rest would have to come from increased contributions from the 40 major corporations already sponsoring the parade, plus donations from small businesses.

In December, 1985, Joseph L. Hudson, Jr., accepted an appointment as president of the Detroit Medical Center Corporation, comprising five major hospitals which treated some 350,000 patients each year. The cluster of hospitals and research facilities included Harper, the hospital to which the Hudson-Webber family and foundation had always been major contributors.

Since May, 1985, when the suburban development company picked up its fourth—and, supposedly, final—option to buy the $2 million Hudson building, plans for the future of the building appeared to be stalemated. The development company's application for an Urban Development Action Grant had been turned down—twice. No pre-lease agreements had been signed by major tenants, and projected costs for the renovating work had escalated from $40 million in 1984 to $60 million in August, 1985.

The 400 employees remaining in the huge Woodward Avenue building had dwindled to 100—office workers and executives—by the end of October, 1986, when at least 360 fires plagued Detroit during a three-night Halloween ritual executed by fire bugs and hoodlums in a senseless siege of igniting dumpsters, cars, garages, and, even, houses. For the remaining Hudson employees, Halloween took on a new significance—their final day of work at Downtown Hudson's. On the first Monday of November, Hudson's corporate headquarters would be housed in remodeled space at Northland.

Using a cart borrowed from a supermarket, one employee moved her personal belongings out the back door. A moving van—packed with typewriters, some office furnishings, and boxes of memorabilia saved by employees—waited at the door to gobble up the last vestiges of activity from a once-glorious Golden Corridor. With a final, protesting belch of exhaust, the van rumbled away on its nine-mile trek to suburbia and Northland Mall, the first shopping mall in the country—alive with arts festivals, health fairs, antique shows, dental clinics, concerts, and Hudson's departments emphasizing their "specialty shops within a store" retailing concept.

But even this "small within big" concept failed to solve some of the problems plaguing Hudson's suburban stores with echoes of earlier troubles afflicting Downtown Hudson's. The problem of oversized buildings, for one . . . the company's Northland unit, its biggest at 500,000 square feet, was four times as large as the 100,000 to 150,000 square feet now considered ideal for this type of store. Another problem was how to impress the 60 to 70 percent of part-time workers making up Hudson's present 10,000 work force with the importance of excellence in customer service. Then there was the increasing problem of crime, impelling Hudson's to expand its valet service and tighter security measures into others of its larger stores.

Under an "up-scale" mandate, Hudson's renovated its larger stores and re-sectioned the bigger departments in each of its 20 branches. By 1987, Hudson's Rainbow—once Basement, then Budget—stores were removed from all units. And in 1988, Hudson's would adopt a "Performance Plus" program putting even more emphasis on the quality of customer service, and reinstating payment of commissions to some of its salespeople—an incentive device not used by Hudson's in many years.

The giant Dayton Hudson—now seventh largest non-food retailer in the country—twitched nervously in June, 1987, when Dart Group Corporation acquired five percent of Dayton Hudson's 97.4 million shares of stock. A battle raged throughout the summer as Dayton Hudson—with 475 retail outlets that included Lechmere, Branden's, Hudson's, Dayton's, and the lucrative discount stores, Target and Mervyn's—resisted Dart's takeover attempt and appealed to the Minnesota governor and legislature to strengthen an anti-takeover law.

By the time Dayton Hudson emerged, unscathed, from the Dart threat, Detroit's cavernous and padlocked Downtown Hudson's still hunkered on Woodward Avenue, oblivious to the sights and sounds of its 1987 progeny—the Thanksgiving Day parade—passing by. The Michigan Thanksgiving Parade Foundation achieved peak success in this, its fifth year, with a 35-float, nearly $1 million re-routed line of march that efficiently wound its way past Hudson's—but barely. A new starting point for the parade, at Grand Circus Park, conveniently eliminated any national televising of more northerly Woodward's weed-infested lots and deserted graffiti-scrawled storefronts. The camera lenses focused only on lower Woodward to East Jefferson and the environs of the self-contained Renaissance Center, the People Mover elevated rails, and other new and lofty buildings near the riverfront.

As a city machine sweeps debris from Woodward curbings after the windswept winter months of 1987–88, the option-burdened developers are, again, as upbeat as spring's refreshing breezes. They anticipate receiving UDAG money, they say. They hope for financial backing from Max Fisher. And then the renovation of Hudson's into an office-shopping-parking complex will begin.

A retired former employee, who pays a late February, 1988, visit to Downtown Hudson's, looks carefully at the corner Woodward Avenue windows as he drives past the deserted building. The two corner windows are alike, boasting only a white, triangular backdrop and a spotlight that seems to await a focus. But at least these two windows remain uncovered to meet provisions of a promise made to Mayor Young by Dayton Hudson to keep the corner windows open until the decrepit Matriarch of Woodward Avenue is either demolished or renovated.

The visitor enters a side door to find only one man on duty in a guard station inside the cavernous building. One man . . . in a ghostly store with 30-year-old memories of as many as 75,000 people—clerks, customers, and office workers—milling about during peak business hours.

Now, two years after the departure of corporate headquarters' people, the sentry tells the retiree that his lonely vigil is broken only by the occasional arrival of a single engineer to check machinery and steam output. The visitor takes a final look at the lofty ceiling, some 21 feet above the first floor, and shakes his head regretfully as he leaves the building and gets into his car. He heads the car into late afternoon traffic jamming the Chrysler freeway, joining swarms of Detroit-made and foreign automobiles funneling into the suburbs, shaking the dust of the city from their shiny fenders.

In the early winter of 1988-89, pizza czar, Mike Ilitch, opens his renovated Fox Theatre on a grimy stretch of Woodward Avenue—just north of Grand Circus Park—now partly transformed with lights and neon. The $6 million restoration has converted the 60-year-old decaying theatre into an opulent, 5,100-seat showcase for major entertainers: Liza Minelli, Frank Sinatra, Sammy Davis and a sparkling array of other stars. Neighboring restaurants and parking facilities open for business and plans are projected for more theatres and a retail mall.

The theatre-district revitalization project brings a spirit of optimism to those who still retain faith in the future of Detroit's Woodward Avenue. But a *Detroit News* article, dated May 1, 1989, provides dispiriting news regarding the future of Downtown Hudson's. A revised plan offered by the Detroit Downtown Development Authority, the article explains, calls for cancelling previously proposed financing to assist with the renovation of Hudson's and for re-directing the money to support several other projects.

Detroit City Councilman Nicholas Hood has no reservations

THE EXODUS—AFTER 102 YEARS

about expressing his opinion that Hudson's downtown store should be demolished so its 14 acres can be used for other development. "Dayton Hudson should be solely responsible for razing expenses," he adds. "They saw fit to leave the city. Let them suffer."

There is another ominous turn of events when, in early October, 1989, CBS notifies Detroit producers of the Michigan Thankgiving Parade that it is cancelling its televising of parade segments. The timing of the parade has failed to meet the precision demands of the major television network. CBS commentators are no longer willing to ad lib cover-ups for lengthy gaps in the line of march and for unexpected appearances of out-of-sequence floats.

The 1989 parade, already in the final stages of production, will proceed without CBS coverage. But with national television coverage lacking, many sponsors—now permitted to flaunt advertising messages to a national audience—can be expected to withdraw further financial support. Although an eleventh-hour reprieve comes through for 1989 as the PBS network agrees to televise the parade, the future of the $1.2 million spectacle is as precarious as is the future of the empty department store occupying one full block at the center of downtown Detroit.

Less than one month later, the Grand Old Lady of Woodward— impassively awaiting her fate—also receives a possible reprieve. A Canadian company buys the building and declares its intention of renovating the first three floors into a department store with six floors converted to parking, and other floors given over to office space.

In February, 1990—the same month in which Joseph L. Hudson, Jr., retires as president and chief executive officer of the Detroit Medical Center—Dayton Hudson records a net income of $410 million on revenues of $13.64 billion as the current fiscal year ends. At this point, Detroiters are saddened to see workmen removing Hudson's signs from the top of the landmark building on Woodward Avenue. Only one month later, the city of Detroit charges that the Canadian owners of the building are gutting the huge store and planning to leave Detroit taxpayers saddled with a towering firetrap—charges denied by the Canadian owners who insist they will carry out their renovation plans.

While the hubbub continues, more changes occur as Dayton-

HUDSON'S: HUB OF AMERICA'S HEARTLAND

Hudson Corporation buys the Chicago-based retailer Marshall Field and Company for $1.04 billion in cash. At this point, Dennis Toffolo, who has come up through the ranks at Hudson's, is named president of the Hudson chain of 20 stores, and plans are set in motion to build new Hudson's stores in 1992 — likely in Traverse City and Troy, Michigan. For the first time since 1984, when Hudson's merged with Dayton's, Hudson's has its own president who must cope with United Auto Workers' organizers. The union people have successfully recruited enough workers to win an election at the Hudson's store in Westland Mall and are now launching organizing drives at other Hudson's stores.

In this changing era, the aged Matriarch of Woodward Avenue may, indeed, be blinded, gutted and, now, nameless, but her twenty thriving offspring Hudson's stores remain committed to treasuring the century-old traditions established by business entrepreneur Joseph L. Hudson when he set up his first downtown Detroit store in 1881. The eldest and largest offspring, Hudson's at Northland Mall, takes over the traditional role of the Grand Old Lady of Woodward by inaugurating a 1990 Christmas extravaganza with more than 100 animated figures participating in a dazzling Cinderella theme complete with a huge pumpkin that changes into a gilded coach.

Today's Hudson's and its cousins — Dayton's and Marshall Field's — make up what is now known as the Department Store Division of Dayton Hudson Corporation. Operating under a credo that circles back 100 years, the entire Department Store Division adheres to a philosphy that embraces the original Joseph L. Hudson's tenet — that a businessman owes a percentage of his earnings to the community in which he lives and works in the same manner that church members tithe to support their churches.

In a single year, 1988, Hudson's contributed $1,657,013 in grants for arts and social action projects in the Indiana, Ohio and Michigan communities where its department stores flourish. In 1989, the Dayton Hudson Foundation contributed more than $22 million for the arts and for economic and social enhancement of the communities in which the corporation conducts its business. As a result, the corporation received two major national awards...America's Corporate Conscience Award from the Council on Economic Priorities and the National Medal of Arts Award presented by President and Mrs. George Bush.

And as the city of Detroit, struggling for its survival as a major metropolis, moves with the rest of the nation into the new decade of the 1990s, the Michigan Thanksgiving Parade—still in debt to the tune of $200,000 from 1989—is once again saved from extinction in November, 1990. This time, the owner of Art Van Furniture stores offers major financing to compensate for overall declining corporate support.

As yet, there is no such financing for the rescue of "Downtown Hudson's." Instead, there is new support expressed by one of the nation's biggest retail developers, A. Alfred Taubman, and by Detroit Mayor Coleman Young for razing the vacant department store.

As the economic recession supposedly "bottoms out" in 1991 and a slow recovery begins, Hudson's representatives and UAW directors await another hearing before the National Labor Relations Board in their continuing union-Hudson's struggle. In August, the Canadian owners of the Downtown Hudson's building, owing money to creditors, prevent a sheriff's auction of the property by filing for Chapter 11 bankruptcy court reorganization. The Canadian group is seeking time to carry out its own negotiations to sell the building to William G. Wizinsky, owner of a suburban Detroit architecture firm, who has plans to convert Downtown Hudson's in much the same way that the Canadian owners had planned.

For now, the hulking, red-brick Downtown Hudson's building—gutted though it may be—remains at the city's hub. As long as it continues to cast its shadow over Woodward Avenue, hope remains in the hearts of Detroiters that the watchtower of Detroit's history will escape the wrecker's ball until the winds of change turn in a more favorable direction.

BIBLIOGRAPHY

BOOKS

Bald, F. Clever, *Michigan in Four Centuries*. Harper & Bros., New York. 1961.
Berman, Connie, *Diana Ross: Supreme Lady*. Popular Library, New York. 1978.
Boardman, Fon W. Jr., *The Thirties: America and the Jazz Age*. Henry Z. Walck, Inc. New York. 1968.
Brough, James, *The Ford Dynasty*. W. H. Allen, London. 1978.
Brunk, Thomas W., *Leonard B. Willeke, Excellence in Architecture*. University of Detroit Press, Detroit, Michigan. 1986.
Detroit Public Library, *Detroit in its World Setting*. Detroit, Michigan. 1953.
Farmer, Silas, *History of Detroit and Wayne County and Early Michigan*. Munsell & Co., New York. 1890.
Furnas, Joseph, *The Life and Times of the Late Demon Rum*. G.P. Putnam's Sons, New York. 1965.
Jenkins, Alan, *The Forties*. Universe Books, New York. 1977.
Lacey, Robert, *Ford: The Men and the Machine*. Little, Brown and Company, Boston-Toronto. 1986.
Lewis, Ferris E., *Michigan Since 1815*. Hillsdale Education Publishing, Inc., Hillsdale, Michigan. 1973.
Lochbiler, Don, *Detroit's Coming of Age, 1873 to 1973*. Wayne State University Press, Detroit, Michigan. 1982.
Rae, John Bell, *American Automobile Manufacturers*. Chilton Company, Philadephia. 1959.
Stampp, Kenneth, *The Peculiar Institution*. Knopf, New York. 1965.
Stark, George W. and Campbell, Anne, *Two Heads Are Better Than One*. Alved of Detroit, Inc., Detroit, Michigan. 1947.

Stark, George W., *In Old Detroit*. Arnold Powers, Inc., Detroit, Michigan. 1939.
Wagenknecht, Edward, *American Profile 1900-1909*. University of Massachusetts Press, 1982.
Woodford, Frank B. and Mason, Philip P., *Harper of Detroit*. Wayne State University Press, Detroit, Michigan. 1964.

PERIODICALS

American Heritage, Vol. 35, No. 5, Aug/Sept. 1984.
Business Week, June 10, 1950 and others.
Crain's Detroit Business, July 6, 1987.
Detroit Historical Society Bulletin, Vol. 23, No. 9. Summer, 1967.
The Detroiter, Nov. 12, 1923, and others.
The Detroit News Magazine, Dec. 16, 1979.
Hudsonian Magazine, April, 1918 and others.
Life Magazine, Vol. 45, Dec. 15, 1958.
Michigan History, Vol. 38, No. 4, Dec. 1954.
Michigan Tradesman, May, 1946.
Newsweek, July 17, 1950.
Time, March 23, 1953 and others.

NEWSPAPERS

Detroit Evening News, Sept. 6, 1891 and others.
Detroit Free Press, Dec. 19, 1889 and others.
Detroit Journal, Aug. 16, 1909.
Detroit News, May 18, 1889 and others.
Detroit Tribune, April 16, 1891.
Hamilton Spectator, May, 5, 1956.
Ionia Sentinel-Standard, Special Edition, 1983.
New York Times, Jan. 24, 1965 and others.

PUBLIC RECORDS and COLLECTIONS

Burton Historical Collections, Detroit Public Library
Business and Finance Collections, Detroit Public Library
Hall-Fowler Memorial Library Archives, Ionia, Michigan
Harper Hospital Archives, Detroit Public Library
Hudson Archives, Detroit Public Library

Hudson Family Tree, Detroit Public Library
Cemetery records, Ionia, Michigan, City Hall

PRIVATE COLLECTIONS

George McCall Archives

GENERAL REFERENCES

Anti-Saloon League Yearbooks, 1911, 1912
Detroit City Directories, 1876 and others
History of Ionia County, Michigan, Vol. II, B.F. Bowen & Co., Inc., Indianapolis, Indiana, 1916
Hudson's 100th Anniversary Appointment Calendar
Ionia City Directories, 1872 and others
Michigan Pioneers, 1837–1937, by the J.L. Hudson Co.
Souvenir of Ionia, Michigan, by Charles J. Seely, Charles J. Seely Publishers, Belding, Michigan, 1907
Statement to the National Advisory Council on Historic Preservation made by Joseph L. Hudson, Jr., 12/18/79

INTERVIEWS

Aimer, Millie
Boutell, Mike
Boutell, Vivian
Clark, Marguerite
Dzialak, Genevieve
Eliot, Sonny
Giss, Clara
Godfrey, Sybil
Gregory, Russ
Hudson, Joseph L., Jr.
Huff, Gladys
Huff, Lewis
Hyatt, Louise Solomon
Justewicz, Helen
Justewicz, John
Kaminski, Mary
Kelly, Susan L.
Kopera, Sophie
Kresik, Eugenia
Mabley, Theodore
Mahoney, Betty
Mellor, Mary
Pawlowski, Diane
Racki, Jean
Roszak, Ed
Speal, Bea

INDEX

Adams, Thomas, 177
Aimar, Millie, 157
alcoholic beverages (also see Prohibition), 24, 37-38, 68, 87, 90, 134-135
Allen, Ray A., 152
Anti-Saloon League, 37, 48-49, 58
Associated Merchandise Corporation, 62
automotive industry, 1-2, 41, 46-47, 61, 66, 69, 85, 91-92, 98-99, 103, 120

Beauvais, Ludger, 159
Bintz, Theodore A., Jr., 166, 174
Blanchard, Paula, 177
Bonner, Carlene, 183
Book Cadillac Hotel, 71
Boyd, William, 124
B'nai B'rith, 152

Cadillac Mall (also Cadillac Square Center), 166-167, 173-174, 176, 180
Cascio, Richard, 181-182
Cavanagh, Jerome, 138, 148, 151
celebrities, 6, 70-71, 94-95, 124, 143, 186
Central Methodist Episcopal Church, 35, 49, 57
Chapin, Roy, 47
child labor, 7-8, 20-21, 40, 63, 83
Cisler, Walter, 151
Civil War, 11, 36
Clark, Marguerite, 120-121, 132, 163, 181
Clay, Eleanor Lowthian (see Ford, Eleanor)
Clay, Eliza (see Hudson, Eliza)
Clay, Frederick, 24
Clay, Josephine (see Kanzler, Josephine)
Clay, William, 24, 33, 38, 43, 46
Cleage, Albert, 152
Coe, Jack, 175
Coe, Madelyn, 158

195

Coffin, Howard E., 47
Colombo, Frank, 127
Continental Development Company, 181, 183, 185
Conyers, John, 152
Crothers, Carol, 101
Crowley, Milner and Company, 45, 92, 128, 165

Dart Group Corporation, 185
Dayton Corporation, 62, 153–154, 168
Dayton family, 153
Dayton Hudson Corporation, 153–154, 168, 171, 174–176, 186–188
    Dayton Hudson Department Store Division, 188
Detroit, city of, 1–2, 6, 15, 19, 21, 27, 34, 38–39, 41, 45–46, 49, 51, 59, 63, 65–69, 71–72, 82–83, 85, 87–88, 90–93, 96–104, 111, 127–128, 134, 138–140, 147–152, 156, 162, 164–167, 180, 184–186
    racial problems in, 67, 93, 100–102, 138, 147–152
Detroit Institute of Arts, 56, 68, 83, 154
Detroit Opera House, 15, 25, 59, 77
Detroit Renaissance, 167, 169, 176–177
Dionne quintuplets, 95–96
discount stores, 3, 156
Dodge Brothers, 41, 67
    John Dodge family, 48
Downtown Detroit Days, 134, 146
Downtown Hudson's, 1–3, 5–6, 39–42, 45–46, 52–54, 59–60, 62–67, 69–95, 98–99, 102–109, 111–121, 124–125, 127–129, 132–140, 143–147, 149, 151–153, 155–168, 173–189
    Basement Store, 2, 62, 80–81, 86–87, 118, 136, 143, 160
    boycotts of (threatened), 152, 160
    bridal registry, 3, 88, 127
    Budget Store, 1, 144, 160
    deaths in, 52, 117, 145–147
    delivery department, 33, 38, 40, 73–74, 106, 148–149, 162–163
    early years of, 33
    financial condition of, 35–36
    employees, number of, 16, 54, 78, 118, 144
    exchange (refund) policies of, 3, 41, 107–109, 127, 132
    expansion of, 38, 45, 52, 60, 62–63, 78, 80–81, 103–104
    first downtown Detroit store (J. L. Hudson Clothier), 6, 15–20, 83, 178
    sales figures for, 21
    flag (world's largest), 4, 78, 112–113, 164
    Fourth of July fireworks (International Freedom Festival), 128–129, 164–165
    Hudson Carolers, 86–87, 93
    Hudson's hospital, 54, 74, 94
    property purchase for, 25–26
    and sales figures for, 33, 40, 48, 57, 60, 70, 84–85, 118, 156, 164
    Santa Claus, 4–5, 80, 98, 122–123, 140, 158, 169

INDEX

Santa Land (see Toyland)
temporary store (second in Detroit), 25
Thanksgiving Day parade, 4–5, 79–80, 86, 97, 102, 121–124, 141–143, 168–169, 177
   Michigan Thanksgiving Day Parade, 177, 182–183, 185, 187, 189
   theft problems at, 46, 114, 118–119, 127, 156, 159–162, 171–172
Toyland, 5, 80, 97–98, 139–140
Dzialak, Genevieve, 132

Eliot, Sonny, 121

Fisher, Max, 151–152, 185
Ford, Clara (Mrs. Henry I), 41
Ford, Edsel, 61, 76, 104
Ford, Eleanor Lowthian (Mrs. Edsel), 35, 43, 46, 48, 56, 61, 76, 104, 125, 154, 159
Ford, Henry I, 41, 46–47, 59, 104
Ford, Henry II, 126, 151–152
Ford Motor Company, 61, 87, 99, 101, 125, 152
   Model T, 46–47
Fortune magazine, 6
Fox Theatre, 186
Frederick, William, 145–146

Giss, Clara, 179–181
Grand Army of the Republic, 28
Grand Rapids, Michigan, 8
Great Depression, 85–89, 91, 96, 111

Hamilton, Ontario, 7–8
Hammond Building, 22, 31, 34
Harper Hospital, 36–37, 49, 57, 82, 183
heat wave, 90–91
Hickey, E. J., 29, 40
Hoover, Herbert, 82, 87
Hudson and Symington, 21, 25, 31
Hudson, Anna (Mrs. Robert Tannahill), 10, 24, 33, 43, 54, 61, 76, 154
Hudson, Eliza (Mrs. William Clay), 10, 24, 33, 35, 40, 43, 46, 54, 61, 81, 102
Hudson, Elizabeth, 7, 9
Hudson, Gilbert, 176
Hudson, James B., 11, 14, 61
Hudson, Jean (Mrs. J. L. Hudson Jr.), 126, 159
Hudson, Joseph Lowthian (founder of The J. L. Hudson Company), 4, 7–26, 29, 31–49, 52–58, 61, 68, 71, 76, 80, 102, 125–126, 144–145, 155, 188
   birth of, 7
   death and funeral of, 55–57
   early life of, 7–9
   education of, 7
   philanthropy of, 36–37, 43–44, 49, 53–55, 57–58, 155
   sense of honor, 25, 38–38, 44
Hudson, Joseph Lowthian, Jr. (great-nephew of store's founder), 3–4, 126–127, 131–137, 142, 148, 151–154, 156, 159–160, 163, 165–168, 174–176, 183, 187
   children of, 126, 135, 167, 181

197

Hudson, Joseph Lowthian Sr. (nephew of store's founder), 56, 81, 126
Hudson, Mary Eleanor (Mrs. J. T. Webber), 10, 24, 42–43, 54, 61, 76
Hudson Motor Car Company, 47, 54, 58, 61–62, 67, 69, 81, 92, 103–104, 120
  "Model 20," 47
  "Model Six-54," 54
  "Six-40 Landau Limousine," 61
  "Super Six," 61–62
Hudson, Dr. Richard, 9, 13, 53, 56, 61
Hudson, Richard Sr., 7–11
Hudson-Webber Foundations, 82, 119, 147, 154, 159, 176, 183
Hudson, William, 12, 16, 24, 32, 57, 61, 76, 81, 126
Hudson's Band, 21, 28, 70
  other musical groups, 70
Hudson's Downtown Detroit store (see Downtown Hudson's)
Hudson's hospital, 54, 74, 94
Hudson's Music Store (also J. L. Hudson Piano and Victrola Store), 60, 63, 69–70
Hudson's Rainbow stores, 160, 185
Hudson's satellite and suburban Detroit stores
  Eastland and Northland Centers, 119–120, 145, 153, 169
  Oakland Mall, 145
  Southland Center, 145
  Westland Center, 145
Budget Stores
  Lincoln Park, 144
  Madison Heights, 144
  Pontiac, 144
Hudson's stores (outside Detroit area),
  Buffalo, New York, 32, 84
  Cleveland, Ohio, 22, 61, 84
  Fort Wayne, Indiana, 172
  Grand Rapids, Michigan, 32, 84
  Ionia, Michigan, 10, 32
  Kalamazoo, Michigan, 169, 172
  Lansing, Michigan, 168
  St. Louis, Missouri, 32, 84
  St. Paul, Minnesota, 32, 84
  Sandusky, Ohio, 32, 84
  South Bend, Indiana, 168
  Toledo, Ohio, 14, 42, 84
Huff, Gladys, 141–143, 163
Huff, Lewis, 115–116, 123, 135–136, 148–149
Hull Brothers Grocery, 33
Humphrey, Hubert, 151

Ilitch, Mike, 186
influenza epidemic, 66
Ionia, Michigan, 8–11

Jackson, Louise (Mrs. Roscoe) see Webber, Louise
Jackson, Roscoe, 47, 56, 69, 77, 81
The J. L. Hudson Company, stock of, 154, 155
Johnson, Arthur, 151
Johnson, Paul, 179–180
Jones, Prophet, 124–125
Joy, Henry B., 22

INDEX

Kanzler, Ernest, 61
Kanzler, Josephine (Mrs. Ernest), 33, 43, 46, 48, 56, 61, 70, 108, 125
Kennedy, John F., 131, 136, 138-139, 147
Kennedy, Robert, 139
Kern's department store, 128
King, Martin Luther, Jr., 138-139
Kmart, 133, 156
Kopera, Sophie, 163
Korean War, 111
Kresge family, 133
Kresge, S. S., 37
Kresge Stores, 133
  Kresge's Woodward Avenue Store, 180
Kresik, Eugenia, 103, 107-108, 126-127, 138

Landry, Albert, 134, 136
Lashley, Pearly, 138
Leland, Henry, 41
Life magazine, 2, 72, 92, 101
Liggett School, 43, 48
Lincoln, Abraham, 10
Lobb, Bonnie, 145
Lodge, John C., 71

Mabley, Catherine (Mrs. Christopher), 12-14, 23-24
Mabley, Christopher S., 8-19, 29, 33-34, 39, 76
  his brothers and sisters, 23-24
Macy's, 2, 4, 84, 126
Mahoney, Betty, 163
Majestic Building, 34, 39
Marshall Field's, 84, 188

Mellor, Mary, 99-100, 119, 179
Michigan State Fair, 13, 43
Mills, Joe, 77-78, 86
Mills, P. Gerald, 175-176, 178, 182
Motown, 137

NAACP, 152
Nation, Carry, 37
National Advisory Council on Historic Preservation, 164, 168
New Detroit, Inc., 151-152, 156, 176
Newcomb, Endicott and Company, 15, 17, 52, 78, 81, 84
newspapers
  Detroit Free Press, 17, 176
  The Detroit News, 23, 142, 151, 180
  The New York Times, 136
  The Plaindealer, 31

O'Brien, Louise, (see Webber, Louise)
Olds, Ransom, 41, 47

Panic of 1873, 11
Panic of 1893, 32-33
Panic of 1920, 69, 82
Pardridge and Blackwell, 34, 45
Penobscot Building, 71
People for Downtown Hudson's, 167-168
Petzold, William A., 20, 83-84
Primettes, 137
Prohibition (also see alcoholic

199

beverages), 54, 58, 68, 72, 87
illegal liquor trade, 72

Quant, Mary, 157

radio and television, 87, 121-122, 124, 182, 187
Ray, Jack, 157
Renaissance Center, 165, 185
Reuther, Walter, 138
riot of 1943 (Detroit), 101-102
riot of 1967 (Detroit), 147-151, 156
Roberts, Edwin G., 159-160, 166
Roche, James M., 151
Romney, George, 149, 151
Roosevelt, Franklin D., 87
Ross, Diana (Diane), 5-6, 137-138
Roszak, Ed, 162
Russell House, 11-12, 28

Sales for Hudson's stores, 32, 164, 167
Sam's Cut Rate, 86
Shannon, Myrtel, 123-124
Sinila, Chester, 142
slave trade, 9-10
Solomon, Louise, 89, 100, 119, 150, 158, 161
Spanish-American War, 36
Speal, Bea, 108-109
Spiers, Catherine (see Mabley, Catherine)
Spiers, William J., 23
State Agricultural Association Fair (see Michigan State Fair)
Stevens, Captain William H., 33

The Stroh Brewery Company, 72, 148, 164-165
Studer, Dr. R. A., 55-56
Supremes, 6, 137
Symington Carpets and Upholstery Goods (see Hudson and Symington)

Tannahill, Anna (Mrs. Robert B., see Hudson, Anna)
Tannahill, Robert B., 12, 16, 33, 43, 54, 61, 76, 154
Tannahill, Robert Hudson, 33, 42, 56, 61, 76, 154
Third National Bank of Detroit, 32, 36
Toffolo, Dennis, 188

unionism, 87, 92-93, 101, 119, 188
University of Michigan, 10, 53, 58

Vietnam War, 1, 139, 150

Watson, Stephen E., 182
Wayne State University, 151
Webber brothers, 60-63, 68, 70-71, 75-78, 80-90, 92-93, 97, 102-103, 106-107, 117-118, 120, 124-125, 131-132, 135, 144, 147
Webber, Eloise Jenks (Mrs. Richard), 60, 77, 135, 159
Webber, George, 10
Webber, James Benson ("Jerry"), 24, 35, 42, 57-58, 107, 117-118, 126, 131

Webber, James Benson, Jr., 107, 117, 120, 125-126
Webber, Joseph Hudson, 77, 100, 107
Webber, Joseph Lowthian ("Tom"), 24, 35, 42, 57-58, 107, 117-118, 126, 148
Webber, Joseph T., 10, 24, 32, 42, 54, 76, 88
Webber, Louise, 24, 30, 35, 56, 77, 81, 88
Webber, Mary Eleanor (see Hudson, Mary Eleanor)
Webber, Oscar, 35, 42, 56-57, 62, 77, 83, 97, 102, 106-107, 118, 120, 122, 125, 127, 131, 148
Webber, Richard, 24-25, 30, 39-40, 42-43, 53, 56-58, 60, 76-77, 82, 89, 100, 106, 115-118, 125, 131, 135, 148
Whitney, David, 25
Willeke, Leonard B., 77, 83
Woodward Avenue, 1, 11-13, 19, 25-27, 33, 45, 49, 51-53, 60, 62-63, 66-68, 72, 86, 91-94, 97, 101-102, 104, 134, 138, 147, 165, 178-180, 186-187, 189
Woolworth's, 92
World War I, 60, 64-66
World War II, 96-103

Yale University, 3, 126, 176
Young, Coleman, 155, 189